Herta Müller

Herta Müller: Politics and Aesthetics

Edited by Bettina Brandt and Valentina Glajar

University of Nebraska Press | Lincoln and London

© 2013 by the Board of Regents of the University of Nebraska

The Nobel lecture by Herta Müller used by permission of the Nobel Foundation.
© The Nobel Foundation 2009.

Text from the collages in *Die blassen Herren mit den Mokkatassen* used by permission of Carl Hanser Verlag. © Carl Hanser Verlag München 2005.

All rights reserved

Manufactured in the United States of America

Library of Congress Cataloging-in-Publication Data

Herta Müller: politics and aesthetics / edited by Bettina Brandt and Valentina Glajar.

pages cm

Includes bibliographical references and index.

ISBN 978-0-8032-4510-5 (pbk.: alk. paper) 1. Müller, Herta, 1953- —Criticism and interpretation. I. Brandt, Bettina, editor of compilation. II. Glajar, Valentina, editor of compilation.

PT2673.U29234Z75 2013

833'.914—dc23   2013017383

Set in Lyon by Laura Wellington.
Designed by J. Vadnais.

Contents

List of Illustrations   viii
Acknowledgments   ix
Introduction   1
    Bettina Brandt and Valentina Glajar

Part 1. Life, Writing, and Betrayal

1. Herta Müller: Writing and Betrayal   15
   Allan Stoekl

2. Nobel Lecture: Every Word Knows Something of a Vicious Circle   20
   Herta Müller

3. Collage Poems   31
   Herta Müller

4. Interview with Ernest Wichner   36
   Valentina Glajar and Bettina Brandt

Part 2. Totalitarianism, Autofiction, Memory

5. When Dictatorships Fail to Deprive of Dignity: Herta Müller's "Romanian Period" 57
   Cristina Petrescu

6. "Die akute Einsamkeit des Menschen": Herta Müller's *Herztier* 87
   Brigid Haines

7. Facts, Fiction, Autofiction, and Surfiction in Herta Müller's Work 109
   Paola Bozzi

8. From Fact to Fiction: Herta Müller's *Atemschaukel* 130
   Olivia Spiridon

Part 3. Müller's Aesthetics of Experimentation

9. "Wir können höchstens mit dem, was wir sehen, etwas zusammenstellen": Herta Müller's Collages 155
   Beverley Driver Eddy

10. In Transit: Transnational Trajectories and Mobility in Herta Müller's Recent Writings 184
    Monika Moyrer

11. Osmoses: Müller's Things, Bodies, and Spaces 207
    Anja Johannsen

12. Herta Müller's Art of Reverberation: Sound in the Collage Books *Die blassen Herren mit den Mokkatassen* and *Este sau nu este Ion* 230
    Arina Rotaru

13. Accumulating Histories: Temporality in Herta Müller's "Einmal anfassen—zweimal loslassen" 252
   Katrina Nousek

Selected Bibliography 273
Contributors 279
Index 285

Illustrations

1. Herta Müller's childhood home in Nitzkydorf   3
2. "Milch ist der Zwilling"   32
3. "Im Gefälle zwischen"   33
4. "Ich gehöre daheim"   34
5. "Als der Abriss des Mondes"   35
6. Herta Müller and Oskar Pastior on former labor camp site in Ukraine, 2004   47
7. Herta Müller and Oskar Pastior in Ukraine, 2004   48
8. "In meinen Schläfen"   154
9. Frontal face view and an undressed lower torso   161
10. A typical sketch in a Herta Müller letter   162
11. Cover *Scherenschnitt* from *Der Wächter nimmt seinen Kamm*   164
12. Cutout from *Im Haarknoten wohnt eine Dame*   168
13. "Adio, patria mea"   242

Acknowledgments

We are greatly indebted to Kristen Elias Rowley, our editor at the University of Nebraska Press, for welcoming our book submission and for her sustained support in getting it published. We thank her and her assistant, Wesley Piper, who provided us with all the materials and answered our many queries. The quality of this book is also indebted to our anonymous readers, who provided us with much appreciated constructive criticism for revisions.

We would also like to thank Herta Müller for allowing us to include five of her newest collages and Beverley Eddy for initiating such an inclusion and for obtaining all the necessary permissions. For permission to reprint Herta Müller's Nobel speech, we are thankful to the Nobel Foundation. Carl Hanser Verlag and Editura Polirom have also been very helpful in allowing us to reprint two collages by Herta Müller, one from the volume *Die blassen Herren mit den Mokkatassen* and one from the Romanian-language volume *Este sau nu este Ion*.

Ernest Wichner provided us with firsthand information on German-language literature from Romania. We are deeply indebted to him for agreeing to be interviewed and for allowing us to reprint two photographs from his personal collection, both taken on his trip with Herta Müller and Oskar Pastior to visit former labor camp sites in Ukraine in 2004.

We are also grateful to the Department of Modern Languages at Texas

State University–San Marcos for its generous aid, which allowed us to provide this book with a professional index.

Finally, we would like to thank our contributing scholars for a wonderful collaboration on this book.

Valentina Glajar and Bettina Brandt

Herta Müller

Introduction
Bettina Brandt and Valentina Glajar

> Literature speaks with everyone individually—it is personal property that stays inside our heads. And nothing speaks to us as forcefully as a book which expects nothing in return, other than that we think and feel.
>
> Herta Müller, speech held at the Nobel banquet in the Stockholm City Hall, December 10, 2009

Two languages inform the writings of Nobel Prize laureate Herta Müller: German as well as Romanian bear on Müller's novels, essays, and collage poetry. Born in 1953 in German-speaking Nitzkydorf—a Banat-Swabian village in southwestern Romania—Müller grew up as part of a linguistic and ethnic minority in a Communist state. Her writing career began with a fictionalized portrayal of the village of her childhood, an isolated backward community deeply influenced by National Socialism and characterized by narrow-minded ethnocentrism. Romanian literary censorship, which had dramatically increased in the 1980s, delayed the publication of Müller's first collection of short stories for several years. When *Niederungen* was finally published in 1982, the censor's fingerprints marked the text.[1] An uncensored *Niederungen* was published by Rotbuch in the Federal Republic of Germany (FRG) in 1984. An English translation, *Nadirs* (published by the University of Nebraska Press), came out in 1999.

In many ways *Niederungen* is a typical *Dorfgeschichte* [village tale], though the defining characteristics of this genre have all been distorted. The idyllic harmony of village life and unspoiled nature turn into a world of alienated relationships due to alcoholism, abuse, cruelty, and hate. The Banat-Swabian environment penetrates Müller's autobiographically inspired writings, but the writer deviates poetically from the facts of her own experiences through a style she calls "sich erfindende Wahrnehmung" [an invented and reinventing perception] that mediates between perception and its refracted form, the invented perception.

Müller's fictionalized stories brutally exposed life in the rural village; hence they offended the Banat-Swabians in Romania as well as the very vocal Banater Schwaben Landsmannschaft (Organization of Banat Swabians) in Germany and led to scathing critiques in the Banat-Swabian press. A few of these reviews had actually been penned by informants of the Securitate (Romanian secret police). In particular the source "Voicu" was instrumental in discrediting her texts. In his review of Müller's *Niederungen*, "Voicu" concludes: "Critică şi iar critică. O critică atît de destructivă, încît te intrebi, ce rost au aceste texte?!" [Criticism and more criticism. This criticism is so destructive that one has to wonder what the purpose of these texts is] (ACNSAS 10).

After an unsuccessful and officially undocumented attempt to recruit Müller for the Securitate, a file on Herta Müller (I233477, "Cristina") was opened in March 1983, a dossier that eventually would grow to an astonishing 914 pages. Müller simply told her recruiting officer: "N-am caracterul" [I don't have the character for this (kind of work)]. This statement apparently infuriated the secret service officer to such a degree that he shredded the recruitment letter that Müller had refused to sign and threw the snippets on the floor, only to gather them all up again when he remembered that the failed recruitment attempt would have to be explained to his superior. This incident, of course, also highlights the moral quality of Müller's writings.

The Communist discourse of Romanian dictator Nicolae Ceauşescu was imposed in all the languages spoken in Romania—Romanian as well

1. Herta Müller's childhood home in Nitzkydorf. (Copyright Valentina Glajar.)

as German and Hungarian, the language of another ethnic and linguistic minority. Müller has a complex relationship not just to (Ceaușescu's) Romanian, which she learned as a teenager as a second language, but also to German, especially the German of her Banat-Swabian village, in which the undefeated discourse of National Socialism seemed to ceaselessly carry on. The result is Müller's characteristic writing style, often associated with the *fremde Blick*, or the "strange gaze."

Faced with increased surveillance, a defamation campaign, and ongoing threats on her life, Müller finally decided to leave Romania. As the result of a bilateral agreement signed in 1978 between the Romanian dictator and the FRG's then chancellor, Social Democrat Helmut Schmidt, Müller was one of the up to twelve thousand ethnic Germans who were granted an exit visa every year for the price of around 8,000 DM (Ash 238). Müller and her husband at the time, the writer Richard Wagner, arrived in the FRG in February 1987. Placed in a transitional camp in Nuremberg, where their paperwork had to be processed for clearance, Müller insisted that they wanted the FRG to accept them as *political refugees*, not as ethnic Germans. Müller and Wagner's application for political asylum complicated and delayed the process of establishing their status in Germany since German officials were looking for proof of German ethnicity, even if it meant disclosing a family member's collaboration with Nazi Germany or looking up the records of the old Deutsche Volkslisten (German People's Lists, created by the Nazis and on which people in German-occupied territories were categorized according to their degree of being German):

> Daß ich 1987 bei der Offenlegung meiner Biographie von der rumänischen Diktatur redete, machte die Beamten nervös. Ich habe eine Diktatur aus politischen Gründen verlassen, und die deutschen Beamten wollten etwas über mein Deutschtum wissen. Als ich die Frage, ob ich mit meiner Haltung auch als Rumänin verfolgt gewesen wäre, mit Ja beantwortete, schickte der Beamte mich zur Ausländerpolizei. Er konstatierte: entweder Deutsche oder politisch Verfolgte. Für beides zusammen gab es kein vorgedrucktes Formular.
>
> [That I was talking about the Romanian dictatorship when disclosing my biography in 1987 made the public official nervous. I left a dictatorship for political reasons, and the German officials wanted to know something about my Germanness. When I answered the question with Yes whether, with my attitude, I also would have been persecuted as a Romanian, the official sent me to the immigration authorities. He stated: either you are German or politically persecuted. He did not have a preprinted form for both categories at once.] (*Hunger und Seide* 25)

Both Müller and Wagner could have easily proved that they were ethnic Germans; indeed, Müller's father and uncle had been in the Waffen-SS during Word War II.

Though Müller's characters are fictional, their stories tend to spring from the author's own life. Müller's writings often focus on the German ethnic minority in Romania with its complex and often duplicitous intertwinement into the two major totalitarian systems of the twentieth century: National Socialism (along with its Romanian fascist variation) and communism. Müller depicts these ethnic Germans simultaneously as perpetrators of Nazi crimes; minority residents under an oppressive Communist regime; and in *Atemschaukel*, her most recent novel, which unfolds in January 1944-49, as victims of Stalinism.

The author herself likes to use the term "autofictional" to describe her writings. Fictionalized accounts of suffering and persecution under the Ceaușescu regime are reflected in novels such as *Herztier* [1995; *The Land of Green Plums*, 1996]; *Der Fuchs war damals schon der Jäger* [1992; The fox was already the hunter]; and *Heute wär ich mir lieber nicht begegnet* [1997; *The Appointment*, 2001], as well as in her collections of essays *Barfüßiger Februar* [1987; Barefoot February]; *Hunger und Seide* [1995; Hunger and silk]; *Der König verneigt sich und tötet* [2003; The king bows and kills], and numerous other essays and interviews.

In these texts, Müller exposes the Romanian Securitate's practices and the trauma of individuals who had to experience death threats that continued even after their immigration into Germany. *The Land of Green Plums*, for example, is based on the experiences of a group of ethnic German writers and exposes the persecution by the Securitate in the 1980s, as well as the atmosphere of fear and hopelessness in an economically and culturally disastrous Communist Romania. The characters are to a large extent based on the real-life writers Rolf Bossert (1952-86), who emigrated from Communist Romania and committed suicide weeks after his arrival in Frankfurt; Richard Wagner (b. 1952); and Roland Kirsch (1960-89), who committed suicide while waiting to emigrate to Germany. In a recent article, however, Müller clarifies that the Securitate most likely killed Kirsch, as neighbors had heard a fight in his apartment before he allegedly hanged himself.

Müller's experimental prose and poetry are exemplified in her literary collages, a radical form of representation based on the transformation of preexisting elements—that is, a form of dislocation in which the familiar becomes surprisingly unfamiliar. Collage making is first described in Herta Müller's short novel *Reisende auf einem Bein* [1989; *Traveling on One Leg*, 1998], a text in which one of the protagonists engages in this activity. A couple of years later Müller started making actual postcard-size collages that were first published in her essay collection *Der Teufel sitzt im Spiegel* [The devil sits in the mirror]. Three German collage collections followed: *Der Wächter nimmt seinen Kamm* [1993; The guard takes his comb]; *Im Haarknoten wohnt eine Dame* [2005; A lady lives in the bun]; and *Die blassen Herren mit den Mokkatassen* [2006; The pale gentlemen with the mocha cups]. In 2005 Müller published her first Romanian-language-bound collage, titled *Este sau nu este Ion* [2005; Is it or is it not Ion]. Müller finds the materials for her collages in the illustrations and in the potent commercial language of advertisements in German and Romanian newspapers, magazines, and catalogues that surround her. She then cuts out letters and entire words or parts of words; sorts them alphabetically; and finally stores them in drawers until they are all posed in front of her on a flat surface, when she is ready to make a new collage postcard. Collage functions in Müller's universe as a device that mediates between art and life.

Thematically divided into three parts, *Herta Müller: Politics and Aesthetics* is addressed to a general English-speaking academic audience with an interest in dissident, exile, migration, experimental, and transnational literature. The book presents a variety of literary, cultural, and historical approaches and covers the major topics of Müller's writings while bringing together Herta Müller scholars from Europe and the United States.

The first part, "Life, Writing, and Betrayal," prefaced by Allan Stoekl, features Müller's Nobel lecture, in which she describes the unlikely story of a little girl herding cows in Nitzkydorf who grew up to become a writer and Nobel Prize laureate; it also includes Müller's own original contribution to our volume: four hitherto unpublished collage poems. The interview with Ernest Wichner, a German-Romanian author, translator, editor, and Müller's personal friend, allows the readers insight into Wichner's fascinating experiences as a founding member of the Aktionsgruppe Banat (a German literary circle of Banat-Swabian authors) and the group's constant surveillance and persecution by the Securitate.

Wichner's early memories of Müller and her literary debut, as well as his close friendship with both Müller and the poet Oskar Pastior, evoke various stages in the life of German-Romanian writers and the intricate web of friendship and deceit under communism.

The essays in the second part of the volume, "Totalitarianism, Autofiction, Memory," focus on the political aspects of Müller's texts and discuss life under the Romanian Communist dictatorial regime of Ceauşescu and his vigilant watchdogs, the Securitate. In a post-Communist Romania, since 2007 a member of the European Union (which has done very little to research its Communist past and the practices of Ceauşescu's secret service), Müller's Nobel Prize has certainly, and finally, struck a chord with Romanians. While Romanian intellectuals have either jumped at the opportunity to share the prize with her on the basis of her Romanianness or rejected it because of her Germanness, Müller continues to ask fundamental questions about totalitarianism and its tools. She writes about the new Securitate, the post-Communist SRI (Serviciul Român de Informaţii—the Romanian Information Service) and claims that 40 percent of the old Securitate members are part of it, while the other 60 percent are either retired and receiving very high pensions or are now in charge of the economy: the new nomenklatura and the nouveaux riches. Müller's poignant discourse of discontent, as well as her personal history as a political writer, allows for a sophisticated perspective on Communist life in Romania, and it reaches a wider audience than most historical texts ever could.

Based on Müller's Securitate file, Cristina Petrescu discusses the author's "Romanian period" as she provides a detailed analysis of the political context of Müller's work before her emigration in 1987. Perversely filed under the category "Fascist German Writers," Müller's file reveals, in Petrescu's words, "an Orwellian world of dictatorship that aimed at total control." Through its elaborate practices and the often voluntary collaboration of its many informants, the Securitate realized a world of fear and opportunism, betrayal and hopelessness, that has profoundly impacted Müller's writing. As Petrescu shows, Müller's refusal to collaborate with the secret police in spite of death threats and interrogations was not a common attitude in Romania. On the contrary, in a much-debated discussion with the Romanian intellectual Gabriel Liiceanu during a post-Nobel visit to Romania, Müller bluntly exposed Liiceanu's claim to "resistance through culture" as futile.

Brigid Haines offers a close reading of Müller's most successful novel to date, *Herztier* [*The Land of Green Plums*], against the political background of the 1980s in Romania. Like most of her previous writings, *Herztier* is deeply rooted in Müller's own biography and her experience of a wide range of Securitate practices, which entailed both physical violence and psychological mind games. Haines focuses on what she calls "an aesthetic of atomization and dispersal," which in her opinion makes Müller's work profoundly political and an appropriate and effective response to repression. With Hannah Arendt, Haines asks relevant questions regarding the very theme of loneliness in a totalitarian society that denies the individual a right to privacy in an attempt to control lives through an ever-present fear.

Drawing on Serge Doubrovsky's and Raymond Federman's useful concepts of "autofiction" and "surfiction" respectively, Paola Bozzi analyzes the writing style in which Müller fictionalizes and transfigures her biographical experiences. As Bozzi pertinently observes, Müller often focuses her attention on experiences that reveal life itself as fiction, or rather as "autofiction." Bozzi challenges the readers to approach Müller's writing style not only as a mode that resists the effacement or erasure of memories, but also as one that attempts to transcend "history."

Müller's latest novel, *Atemschaukel* [*The Hunger Angel*], represents a break from her direct personal biography as it addresses the deportation of ethnic Germans from Romania to Ukrainian labor camps in January 1945 in the fictionalized story of another famous German-Romanian writer, Oskar Pastior. Olivia Spiridon argues that Müller creates a site of memory for the ethnic Romanian community as it focuses on this understudied historical event. As Spiridon shows, the representation of this particular historical event raises questions about the relationship between literary texts and historiography, and it also allows various groups to appropriate this highly successful novel for their own political purposes. None other than the controversial Zentrum gegen Vertreibungen (Center against Expulsions, a yet-to-be built site closely associated with the Banater Schwaben Landsmanschaft), for instance, has awarded Müller the Franz Werfel Humanitarian Award for *Atemschaukel*.[2]

The essays in the third part of this volume, "Müller's Modes of Writing and the Aesthetics of Experimentation," stress key elements of the Nobel laureate's avant-garde poetics, an aesthetics that promises both self-conscious formal experimentation and political intervention. Beverley Driver Eddy, Monika Moyrer, and Arina Rotaru analyze different aspects of Müller's collages, a particular form of modernist writing that increasingly dominates the author's style. In the collages a critical mode explicitly comes to the fore that can be said to be the driving force behind Müller's writing as a whole: a formal radicalism combined with a highly politicized content.

Eddy examines Müller's collections of collages as total works of art in which cutout picture meets cutout text. She indicates how Müller's collages relate to her prose texts, traces their origins, and shows their thematic and artistic development through Müller's three German collage collections: *Der Wächter nimmt seinen Kamm*, *Im Haarknoten wohnt eine Dame*, and *Die blassen Herren mit den Mokkatassen*. Finally, Eddy's essay acknowledges the ongoing popularity of collages as marketed items of popular culture.

Monika Moyrer examines one particular cutout, the *Mokkatasse*, or mocha cup, which circulates in Müller's German collages also as *Knorpeltasse* or MOKKATASSE and in her Romanian collages as *Ceașca de moca*. Analyzing the textual and linguistic border crossings within the context of Müller's close collaboration with Oskar Pastior and focusing on both the visual and the tactile aspects of these cutouts, Moyrer reads Müller's textual collection of mocha cups as textual *Vitrinen* [glass cabinets] in which the possibility of assuming agency over recollected transnational memories is on display.

Arina Rotaru stresses the aesthetics of sound and reverberation in a number of Müller's collage poems and prose texts, thus offering an alternative interpretation of Müller's relationship with the Western world and its exaltation of the image. Analyzing Müller's use of Surrealist and Dadaist techniques, Rotaru comes to the conclusion that Müller's collages are not only an attempt at validating her writing identity beyond gender, but also an attempt at transcending ethnicity in the name of the globalized practices of the avant-gardes and their use of sounds and performance. Indeed, the accented German and Romanian voices present in Müller's poems form a distinct, fragmented sonoric spectrum "that echoes in the past and chimes in the present."

Anja Johannsen's and Katrina Nousek's essays shed light on Müller's complex literary strategies. Drawing on the theories of the Russian formalist Viktor Shklovsky and focusing on selected passages from Müller's prose works (mainly *Herztier*, *Heute wäre ich mir lieber nicht begegnet*, and *Atemschaukel*), Johannsen presents Müller as an author whose literature irritates and captivates its readers by continually challenging the patterns of perception. Nousek focuses on Müller's poetics lecture held at the University of Tübingen "to demonstrate the inadequacy of representing subjective experience within a temporal structure divided into past, present, and future." In this same lecture Müller addressed the critique that her writings, after more than two decades in Germany, continued to address the Romanian past:

> Wenn ich über zehn Jahre zurückliegendes aus Rumänien schreibe, heißt es, ich schreibe (noch immer) über die Vergangenheit. Wenn ein hiesiger Autor über die Nachkriegszeit, das Wirtschaftswunder oder die 68er Jahre schreibt, liest man das als Gegenwart. Das hiesig Vergangene, wie weit es auch zurückliegen mag, bleibt Gegenwart, weil es sich hier zugetragen hat, weil es durch Zugehörigkeit bindet. Bei Autoren wie ... Imre Kertész wird das zeitliche Kriterium nicht verhandelt, weil die räumliche Trennung klarstellt, dass sie nicht dazugehören. Ich bin aber in dieses Land gekommen, meine Zugehörigkeit muß verhandelt werden.
>
> [When I write about something that happened in Romania ten years ago, people say that I am still writing about the past. If a local German writes about the postwar period, about the economic miracle, or about 1968, this is read as having to do with the present. The local past, however far back it might go, remains present because it happened here, because it connects through a form of belonging. When talking about authors such as ... Imre Kertész the time criterion is not brought up because the spatial distance makes clear that they don't belong. But I have come to this country; my belonging needs to be negotiated.] (37)

The award of the Nobel Prize committee affirms that Herta Müller's writing is not trapped either in Romanian or German local histories but speaks to a broader cosmopolitan, politically engaged audience.

Notes

1. In the summer of 2011 the University of Nebraska Press published a new edition of *Niederungen* with four additional chapters that had been part of the original manuscript.

2. While the debate over the location of the Center against Expulsions is still ongoing, it will most likely be built, despite considerable political opposition against the project because it memorializes the fate of German expellees without simultaneously addressing the *causes* of World War II; the mass killings of Jews, Poles, Roma and Sinti, homosexuals, Soviet prisoners of war, and other persecuted groups is an affront. Herta Müller, one of the vocal opponents of the center, therefore recently wrote an open letter to the German chancellor, Angela Merkel; published in the *Frankfurter Allgemeine Zeitung*, a national newspaper with a conservative readership, the letter demanded that a Center for Exile should be built in Germany as well—a space in which the experience of exile, what Müller calls "the very first expulsion," can be properly commemorated.

Works Cited

ACNSAS (Archive of the National Council for the Study of the Securitate). File 1233477, "Cristina."
Ash, Timothy Garton. *In Europe's Name*. New York: Random House, 1993.
Müller, Herta. *The Appointment*. Trans. Michael Hulse and Philip Boehm. New York: Metropolitan Books, 2001.
———. *Atemschaukel*. Munich: Hanser, 2009.
———. *Barfüßiger Februar*. Berlin: Rotbuch, 1987.
———. *Der Fuchs war damals schon der Jäger*. Reinbek: Rowohlt, 1992.
———. *Der König verneigt sich und tötet*. Munich and Vienna: Hanser, 2003.
———. *Der Wächter nimmt seinen Kamm: Vom Weggehen und Ausscheren*. Reinbek: Rowohlt, 1993.
———. *Die blassen Herren mit den Mokkatassen*. Munich: Hanser, 2005.
———. *Este sau nu este Ion*. Iași: Polirom, 2005.
———. *Herztier*. Reinbek: Rowohlt, 1994.
———. *Heute wäre ich mir lieber nicht begegnet*. Reinbek: Rowohlt, 1997.
———. *The Hunger Angel*. Trans. Philip Boehm. New York: Metropolitan Books, 2012.

———. *Hunger und Seide*. Reinbek: Rowohlt, 1995.

———. *Im Haarknoten wohnt eine Dame*. Reinbek: Rowohlt, 2000.

———. *The Land of Green Plums*. Trans. Michael Hofmann. New York: Metropolitan Books, 1996.

———. *Nadirs*. Trans. Sieglinde Lug. Lincoln: University of Nebraska Press, 1999.

———. *Niederungen*. Berlin: Rotbuch, 1984.

———. *Reisende auf einem Bein*. Berlin: Rotbuch, 1989.

———. *Traveling on One Leg*. Trans. Valentina Glajar and André Lefevere. Evanston: Northwestern University Press, 1998.

Part 1 Life, Writing, and Betrayal

1 Herta Müller
Writing and Betrayal
Allan Stoekl

Herta Müller's is a poor writing, or a writing that uses the poverty of means to escape, momentarily, a greater and much more profound poverty. The world presented in her writing, in a collision of verisimilitude and surrealism, is a world in which one makes do with very little; Müller's Nobel Prize speech (titled "Every Word Knows Something of a Vicious Circle"), for example, is an extended meditation on words and things, starting from, and always coming back to, the handkerchief.[1] In a world outside of, or below, the consumer economy, small objects, passed from parent to child, assert themselves.

For Müller the handkerchief is a marker, a badge, of her mother's love—a love that is expressed with difficulty in the harsh, stripped-bare existence of the village, but the love that surfaces is the mother's constant concern for her daughter's possession of a thing—a single, small thing—with which she can carry out any number of tasks. It's a micro-survival tool and at the same time the metonym for a much larger strategy of survival. And as often happens with metonyms, Müller's handkerchief joins, melds with, leads into and out of any number of other metonyms that make up her writing. After the powerful initial question—Do you have your handkerchief?—we see the morphing of the handkerchief into any number of other objects, through contiguous contact.

Müller's uncle—whom she characterizes only as "the son" of her grandparents—is, as a young man, won over by the Nazis when he goes to study business at a school in Timişoara in the 1930s. More Nazi than the Nazis, Uncle Matz inevitably finds himself in the ss, fighting—along with Müller's father—on the Eastern Front. And soon enough he is killed, and his photo—or rather the grisly photo of his body lying on a tarp—is sent back to his grieving parents. Müller writes: "The death-photo is hand-sized: in the middle of a black field a little gray heap of human remains can be seen resting on a white cloth. Against the black field the white cloth looks as small as a child's handkerchief, a white square with a strange design painted in the middle. For my grandmother this photo was a combination too: on the white handkerchief was a dead Nazi, in her memory was a living son" (6).

What first seemed merely a symbol of parental concern thus quickly becomes a framing device for something much larger. The handkerchief is now a setting for a memento mori that is also a reminder and stark indictment of the complicity and guilt of many members of the Banat German community. As Matz's father, Müller's grandfather, puts it: "When the flags start to flutter, common sense slides right into the trumpet" (8). And one metonym slides right into another: handkerchief as care; handkerchief as death-frame, as indictment; handkerchief as trumpet announcing; trumpet as alimentary or excretory canal swallowing and excreting; canal as toilet in which deluded idealism, as well as cynical commitment, are swept away, down and out: "[My grandfather's] warning also applied to the following dictatorship, which I experienced" (7). Later, Müller as a child learns to play that beloved folk instrument, the accordion; the instrument is her dead Uncle Matz's, its straps way too large to hang from her shoulders—so they are tied together behind her back, with a handkerchief.

Müller's style, then, is comprised of series of metonyms, circling, indicating a whole, indicating each other, indicating the impossibility of a total indication. A metonymic cloud. Müller herself has another name for it: a devil's circle.[2] "Can we say that it is precisely the smallest objects—be they trumpets, accordions, or handkerchiefs—which connect the most disparate things in life? That the objects are in orbit and that their deviations reveal a pattern of repetition—a vicious circle, or what we call in German a devil's circle" (7).

The devil's circle is that of writing and all it implies in a repressive dictatorship, where independent expression tends to land its author in a captain's office, undergoing psychological and physical torture—if not death. But there is a larger devil's circle, which itself is a function of the circulation of metonyms *as* writing. Müller writes because speech is incapable of expressing what writing *does*. "On the stairs"—in the factory after she has been sacked, sitting on the stairs, refusing to leave, refused an office, Müller tells us that she realized the futility of talking. A nonperson in the factory, a nonperson everywhere, she was fired for refusing to spy on her friends. The devilish response on the part of the Securitate was to spread the rumor that, precisely, she was a spy. She writes: "I talked a great deal during the dictatorship, mostly because I decided not to blow the trumpet. Usually my talking led to excruciating consequences. But the writing began in silence, there on the stairs, where I had to come to terms with more than could be said. What was happening could no longer be expressed in speech" (7).

Jacques Derrida famously argued that speech, rather than purer, more real, more authentic than writing, was itself a function of writing. Müller, under the constant gaze of the dictatorship, realizes that the devil's circle is alone adequate to rendering "the totality of events themselves" (7). Speech is now and can be only silence, the spaces between the circles of words spinning in the head—and then on paper. "The mouth is skipped over," she writes and goes on to state, "The subject is there implicitly, but the words are what take possession of me. They coax the subject anywhere they want" (7). Touching on surrealist automatic writing, the circulation of words is also the movement of a double bind into which falls any person who refuses to blow the trumpet. Another devil's circle: one writes because that alone is adequate to the all-swallowing trumpet, that alone is the possible resistance to the trumpet, the escape from its double bind of resister and traitor, spy and spied upon, but by doing so, by writing silently, one nevertheless brands oneself a traitor and is all the more liable to being engulfed by the trumpet. The many sessions in the captain's office are, after all, the regime's response to Müller's defiant act of writing. Writing is both poison and cure, the *pharmakon*, and in a dictatorship of the sort Müller faces it is impossible even to separate the two: poison-cure, metonyms of each other, they circle like an accursed double star in the profound loneliness of the devil's staircase.

This to me is one of the strongest elements in Müller's project: writing is resistance, to be sure, in a sense the only resistance, and it is, it becomes, one's "life," yet it is never predicated on some fundamental innocence, some primary victimhood that graces writing with unshakeable virtue. Writing is betrayal, not only of the regime, but also of one's own sanity, of one's self-certainty, self-confidence, one's own authority. There is no truth in writing; that only belongs to speech, to the wit of the staircase. Terms circulate and always *implicate* each other. There is no community whose virtue or veracity will be or can be redeemed by Müller's writing. She "speaks" for no "minority" whose "rights" are to be guaranteed or asserted. Her "minority," if one can even call it that, is a disrupted, dispirited one: it seems all the fathers, all the uncles, are former members of the SS; the very ideal of a coherent and virtuous linguistic or cultural community has been flushed down the trumpet long ago. Nor is there any ideal in Germany, a country in which she has never lived, whose own history is hardly an innocent one; she cannot base her love of writing, mostly in German (but sometimes in Romanian), on some national essence. That has all been done before, to disastrous effect. At most she can read contemporary German writing as an example of what writing might be outside of a dictatorship, but once she actually gets to Germany, she realizes that its citizens are even more hungry than those of Romania under Ceaușescu—the only difference is that they don't know what they are hungry for. Müller is a "fascist whore" German in Romania, a totally marginal Romanian in Germany, shunned from the first by her own peasant-Nazi community for "shitting in her own nest," and her writing is most certainly not a home, not a place of stability or repose.

Perhaps in her writing Müller is tending toward another community; her devil's circle propels her out of or at least alongside the trumpet and toward a "coming community," as Agamben calls it, a community for whom identity is only a reference of partial, floating metonyms, as the space of the left-behind, stripped of any general validity or truth-value. A community of readers and of writers, a community of those who have nothing in common.

Agamben writes: "[If] instead of continuing to search for a proper identity in the already improper and senseless form of individuality, humans were to succeed in belonging to this impropriety as such, in making of the proper being-thus not an identity and an individual property but a singularity without identity . . . then they would for the first time enter into a community without presuppositions and without subjects, into a communication without the incommunicable" (64).

But could they enter into the community of the handkerchief? Into the community of care, against the community?

Notes

1. Müller's 2009 Nobel Prize lecture, from which I quote below, is available online from the Nobel Foundation at: http://nobelprize.org/nobel_prizes/literature/laureates/2009/muller-lecture_en.html.

2. While the translator of the Nobel Prize speech into English (Philip Boehm) uses the term "vicious circle" in the title ("Every Word Knows Something of a Vicious Circle"), in German the devil makes an appearance: "Jedes Wort weiß etwas vom Teufelskreis."

Works Cited

Agamben, Giorgio. *The Coming Community*. Trans. Michael Hardt. Minneapolis: University of Minnesota Press, 1993.

2 Nobel Lecture
Every Word Knows Something of a Vicious Circle

Herta Müller

"Do you have a handkerchief?" was the question my mother asked me every morning, standing by the gate to our house, before I went out onto the street. I didn't have a handkerchief. And because I didn't, I would go back inside and get one. I never had a handkerchief because I would always wait for her question. The handkerchief was proof that my mother was looking after me in the morning. For the rest of the day I was on my own. The question "Do you have a handkerchief?" was an indirect display of affection. Anything more direct would have been embarrassing and not something the farmers practiced. Love disguised itself as a question. That was the only way it could be spoken: matter-of-factly, in the tone of a command, or the deft maneuvers used for work. The brusqueness of the voice even emphasized the tenderness. Every morning I went to the gate once without a handkerchief and a second time with a handkerchief. Only then would I go out onto the street, as if having the handkerchief meant having my mother there, too.

Twenty years later I had been on my own in the city a long time and was working as a translator in a manufacturing plant. I would get up at five a.m.; work began at six-thirty. Every morning the loudspeaker blared the national anthem into the factory yard; at lunch it was the workers' choruses. But the workers simply sat over their meals with empty tinplate eyes and hands smeared with oil. Their food was wrapped in newspaper. Before they ate their bit of fatback, they first scraped the newsprint off the rind. Two years went by in the same routine, each day like the next.

In the third year the routine came to an end. Three times in one week a visitor showed up at my office early in the morning: an enormous, thick-boned man with sparkling blue eyes—a colossus from the Securitate.

The first time he stood there, cursed me, and left.

The second time he took off his windbreaker, hung it on the key to the cabinet, and sat down. That morning I had brought some tulips from home and arranged them in a vase. The man looked at me and praised me for being such a keen judge of character. His voice was slippery. I felt uneasy. I contested his praise and assured him that I understood tulips, but not people. Then he said maliciously that he knew me better than I knew tulips. After that he draped his windbreaker over his arm and left.

The third time he sat down but I stayed standing, because he had set his briefcase on my chair. I didn't dare move it to the floor. He called me stupid, said I was a shirker and a slut, as corrupted as a stray bitch. He shoved the tulips close to the edge of the desk, then put an empty sheet of paper and a pen in the middle of the desktop. He yelled at me: *Write*. Without sitting down, I wrote what he dictated—my name, date of birth and address. Next, that I would tell no one, no matter how close a friend or relative, that I . . . and then came the terrible word: *colaborez—I am collaborating*. At that point I stopped writing. I put down the pen and went to the window and looked out onto the dusty street, unpaved and full of potholes, and at all the humpbacked houses. On top of everything else this street was called Strada Gloriei—Glory Street. On Glory Street a cat was sitting in a bare mulberry tree. It was the factory cat with the torn ear. And above the cat the early morning sun was shining like a yellow drum. I said: *N-am caracterul—I don't have the character for this*. I said it to the street outside. The word "character" made the Securitate man hysterical. He tore up the sheet of paper and threw the pieces on the floor. Then he probably realized he would have to show his boss that he had tried to recruit me, because he bent over, picked up the scraps and tossed them into his briefcase. After that he gave a deep sigh and, defeated, hurled the vase with the tulips against the wall. As it shattered it made a grinding sound, as though the air had teeth. With his briefcase under his arm he said quietly: *You'll be sorry, we'll drown you in the river.* I said as if to myself: *If I sign that, I won't be able to live with myself anymore, and I'll have to do it on my own. So it's better if you do it.* By then the office door was already open and he was gone. And outside on the Strada Gloriei the factory cat had jumped from the tree onto the roof of the building. One branch was bouncing like a trampoline.

The next day the tug of war began. They wanted me out of the factory. Every morning at 6:30 I had to report to the director. The head of the official labor union and the party secretary were also in his office. Just like my mother once asked: "Do you have a handkerchief?" the director now asked every morning: *Have you found another job?* Every morning I gave the same answer: *I'm not looking for one, I like it here in the factory, I'd like to stay here until I retire.*

One morning I came to work and found my thick dictionaries lying on the floor of the hall outside my office. I opened the door; an engineer was sitting at my desk. He said: *People are supposed to knock before they enter a room. This is my place, you have no business here.* I couldn't go home; any unexcused absence would have given them a pretext to fire me. I no longer had an office, so now I really had to make sure I came to work; under no circumstances could I fail to be there.

My friend, whom I told everything as we walked home down the pitiful Strada Gloriei, cleared a corner of her desk for me, at first. But one morning she stood outside her office and said: *I can't let you in. Everyone is saying you're an informer.* The harassment was passed down; the rumor was set into circulation among my colleagues. That was the worst. You can defend yourself against an attack, but there's nothing you can do against libel. Every day I prepared myself for anything, including death. But I couldn't cope with this perfidy. No preparation made it bearable. Libel stuffs you with filth; you suffocate because you can't defend yourself. In the eyes of my colleagues I was exactly what I had refused to become. If I had spied on them they would have trusted me without the slightest hesitation. In essence they were punishing me because I had spared them.

Since now I really had to make sure I came to work, but no longer had an office, and since my friend could no longer let me into hers, I stood in the stairwell, unable to decide what to do. I climbed up and down the stairs a few times and suddenly I was again my mother's child, because I *had a handkerchief*. I placed it on one of the stairs between the second and third floors, carefully smoothed it out and sat down. I rested my thick dictionaries on my knee and translated the descriptions of hydraulic machines. I was a staircase wit and my office was a handkerchief. My friend joined me on the stairs at lunchtime. We ate together as we had in her office, and before that in mine. From the loudspeaker in the yard the workers' choruses sang about the happiness of the people, as always. My friend ate her lunch and cried over me. I didn't cry. I had to stay tough. For a long time. A few never-ending weeks, until I was dismissed.

During the time that I was a staircase wit, I looked up the word "stair" in the dictionary: the first step is the "starting step" or "curtail step" that can also be a "bullnose." "Hand" is the direction a stair takes at the first riser. The edge of a tread that projects past the face of the riser is called the "nosing." I already knew a number of beautiful words having to do with lubricated hydraulic machine parts: "dovetail," "gooseneck," "acorn nuts," and "eyebolts." Now I was equally amazed at the poetic names of the stair parts, the beauty of the technical language. "Nosing" and "hand"—so the stair has a body. Whether working with wood or stone, cement or iron: why do humans insist on imposing their face on even the most unwieldy things in the world, why do they name dead matter after their own flesh, personifying it as parts of the body? Is this hidden tenderness necessary to make the harsh work bearable for the technicians? Does every job in every field follow the same principle as my mother's question about the handkerchief?

When I was little we had a handkerchief drawer at home, which was always partitioned into two rows, with three stacks apiece:

On the left the men's handkerchiefs for my father and grandfather.

On the right the women's handkerchiefs for my mother and grandmother.

In the middle the children's handkerchiefs for me.

The drawer was a family portrait in handkerchief format. The men's handkerchiefs were the biggest, with dark stripes along the edges in brown, gray or Bordeaux. The women's handkerchiefs were smaller, and their edges were light blue, red, or green. The children's handkerchiefs were the smallest: borderless white squares painted with flowers or animals. All three handkerchief types were divided into those for everyday use, in the front row, and those reserved for Sunday, in the back. On Sundays your handkerchief had to match the color of your clothes, even if it wasn't visible.

No other object in the house, including ourselves, was ever as important to us as the handkerchief. Its uses were universal: sniffles; nosebleeds; hurt hand, elbow or knee; crying, or biting into it to suppress the crying. A cold wet handkerchief on the forehead for headaches. Tied at the four corners it protected your head against sunburn or rain. If you had to remember something you made a knot to prompt your memory. For carrying heavy bags you wrapped it around your hand. When the train pulled out of the station you waved it to say good-bye. And because the word for tear in our Banat dialect sounds like the Romanian word for train, the squeaking of the railcars on the tracks always sounded to me like crying. In the village if someone died at home they immediately tied a handkerchief around his chin so that his mouth stayed closed when the rigor mortis set in. In the city if a person collapsed on the side of the road, some passerby would always take a handkerchief and cover his face, so that the handkerchief became the dead man's first place of peace.

On hot summer days the parents would send their children to the cemetery late in the evening to water the flowers. We stayed together in groups of two or three, quickly watering one grave and then the next. Afterwards we would huddle together on the steps of the chapel and watch wisps of white mist rise from some of the graves. They would fly up a little ways and disappear in the darkness. For us they were the souls of the dead: animal figures, glasses, little bottles and cups, gloves and stockings. And here and there a white handkerchief bordered by the black night.

Later, when I was meeting with Oskar Pastior so I could write about his deportation to the Soviet labor camp, he told me that an elderly Russian mother had given him a handkerchief made of white batiste. Maybe you will both be lucky, said the Russian woman, and you will come home soon and so will my son. Her son was the same age as Oskar Pastior and as far away from home as he was, but in the opposite direction, she said, in a penal battalion. Oskar Pastior had knocked on her door, a half-starved beggar wanting to trade a lump of coal for a little bit of food. She let him in and gave him some hot soup. And when she saw his nose dripping into the bowl, she gave him the white batiste handkerchief that no one had ever used before. With its a-jour border, and stems and rosettes precisely stitched with silk thread, the handkerchief was a thing of beauty that embraced as well as wounded the beggar. It was a combination: consolation made of batiste, and a silk-stemmed measure of his decrepitude. For the woman, Oskar Pastior was also a combination: an unworldly beggar in her house and a lost child in the world. Both of these personae were delighted and overwhelmed by the gesture of a woman who was two persons for him as well: an unknown Russian woman and the worried mother with the question: "Do you have a handkerchief?"

Ever since I heard this story I have had a question of my own: is "Do you have a handkerchief?" valid everywhere? Does it stretch halfway across the world in the snowy sheen between freezing and thawing? Does it pass between mountains and steppes to cross every border; can it reach all the way into a gigantic empire strewn with penal and labor camps? Is the question "Do you have a handkerchief?" impossible to get rid of, even with a hammer and sickle, even with all the camps of Stalinist re-education?

Although I have spoken Romanian for decades, it was only while talking with Oskar Pastior that I realized that the Romanian word for handkerchief is *batistă*. Another example of how sensual the Romanian language is, relentlessly driving its words straight to the heart of things. The material makes no detour, but presents itself ready-made as a handkerchief, as a *batistă*. As if all handkerchiefs, whenever and wherever, were made of batiste.

Oskar Pastior kept that handkerchief in his trunk as a reliquary of a double mother with a double son. And after five years of life in the camps he brought it home. Because his white batiste handkerchief was hope and fear. Once you let go of hope and fear, you die.

After our conversation about the white handkerchief I spent half the night pasting up a word collage for Oskar Pastior on a white card:

Dots are dancing here says Bea
you're coming into a long-stemmed glass of milk
linens in white gray-green zinc tub
nearly all materials
correspond upon delivery
look here
I am the trainride and
the cherry in the soapdish
never talk to strange men
or speak over the switchboard

When I went to see him later in the week to give him the collage, he said: *You have to paste on "For Oskar" as well.* I said: *Whatever I give to you is yours.* He said: *You have to paste it on, because the card may not know that.* I took it back home and pasted on: For Oskar. And then I gave it to him the following week, as if I had left the gate first without a handkerchief and now was back the second time with a handkerchief.

Another story also ends with a handkerchief:

My grandparents had a son named Matz. In the 1930s he was sent to study business in Timișoara, so that he could take over the family grain trade and grocery store. The school had teachers from the German Reich, real Nazis. Matz may have been trained as a merchant on the side, but mainly he was taught to be a Nazi—brainwashed according to plan. After he finished, Matz was a passionate Nazi, a changed person. He barked out anti-Semitic slogans, and was as unreachable as an imbecile. My grandfather rebuked him several times: he owed his entire fortune to the credit advanced by Jewish business friends. And when that didn't help, he boxed Matz on the ears several times. But the young man's faculty of reason had been erased. He played the village ideologue, bullying his peers who were dodging the front. Matz had a desk job with the Romanian army. Nevertheless he felt an urge to move from theory to practice, so he volunteered for the SS and asked to be sent to the front. A few months later he came home to marry. Wiser for having seen the crimes at the front, he used a then-current magical formula to escape the war for a few days. The magical formula was called: wedding leave.

My grandmother kept two photos of her son Matz far back in a drawer: a wedding photo and a death photo. The wedding picture shows a bride in white, taller than he by a hand, thin and earnest—a plaster Madonna. On her head was a wreath made of wax that looked like snow-flocked leaves. Next to her was Matz in his Nazi uniform, a soldier instead of a husband, a brideguard instead of a bridegroom. No sooner had he returned to the front, the death photo came. It shows a poor soldier torn to shreds by a mine. The death photo is hand-sized: in the middle of a black field a little gray heap of human remains can be seen resting on a white cloth. Against the black field the white cloth looks as small as a children's handkerchief, a white square with a strange design painted in the middle. For my grandmother this photo was a combination, too: on the white handkerchief was a dead Nazi, in her memory was a living son. My grandmother kept this double picture inside her prayer book for all her years. She prayed every day, and her prayers almost certainly had double meanings as well. Acknowledging the break from beloved son to fanatic Nazi, they probably beseeched God to perform the balancing act of loving the son and forgiving the Nazi.

My grandfather had been a soldier in the First World War. He knew what he was talking about when he said, often and embittered, in reference to his son Matz: *When the flags start to flutter, common sense slides right into the trumpet.* This warning also applied to the following dictatorship, which I experienced. Every day you could see the common sense of the profiteers, both big and little, sliding right into the trumpet. The trumpet I decided not to blow.

As I child, however, I did have to learn to play the accordion—against my will. Because at home we had the red accordion that had belonged to the dead soldier Matz. The straps were much too long for me. To keep them from slipping off my shoulders, the accordion teacher tied them together on my back with a handkerchief.

Can we say that it is precisely the smallest objects—be they trumpets, accordions, or handkerchiefs—which connect the most disparate things in life? That the objects are in orbit and that their deviations reveal a pattern of repetition—a vicious circle, or what we call in German a devil's circle. We can believe this, but not say it. Still, what can't be said can be written. Because writing is a silent act, a labor from the head to the hand. The mouth is skipped over. I talked a great deal during the dictatorship, mostly because I decided not to blow the trumpet. Usually my talking led to excruciating consequences. But the writing began in silence, there on the stairs, where I had to come to terms with more than could be said. What was happening could no longer be expressed in speech. At most the external accompaniments, but not the totality of the events themselves. That I could only spell out in my head, voicelessly, within the vicious circle of the words during the act of writing. I reacted to the deathly fear with a thirst for life. A hunger for words. Nothing but the whirl of words could grasp my condition. It spelled out what the mouth could not pronounce. I chased after the events, caught up in the words and their devilish circling, until something emerged I had never known before. Parallel to the reality, the pantomime of words stepped into action, without respect for any real dimensions, shrinking what was most important and stretching the minor matters. As it rushes madly ahead, this vicious circle of words imposes a kind of cursed logic on what has been lived. Their pantomime is ruthless and restive, always craving more but instantly jaded. The subject of dictatorship is necessarily present, because nothing can ever again be a matter of course once we have been robbed of nearly all ability to take anything for granted. The subject is there implicitly, but the words are what take possession of me. They coax the subject anywhere they want. Nothing makes sense anymore and everything is true.

When I was a staircase wit, I was as lonely as I had been as a child tending the cows in the river valley. I ate leaves and flowers so I would belong to them, because they knew how to live life and I didn't. I spoke to them by name: "milk thistle" was supposed to mean the prickly plant with milk in its stalk. But the plant didn't listen to the name "milk thistle." So I tried inventing names with neither "milk" nor "thistle": "thornrib," "needleneck." These made-up names uncovered a gap between the plant and me, and the gap opened up into an abyss: the disgrace of talking to myself and not to the plant. But the disgrace was good for me. I looked after the cows and the sound of the words looked after me. I felt:

Every word in your face,
Knows something of the vicious circle
But doesn't say it

The sound of the words knows that it has no choice but to beguile, because objects deceive with their materials, and feelings mislead with their gestures. The sound of the words, along with the truth this sound invents, resides at the interface, where the deceit of the materials and that of the gestures come together. In writing, it is not a matter of trusting, but rather of the honesty of the deceit.

Back then in the factory, when I was a staircase wit and the handkerchief was my office, I also looked up the beautiful word "treppenzins" or "ascending interest rate," when the interest rate for a loan ascends as if climbing a stair. (In German this is called "Stair Interest.") These ascending rates are costs for one person and income for another. In writing they become both, the deeper I delve into the text. The more that which is written takes from me, the more it shows what was missing from the experience that was lived. Only the words make this discovery, because they didn't know it earlier. And where they catch the lived experience by surprise is where they reflect it best. In the end they become so compelling that the lived experience must cling to them in order not to fall apart.

It seems to me that the objects don't know their material, the gestures don't know their feelings, and the words don't know the mouth that speaks them. But to be certain of our own existence, we need the objects, the gestures, and the words. After all, the more words we are allowed to take, the freer we become. If our mouth is banned, then we attempt to assert ourselves through gestures, even objects. They are more difficult to interpret, and take time before they arouse suspicion. They can help us turn humiliation into a type of dignity that takes time to arouse suspicion.

Early one morning, shortly before I emigrated from Romania, a village policeman came for my mother. She was already at the gate, when it occurred to her: "Do you have a handkerchief?" She didn't. Even though the policeman was impatient, she went back inside to get a handkerchief. At the station the policeman flew into a rage. My mother's Romanian was too limited to understand his screaming. So he left the office and bolted the door from the outside. My mother sat there locked up the whole day. The first hours she sat on his desk and cried. Then she paced up and down and began using the handkerchief that was wet with her tears to dust the furniture. After that she took the water bucket out of the corner and the towel off the hook on the wall and mopped the floor. I was horrified when she told me. *How can you clean the office for him like that* I asked. She said, without embarrassment: *I was looking for some work to pass the time. And the office was so dirty. Good thing I took one of the large men's handkerchiefs with me.*

Only then did I understand that through this additional, but voluntary, humiliation she had created some dignity for herself in her detention. I tried to find the words for it in a collage:

> I thought about the sturdy rose in my heart
> about the useless soul like a sieve
> but the keeper asked:
> who will gain the upper hand
> I said: saving the skin
> he shouted: the skin is
> nothing but a scrap of insulted batiste
> with no common sense

I wish I could utter a sentence for all those whom dictatorships deprive of dignity every day, up to and including the present—a sentence, perhaps, containing the word "handkerchief." Or else the question: "Do you have a handkerchief?"

Can it be that the question about the handkerchief was never about the handkerchief at all, but rather about the acute solitude of a human being?

Translated by Philip Boehm

3 Collage Poems
Herta Müller

2. "Milch ist der Zwilling." (Copyright Herta Müller. Collages by Herta Müller can be purchased from www.DrNice.net in various sizes as posters or wallpaper.)

3. "Im Gefälle zwischen." (Copyright Herta Müller.)

4. "Ich gehöre daheim." (Copyright by Herta Müller.)

5. "Als der Abriss des Mondes." (Copyright Herta Müller.)

4 Interview with Ernest Wichner

Valentina Glajar and Bettina Brandt

Ernest Wichner (b. 1952, Guttenbrunn, Romania) is a founding member of the Aktionsgruppe Banat. Wichner left Romania in 1975 and has been living in Berlin ever since. He is a writer, translator, and editor, and he has served as the director of the Literaturhaus (Literary Institute, Berlin) since 2003. In 2004, Wichner accompanied Herta Müller and the poet Oskar Pastior on a research trip to the Ukraine, where they visited the remainders of a campsite to which Pastior had been deported in 1945 and where he worked as a forced laborer until 1949. The interview was conducted in German via e-mail in March 2011 and then later translated into English.

Valentina Glajar: Mr. Wichner, Bettina and I would like to thank you for agreeing to participate in this interview and for sharing your experiences with our readers. As German writers from Banat, Romania, you and Herta Müller seem to have had a similar trajectory. You come from the same region, grew up in traditional ethnic German households, left your birthplaces to get an education, and studied German language and literature at the University of Timișoara. Do you recall when your paths first crossed? What was your impression of Herta Müller at the time?

Ernest Wichner: In September 1968, I went for a weekend to a parish festival in Nitzkydorf with a friend from high school; we were both attending the (German-language) Lenau Lyzeum in Timișoara, and on Sunday night at the ball this friend introduced me to Herta Müller. We danced together and talked about how we liked literature and both were writing poems. I remember clearly how Herta Müller complained that her girlfriends were teasing her because she wrote poetry. At the time, that came as a surprise to me because until then I had thought that only boys were picked on and ridiculed when they wrote poetry, that it was not considered very masculine. That girls or young women (Herta was fifteen and I was sixteen years old at the time) could be mocked for the same reason was news to me.

VG: You are one of the founding members of the Aktionsgruppe Banat, a group of German-Romanian writers that also included Richard Wagner, William Totok, Johann Lippet, Gerhard Ortinau, and Rolf Bossert. In 1992 you compiled and published texts by these authors from the early years in Romania in *Ein Pronomen wurde verhaftet*. Müller was not a member of your group but was closely associated with it. In what ways did Müller interact with the Aktionsgruppe? In what kind of group activities did Müller not participate—that is, what made her not a "member"? Please tell us about your first impressions regarding her very early poetic writings.

EW: Indeed, Herta Müller was not a member of the Aktionsgruppe Banat. That might have had to do with the fact that we were a group of young men who were regularly discussing politics, talking about the relationship between literature and society, about Marxism and Neomarxism. That is why we called ourselves the "Aktionsgruppe": we did indeed think that literature should have an activist impulse on society, should be willing to intervene. We wanted to change society's structures through literature's ability to change the structure of consciousness. These kinds of thoughts were not on Herta Müller's mind at the time. She came to our meetings and listened but never said anything. We also thought that her early poems, from the end of the sixties and the beginning of the seventies, were a little naive—were not what we called and considered "engaged." Besides, she probably thought that we were male chauvinists, know-it-alls. What we were saying was very interesting to her, but our attitude must have alienated her. A few years later—the Aktionsgruppe had been broken apart in the fall of 1975—they arrested Richard Wagner, Gerhard Ortinau, William Totok, and Gerhard Csejka, the literary critic from Bucharest who had been our editor at the *Neue Literatur* journal, and the Securitate in Timişoara interrogated them for several days. After they were released, they rearrested William Totok and detained him for eight months. These arrests were a clear signal that we could not carry on with the Aktionsgruppe as before. So my friends stopped using the name "Aktionsgruppe" and ceased all activities related to the literary circle. In January of that year, I emigrated to Germany. [Anton Sterbling came a few months later.]

Following these occurrences Herta Müller encountered the former members of the Aktionsgruppe at the Adam-Müller-Guttenbrunn society, the official literature circle of Timişoara which the Aktionsgruppe, until then, had not frequented because the society's discussions seemed provincial and narrow-minded to us. Friendships started that became important for Herta Müller's further development. Friendships with Richard Wagner, Rolf Bossert, Gerhard Ortinau, William Totok, and Johann Lippet. These friends made suggestions and supplied her with books. Richard Wagner helped her first prose publication along, gave her advice, occasionally served as an editor as well. Herta Müller can corroborate all of this. In fact, she talked about it at a crucial point during her talk at the [Nobel] banquet.

Bettina Brandt: From Herta Müller's early writings we get the sense that the ethnic German community in Romania kept very much to itself. Did this separation along ethnic lines determine the overall literary scene as well? Did German- and Romanian-language poets exclusively read at separate forums and publish in different journals? Was there no overlap at all? How did this develop over the decades?

EW: Yes, it determined other areas as well. The living conditions of the German minority were different from those of the Romanians—at least this was the case in the villages of the Banat where we all came from—and this difference affected the literary sector as well—that is, it produced different notions of literature. We young people came from the tradition of German literature and were concerned with Brecht and Gottfried Benn, the Wiener Gruppe (H. C. Artmann, Konrad Beyer, Gerhard Rühm, Ernst Jandl), Thomas Bernhard, Günter Grass, and Hans Magnus Enzensberger. We read American Beat poets along with Walter Benjamin [and] Ludwig Marcuse, as well as the literary correspondence between Heinrich Vormweg and Helmut Heißenbüttel. Meanwhile the Romanian authors of our generation wrote heavy-handed, metaphysically oriented literature that they themselves probably did not understand either. And their literary discussions (I once or twice attended a meeting of a literary circle of Romanian students) did not have a dialogical character; they were not communicating with each other but were simply promoting themselves. They were, or so it seemed to me, overloaded with cultural baggage that they could not grasp and were far removed from the reality in which they were living. They were creating a parallel universe for themselves, whereas we were trying to capture our reality in words and to have an impact with our texts. This was something that the Romanian intellectuals of those days simply despised. It was not until a generation later that the Romanians noticed what we had been trying to do in those days. Then, they too started to objectify poetic language, turned to daily concerns, and, occasionally, gave a critique of the political situation. From where I stand now I can fully understand this. The German tradition of Enlightenment, of bourgeois Realism, of the avant-garde movements of the first two decades of the twentieth century, of expressionism and the literature after 1945—Gruppe 47, concrete poetry, the politicization of literature in the second half of the sixties—all that had left a deep impression on us, but our Romanian colleagues came from a very different tradition. The only thing that connected us in those days was a comparable global youth culture: the Beatles, Rolling Stones, Jimmy Hendrix, Janis Joplin, long hair, and jeans—and, in Timișoara, the rock band Phoenix. Otherwise, we did not have much in common at all.

BB: You are not only a writer and an editor but, like Oskar Pastior, an important translator of Romanian literature into German as well. Both you and Pastior started translating only after having left Romania, correct? What role did and could literary translation play in Communist Romania? How did the official policy vis-à-vis translation change over the various decades of Communist rule?

EW: Oskar Pastior had already started translating in Romania. He translated one of Tudor Arghezi's collections of poetry, a volume of poetry by Lucian Blaga, and a prose collection by Panait Istrati. After 1968, when he did not return to Romania after a visit to Austria and Germany, he continued translating from the Romanian: Marin Sorescu, the early Romanian poems of Tristan Tzara, the oeuvre of the Romanian pre-avant-gardist Urmuz, almost all of Gellu Naum, and others. Pastior understood translating (particularly the texts that he loved such as the ones mentioned above or those of Velimir Chlebnikov, Gertrude Stein, Charles Baudelaire) as an integral part of his poetic writings. That is why he preferred translating poetry. This is also how and why I started to translate Romanian literature. In the early eighties Pastior was asked to translate the prose texts of Ștefan Bănulescu; then he asked me whether I would like to translate with him, the assumption being that he would translate two or three of the stories and that I would do the rest. I said yes and for the first time translated something while being under contract with a publisher. Soon thereafter Pastior was asked to translate M. Blecher. That request he immediately sent my way. That's how I started reading M. Blecher, really discovered the author for myself, and then edited and translated his three volumes of prose writings.

I am not really sure what the meaning of translation was in Communist Romania. It might have been a cultural alibi: a way to promote Romanian authors in the languages of the minorities. For a while there existed a certain cooperation between Romanian publishing houses and the German Democratic Republic (GDR). That meant that Romanian literature that was part of the official literary canon was first translated in Romania and then was published simultaneously in Romania and the GDR. Most of these publications were classics: Mihail Sadoveanu, Camil Petrescu, Liviu Rebreanu, George Călinescu, etc.

Some contemporary Romanian literature (books that were published after the dictatorship ended) is currently being translated in Germany and Austria; by contrast, interest in the quite substantial Romanian literature of the twentieth century is minor. As editor of the Romanian Library, planned as a series of twenty-four elegant, annotated volumes (prose, poetry, essays, theater), I would like to counteract this trend. The goal of the library, the first two volumes of which are scheduled for publication next year, is to serve as an introduction to Romanian literature from its beginnings until the year 2000. I am keen to find out whether there are still enough buyers for a series of books designed as a library in our digital age.

BB: The epigraph to Herta Müller's *Herztier* is a poem by Gellu Naum (1915–2001). Naum was one of the members of Infra Noir, a Romanian surrealist group that was operative until the early 1950s and wrote predominantly in French. Did the crackdown on the postwar avant-garde ring in the end of multilingual literature in Romania? If so, for how long?

EW: Gellu Naum, who was a very good friend of mine during the last fifteen years of his life, was the one who, with his moral attitude, his integrity, his seriousness, and his unassuming yet absolutely determined insistence on cultural and human standards, drew me close to Romania again once the dictatorship was overthrown; this Gellu Naum is in my eyes the most important poet of Romanian surrealism. He knew how to transform a literary and artistic movement from the beginning of the twentieth century into a mandatory way of life. He did so by opening himself up to the utopian demands the surrealists had had for humanity while simultaneously probing all that which opposed this humanity on a political and societal level and making this extreme standard part of his daily life. That's why he was for me, and probably also for Oskar Pastior and Herta Müller, the Romanian poet and intellectual whose actions knew no inconsistencies, who lived—in wretched poverty—and who thought as his free mind demanded it.

BB: Pastior translated the Naum fragment as follows:

... jeder hatte einen Freund in jedem Stückchen Wolke
so ist das halt mit Freunden wo die Welt voll Schrecken ist
auch meine Mutter sagte das ist ganz normal
Freunde kommen nicht in Frage
denk an seriösere Dinge

[... everybody has a friend in every little bit of cloud
that's how it is with friends when the world is full of terror
even my mother said that's pretty normal

friends are out of the question
consider more serious things]

Friendship and betrayal by friends are important themes in Herta Müller's writings. Was friendship also what kept Infra Noir together and betrayal what broke it apart?

EW: Yes, it was a similar situation, but based on what Gellu Naum told me, I daresay that he did not morally condemn that betrayal. He had significant problems and big arguments with Gherasim Luca; they were rivals, competitors, and yet also friends. Gherasim Luca must have deceived and betrayed him on more than one occasion, but Gellu Naum never gave up his underlying sympathy or his appreciation for a very special mind. He often talked about the highly problematic character of his friend but always added that I should not misunderstand him, that he did not blame Luca (whom he called "Zola," by the way) for that. Luca simply was the way he was; he, Naum, had to try to understand and accept that. *Basta.* What broke up the Bucharest surrealists was the barbaric regime, the illiteracy, the aggressive ignorance of the Communist cultural functionaries.

BB: Herta Müller combines literary and visual elements in her collages; in fact the principle of collage can be said to define Müller's writings in a certain way. Was there much interaction between the literary and the art scene in Communist Romania?

EW: No; when we were young, there was no interaction between the visual and the literary arts in Romania. Under Communist rule the visual arts were even more strictly regulated and, as a result, were of poorer quality, more amateurish than the literary arts. There would have been no point in trying to get out of our isolation by going down that particular road. For a while, though, Herta Müller wrote song texts for a rock band in Timișoara. But these texts had all been forbidden. To this day, I am not sure that the Securitate knew that the lyrics—written in Romanian—were actually hers. The rock band had submitted them to the examining authorities without providing the name of the author.

VG: One of the main themes in Müller's work is the repressive regime of Ceaușescu and the constant surveillance of the Communist secret police, the infamous Securitate. In a recent Romanian interview with Eugenia Vodă, Herta Müller states that the Securitate began to follow her because of her association with the Aktionsgruppe, although the first report in her file is dated March 1983. Among her friends and members of the Aktionsgruppe, you were the first one to leave Romania in 1975. Can you tell us how and why your group drew the attention of the Securitate?

EW: The simple fact that a bunch of high school graduates created a literary group was highly suspicious to the Securitate. On top of that, the group chose to call itself "Aktionsgruppe Banat"; they surely must have wondered what kind of "actions" such a group had in mind. The Securitate could not have known that by "action" we meant literature as an intervention. That our reference was Brecht and his idea of literature as something that intervenes in social processes, that we saw literature as a medium through which we hoped to achieve a change in consciousness, which in turn would provoke a changed worldview, and that only in a next step did we aim for actions and behaviors to match these views. Self-enlightenment, in other words, that should lead to enlightenment of the society as a whole and finally result in a critical attitude. The Securitate must have thought that we wanted to build bombs like West European terrorists. But soon they understood that we were talking about literature and that we were serious about it and were not going to be stopped.

Herta Müller appeared on the radar screen of the Securitate when she was not even writing; after graduation, when she worked as a translator in a factory (Technometal) in Timișoara, the Securitate attempted to recruit her as an informant, but Müller refused. That enraged them. How could this insignificant person simply say no and not give in? Almost everybody else was simply scared stiff. That was around 1977/1978. And because the Securitate really started terrorizing her after that, she began writing short prose texts to affirm her existence. In order not to lose herself, to understand what was happening to her. With these prose texts in hand she approached those few former members of the Aktionsgruppe Banat who remained in Timișoara—Richard Wagner, Gerhard Ortinau, Johann Lippet, and William Totok—and they encouraged her to write more, suggested titles of books, and persuaded her to read from her writings in public. Her first collection of stories, *Niederungen* [*Nadirs*], was published with Kriterion Publishers (in a censored version) in Bucharest in 1982. After the book was published, certain Banat Swabians felt that they had been vilified (in the story "The Swabian Bath," for instance), exposed as former Nazis ("The Funeral Sermon"), or that their lived reality had been disrespected and ridiculed. So they wrote letters to the local newspaper, *Neue Banater Zeitung*, that were promptly published. The Securitate was, of course, following it all and likely had something to do with it. Be that as it may, the Securitate then asked one of its informers, Thomas Schleich, who was himself an author and who wrote for the *Neue Banater Zeitung*, to critically evaluate the *Niederungen* collection. He delivered exactly what the Securitate had been hoping for: a statement proclaiming that *Niederungen* was the product of an anti-socialist attitude. It ridiculed not just the Banat Swabians (that would have suited the Securitate just fine, in fact), but also the village functionaries, the state, the party, and its institutions. Herta Müller's Securitate file starts with the evaluation of this book, written shortly after its publication, and keeps track of her until the very end of the Communist regime. That is, even after 1987, after her emigration to Germany, Herta Müller continued to be on their radar screen and in their radius of action. They sent a girlfriend to her in Berlin who had been given the assignment to spy out her Berlin apartment, and she showed up equipped with a second house key.... Müller was sent threatening letters, and during her readings in Germany people showed up who were verbally abusive. Herta Müller was an extremely important person for the Securitate. Mostly because she would time and again speak up in Germany about the criminal and inhumane activities of the Romanian regime. She helped organize the Aktionstage Romania, was one of the speakers at that event, was successful in getting protest and informational meetings of this kind into the West German news. That shocked the rulers in Bucharest and hurt them. So they did everything they could to silence this person. Luckily, the regime did not last that much longer. The Romanians silenced Ceaușescu, and Herta Müller, somewhat relieved, could dedicate herself to her literary projects.

VG: Herta Müller and her then husband Richard Wagner left Romania in February 1987, about twelve years after your emigration. How difficult was it to stay in touch during this period?

EW: During those years, I visited Romania a couple of times; in 1983 my wife and I brought Herta Müller's *Niederungen* out of the country and passed it along to the Rotbuch Verlag Berlin, which then published the collection in 1984. That same year, Herta Müller was awarded the Aspekte Prize for the best literary debut in Germany and was given permission to travel to Germany to accept the prize. The next year, the Romanian authorities did not allow her to participate in the Ingeborg Bachmann Prize competition, and as a result Herta Müller put pressure on the Securitate in Timișoara; she reasoned that if they did not let her travel to Germany, the German journalists would travel to Romania, and then she asked the Securitate whether that would be preferable. It was obvious that this would be far worse. If journalists were to actually show up in Timișoara, they would be able to see a lot more than what they would learn from Herta Müller. So they gave her permission to travel a couple more times. On these occasions, we would always get together. Sometimes she also would stay with us in Berlin.

BB: Can you tell us about events and exhibits at your Literaturhaus that have addressed Herta Müller's traumatic experience with the Securitate for a German audience? What has the reception been of these exhibits and events?

EW: Whenever Herta Müller published a new book, we invited her to do a reading at the Literaturhaus. In 2010 we held an exhibition that portrayed the milieu from which Herta Müller came, showed the trajectory of her personal and literary development, her relation to authors of the Aktionsgruppe, and her friendship with Roland Kirsch, who remained in Timișoara after Herta Müller left the country and was probably killed by the Securitate in 1989. The exhibition placed her books within the political situation in Communist Romania and in the context of her commitment to those discriminated against (like the Roma) after the so-called revolution—in short it portrayed Herta Müller as a political writer. On the audio guide for the exhibition Herta Müller herself explained most of the exhibited items and led the visitors through her life and her works.

VG: Both you and Müller decided to settle down in Berlin. What is Berlin's special fascination for German writers from Romania?

EW: When I came to [West] Berlin, I was interested in the political and cultural situation in East Berlin as well; I wanted to know how GDR authors of my generation were thinking, if they were critical vis-à-vis the regime, what shape their criticism took, whether there was a possible generational affinity between us, those who had grown up under communism in Romania and the younger GDR writers. I often went to East Berlin and knew, for instance, Uwe Kolbe, from those days, but also Sascha Anderson, who organized a reading for me once in somebody's home, to which almost one hundred people came. That was one reason. The other reason was that after arriving in Berlin, I decided I wanted to study German literature and political science at the Free University. In those years West Berlin was much more open than other cities in Germany. Most writers actually lived in Berlin, and there were always many interesting cultural events. For anybody interested in contemporary culture, West Berlin was the obvious place to be. That's how my friends in Romania saw it as well. It was an easy decision. Berlin was the metropolis, and that's still true today, though in a different way, of course, then in the seventies and eighties.

VG: Enter Oskar Pastior. He was your dear friend until his death in 2006. He is also considered one of the most important German writers from Romania next to Herta Müller. If you were to describe Pastior's influence on German-Romanian writers, what would stand out in your mind?

EW: Oskar Pastior was the poet who showed us the possibilities inherent in language, what can be thought and formulated when you take the singularity of language seriously and don't simply reduce language to a means of communication and representation. If you go beyond mimesis. Pastior, in his very own way, did not reproduce the world but created it through his poetry. That was his explicit goal because reproduction—that's how he saw it—is always false, implies a lie—namely, the belief in the possibility to reproduce or duplicate an extra-linguistic entity in language without producing difference or while only introducing minimal difference. This is true even though the arbitrary character of language, as well as its material side (sign, sound), point in a completely different direction—namely, to musicality, to a free form that gives shape to itself as it arises out of the material. As an OULIPO-author, he loved the constraints of poetic rules and was aware that these could only stay productive and fresh if he also went against these constraints or outsmarted them.[1] From Pastior one could learn how to catch thinking by the tail the very moment

6. Herta Müller and Oskar Pastior on former labor camp site in Ukraine, 2004. (Copyright Ernest Wichner.)

thinking was changing direction. That was liberating and encouraging. And now, when I am reading his texts, I am dealing with something altogether different from *l'art pour l'art*. I always see Pastior himself in these texts. I see that this was also a way to transform a life into a text.

VG: When Müller expressed interest in writing about the deportation of German-Romanians to the Russian labor camps, you proposed a meeting with Pastior, who had been himself deported and spent five years in a camp in Ukraine. Can you recall the beginning of their collaboration on Müller's latest novel, Atemschaukel [*The Hunger Angel*]?

EW: Herta Müller had talked with a number of people about their deportations but was disappointed or frustrated because they could not recall the specifics. Their experiences had been superseded by others or had simply been repressed. In Romania it had after all been forbidden to talk about the deportations.

I knew that Oskar Pastior remembered his time in the camp in great detail—those five years were extremely important to him. He was seventeen, a high school student, when he was sent to the camp. He experienced the camp not just as a labor slave, but also as someone who was learning

7. Herta Müller and Oskar Pastior in Ukraine, 2004. (Copyright Ernest Wichner.)

something. His memories were shaped in a different way than those of people who did not want to learn anything anymore, who did not want to experience the world any longer, who simply wanted to survive the camps. And when the three of us were on our way to Lana [southern Tirol/Italy] for some literary events, I moderated their discussion about his deportation. Thereafter, they met every week until Oskar's death and worked together for several hours. That's how the idea to write a book together came about, although that project was not realized because of Oskar Pastior's sudden death on October 4, 2006, in Frankfurt am Main.

VG: You witnessed the unfolding of the Müller-Pastior collaboration and even accompanied them on a trip to Ukraine in 2004. There is an intriguing photograph you took of Pastior and Müller on this trip, presumably in the vicinity of a former camp site. Müller and Pastior seem to be in perfect harmony with the environment, smiling and picking flowers on a beautiful green meadow. Can you describe the circumstances of this photograph and place it in the larger context of the trip?

EW: This picture shows a part of the former camp site with the wooden barracks in which the deportees used to sleep. A local told us that the barracks were still in use as housing for laborers working in a nearby coke factory as late as the 1970s. The relatively young vegetation confirms that. Those trees are not very old. And in the background you see a slanted pole to which electric wires were once attached. We had been looking for quite some time for this particular part of the camp, which must have been no more than eight or ten minutes from the factory. And as soon as we found it, Herta Müller and Oskar Pastior walked straight into the high grass, started scanning the ground in the hopes of finding something that had been left behind. Of course, they did not find anything anymore. So they just picked some flowers.

VG: Günter Grass's *Im Krebsgang* [*Crabwalk*] was credited with making it acceptable to talk about German suffering in the aftermath of World War II, especially about the flight and expulsions from Poland and Czechoslovakia. Do you think Müller's book will have a similar effect of shining light on the deportation of German-Romanians? What do you think would be the shortcomings and traps of such a reception?

EW: Independent of the theme or the material, Herta Müller's book *Atemschaukel* is an eminently important book for literary reasons, simply because of the way in which it is narrated. Of course, I don't want to separate the sentence structure from the theme of the narrative. The book talks about a historical event, fills it in with details, the suffering, the hunger, the cold, the humane and the inhumane. To address this topic was perhaps taboo while the systems were still confronting each other, certainly under communism. Today, it is no longer taboo. For Herta Müller this historical event had been transformed into literature because of her mother, who, like Oskar Pastior, was deported for five years. And because this mother acquired maxims from her camp experience that she applied later in life, including educational principles to which her daughter was then exposed. That's how that historical event became a very personal topic about which she wanted to write, independent of how a literary or political public might feel about this.

Many times elderly people have come up to Herta Müller after one of her readings to thank her for having given them back their history and their experiences. That might be true, but probably the book tells more because it depicts people in extreme situations, presents basic survival strategies, scenes of comfort and of hate, affections and indifferences, and gives you an idea of the whole spectrum of human behavior in all its variations. And this level of experience applies to many different terrible places in many countries. You can see that in the reception of the book, for example, in Poland, in Hungary, but also in Spain and in other countries. Probably even those who were locked up in camps during the Chinese Cultural Revolution might find something of their own stories in it here and there. And in these post-ideological times, the question of whether the book was abusively appropriated fades into the background; it is finally allowed to be what it is: further testimony of the barbaric challenge to the human condition, as it happened so often in all kinds of camps, political camps.

VG: Two of Müller's most important losses in recent years relate to Pastior: his death before they could conclude this project and then the Oskar Pastior she knew when she found out that Pastior had been a Securitate informer in the 1960s. By the time Stefan Sienerth's study revealed that IM [informer] "Stein Otto" was indeed Oskar Pastior, you and Müller had known about Pastior's collaboration for some time. How did you find out, and why did you keep silent about it?

EW: We did not know that Oskar Pastior had been working as the informant "Stein Otto" for the Romanian secret service since June 1961. We only found out about it through the research of Stefan Sienerth. Then I immediately set out for Bucharest and looked at the file myself in order to learn what Oskar Pastior had not told us. But also to understand the circumstances that finally lead to Oskar Pastior's signing of a formal obligation in 1961. Herta Müller and I did not keep to ourselves what we found out but talked about it publicly as soon as we knew. I immediately wrote a long article in the *Frankfurter Allgemeine Zeitung* and described what I had learned from the files. And I will continue with my research until I have learned everything that there is to know. As matters stand right now though, this is not a final assessment; I have the impression that Oskar Pastior was a rather harmless informant. He had been pressured into service; was afraid that if he said no, he would go to jail; and produced rather meaningless reports. Currently, I am familiar with four of his reports. While reading through the files, though, I have become acquainted with eager informants who wrote dozens of reports. This whole situation has still to be explained in more detail.

VG: While Müller's initial reaction to this news was shock and grief, she was also apologetic as she referred to her friend's sexual orientation and his fear of being imprisoned as explanation or justification for his collaboration. She is, however, known for being a strong and severe critic of those who collaborated with the Securitate. In fact, she has revealed the identity of several of her informers, who now live in Germany. You have now taken several trips to CNSAS [Consiliul Național pentru Studierea Arhivelor Securității; the National Council for the Study of the Archives of the Secret Service] to research Pastior's file. Why and how is Pastior's file different? Should it be treated differently?

EW: This question would require a very long answer that would go beyond this context. An abbreviated version: through intensive study of the dossier I learned things that ought to be considered and brought to light. A small example that has to do with us—those born after 1950. We who grew up in the so-called period of thaw at the end of the sixties were relatively untouched by Stalinist terror. If somebody of our generation became an informer, then this was no longer done with the fear and under the same conditions of terror that had existed in the fifties and sixties. Somebody who became an informant in 1970 or in the mid-seventies did this because of his own interests as well (career, apartment, potential travel); if you refused to cooperate, you were not even removed from the university. The only disadvantage you might have had was that your career did not take off or that you did not get a certain job that you would have liked or you would not be allowed to travel abroad. An informant from this period is, in my eyes, more reproachable than one who was recruited a decade earlier, when he still had to fear that saying no would result in drastic punishment. From that point of view, Werner Söllner, who became an informant at the beginning of the seventies, is in my eyes more morally compromised than Oskar Pastior. I am not saying that to make excuses for Oskar Pastior but in order to point out that not all IMs are necessarily the same. There were different laws and different types of threatening situations at different times. In the eighties, the repressive apparatus started to develop striking similarities with that of the fifties again. In those years, the dangers associated with not collaborating grew again. The methods of the Securitate became more drastic as well. Of course, then we also have to look at what each particular informant did, with what ethos he did it, and what he actually did. Was he remunerated for it? Did he suffer under it? How did others in his position—other informants, for instance—act? That will produce a rough sketch of what happened in a certain time period, how it happened, and what it might mean from a moral point of view. But in this realm it is easier for me to sketch an outline of the problem than to provide conclusive answers.

VG: From Nitzkydorf to Stockholm 2009: You were there when Herta Müller received the highest honor in literature. One cannot help but imagine the long and improbable road from the small isolated Banat-Swabian village of Nitzkydorf to Stockholm to receive the Nobel Prize. What went through your mind as you witnessed this extraordinary event?

EW: I remember being very impressed with the seriousness and the intellectual presence with which Herta Müller mastered it all. Müller pretty much spoke in her talk about what went through my head in that moment. That the road from herding cows in a valley to Stockholm's City Hall had been bizarre and that she saw the Nobel Prize winner standing next to the cowherd. Something else went through my mind as well: we set out at an early age to enlighten ourselves, to do what we were doing in a responsible way and as best we could. We did not intend to meet the king of Sweden. Had we ever wanted that, we would not be standing here now.

Translated by Bettina Brandt

Notes

1. OULIPO (Ouvroir de Littérature Potentielle, or Laboratory of Potential Literature) is a collective of writers, mathematicians, engineers, and "pataphysicians" founded by Raymond Queneau in 1960. Though most OULIPO members write in French (Georges Perec, Jacques Roubaud, Queneau, Valerie Beaudouin), the group has also included Oskar Pastior, Harry Mathews, and Italo Calvino. The group's official French website can be found under www.oulipo.net.

Works Cited

Müller, Herta. *The Hunger Angel*. Trans. Philip Boehm. New York: Metropolitan Books, 2012.

———. *Nadirs*. Trans. Sieglinde Lug. Lincoln: University of Nebraska Press, 1999.

Sienerth, Stefan. "Ich habe Angst vor unerfundenen Geschichten. Zur *Securitate*-Akte Oskar Pastiors." *Spiegelungen. Zeitschrift für deutsche Kultur und Geschichte Südosteuropas* 3 (2010): 236–71.

Wichner, Ernest, ed. *Ein Pronomen wurde verhaftet: Die frühen Jahre in Rumänien—Texte der Aktionsgruppe Banat*. Frankfurt: Suhrkamp, 1992.

Part 2 Totalitarianism, Autofiction, Memory

5 When Dictatorships Fail to Deprive of Dignity

Herta Müller's "Romanian Period"

Cristina Petrescu

Twenty years after the demise of Communist regimes in Eastern Europe, Herta Müller still dedicates her writings to "all those whom dictatorships deprive of dignity every day," as she declared in her Nobel Prize lecture. While her adopted country, the Federal Republic of Germany, proposed Müller for the award, it was her country of birth, Romania, that had inspired the writings that made her worthy of such a prize. Indeed it is her traumatic past under Nicolae Ceaușescu's Communist yet nationalist dictatorship that this internationally acclaimed author constantly and obsessively revisits in her writings. This chapter aims at reconstructing the "Romanian period" in Herta Müller's life and its significance for her development as a writer. In other words, it explores her identity-shaping experiences growing up under a non-democratic regime that imposed and maintained its political dominance—as all non-democratic regimes do—with the instrumental support of its secret police, the Securitate.

The chapter consists of two parts, which chronologically correspond to the successive sociocultural environments with which Müller primarily interacted while in Romania: the Swabian rural community of Nitzkydorf in the Banat and the group of ethnic German writers in Timişoara, the capital city of this region. Both environments shaped Müller's identity as a person and a writer, but each in a radically different way: while she became alienated from the first, she developed a lifelong solidarity with individuals with whom she intensely related in the second. Two types of sources contribute to this analysis: Müller's autobiographically inspired writings and her Securitate file. I argue that the author's relocation to another sociocultural environment did not terminate her relation with the earlier identity-conferring milieu: it was after moving to the urban setting of Timişoara that she wrote on her incompatibility with the rural Banat-Swabian village, and it was after immigrating to Germany that she authored most of her works inspired by the "Romanian period." Furthermore, I analyze Müller's entanglements with the Securitate as repeated intrusions into her life beginning in 1983, as well as retroactive and successive reevaluations of her past as it is emerging from the secret police documents.

Perhaps the concept of *eccezionale normale* [normal exception], developed by the Italian school of microhistory, can best describe Müller's "Romanian period."[1] According to proponents of this school, among them prominent historian Carlo Ginzburg, a small-scale analysis focusing on an individual atypical for his time and culture allows for large-scale assumptions precisely because the exceptionality of such an individual reveals normal social practices or cultural belief systems otherwise obscured.[2] Although the microhistorical approach was designed for and applied to remote periods of the past with scarce sources, this method can equally be used to study the recent past. Most cases analyzed by microhistorians have examined individuals whose deviations from the average stirred the attention of the authorities. Thus these small-scale analyses focusing on such out-of-the-ordinary individuals shed light on the institutions of power and their practices.[3] Similarly Müller's case—an atypical personality among intellectuals in Romania whose conduct attracted the interest of the Securitate—can reveal the routine practices of the Romanian secret police usually obscured in the documents produced by this institution.

Although not openly critical of Ceauşescu's dictatorship, Müller and her fellow German writers in Timişoara took an active stance in defending the liberty of expressing their ideas. Her case was a double "normal exceptional" one: she was not only atypical among the writers in the German minority, but she was atypical among all intellectuals in Romania as well. Even when refraining from supporting the regime, most such individuals limited themselves to remaining good professionals who tackled issues that did not challenge official dogmas. They withdrew into culture in order to avoid politics and, implicitly, troublesome entanglements with the Securitate, as Müller expressed it in a recent public debate with prominent Romanian intellectuals that turned into a cultural reference moment of post-communism.[4] Toward the end of Romanian communism, the regime no longer employed large-scale repression to destroy any resistance as it had done in the late 1940s and 1950s. After the mid-1960s such measures were gradually replaced with softer but more perverse methods of control: a huge network of undercover informants worked with the secret police in order to put an end to any revolt before it ever had time to develop.[5] Terror was no longer necessary to keep the new regime in power since most individuals simply had learned to conform and thus assured the functioning of the system.[6]

Nowadays, when Ceauşescu has ironically emerged as a symbol of Romania (like Dracula, with whom he is frequently compared), it has become commonplace to criticize his dictatorship. Few, however, can actually bear witness to the monstrousness of his regime on the basis of their personal traumas. Müller's direct and unmediated experience has given her a personal insight into the perverse blend of coercion and cooptation that characterized Romanian communism in the 1980s. While documents of the secret police never recorded acts of harassment or brutality, Müller's exceptional case illustrates that such selectively applied brutality epitomized the repressive essence of all Communist regimes, and it did not actually disappear once control was assured through methods other than sheer terror. Moreover, as this chapter aims to show, she is a testifying witness to the barbarities committed by all dictatorships, which arbitrarily erase the universal values of humanity and transform some human beings into accomplices ready to violate the liberty of others.

An Identity Rejected: The Banat Swabian Community

Müller's writings epitomize a troublesome relation with both of her homelands: the Banat-Swabian and the Romanian Communist state. It was the double rejection of both the false pretenses of her native community and the duplicity of the existence under dictatorship that deprived Müller of a homeland, pushing her to emigrate to a country where she could freely write about the trauma of the dispossessed. This trauma has become a leitmotif of her writings, while German has remained the main language in which she expresses it. "Beide Heimatbegriffe waren provinziell, xenophobisch und arrogant" [Both notions of homeland were provincial, xenophobic, and arrogant] (König 29). Yet Müller agrees with Jorge Semprún that the native language cannot be a homeland either if there is no shared meaning of its words: "Er weiß um das minimale innere Einverständnis mit den gesagten Inhalten, das man braucht, um dazuzugehören" [He (Semprún) knows about the minimal interiorized consensus one needs in order to belong] (König 30).[7]

Müller's native community descends from the German-speaking colonists who settled in the Banat in the eighteenth century. Currently part of Romania, this region had a history marked by successive border changes that occurred since the middle of the sixteenth century as a result of military confrontations between the Ottomans and the Austrians. After the inclusion of the Banat in the Habsburg empire in 1718, the new authorities encouraged the establishment of German-speaking colonists in this border region. Ever since, these settlers have referred to themselves as Swabians, while carefully preserving a distinct cultural identity through maintaining specific customs and traditions.[8] In the Banat, Swabians lived alongside, but not together with, Romanians, Serbs, or Hungarians, mostly in villages overwhelmingly if not entirely dominated by their own ethnic group. The cultural heterogeneity of this region was severely affected by the policies of the Communist regime, which aimed at homogenizing the nation by all means, ranging from forced assimilation to the encouraged emigration of minority groups. Thus by 1989 almost the entire German community of the Banat (and in the rest of Romania) had immigrated to the FRG. Today it survives only in the memory of the local people.[9]

Inspired by her personal experience of the native village universe, much of Müller's early fiction symbolizes her departure from the rural Swabian community with which she no longer identified. She made the discrepancy between essence and appearance, generated by a manifold and mutilating transformation of these villages, the focus of her early writings. The Swabian rural community in the Banat that she depicts was trapped between its own conservatism and the changes imposed from Bucharest; between its past, marked by Nazi collaborationism, and its present, marked by yet another dictatorship; between its ostentatious traditions and a distorted modernization promoted by the Communist regime. With such a perception of "socialist reality," Müller's literary debut, *Niederungen*, a prose collection published in a censored version in 1982, annoyed the Communist authorities despite the fact that it was written in German, a language little understood by the Romanian majority. From the early eighties onward her private and professional life was entangled with the Securitate, an institution that over time became an everyday presence in her existence.[10]

Müller's pessimistic perspective and critical fictionalized observations about her native rural community stood in sharp contrast to all other postwar literary writings dedicated to the rural world in Romania. The genre of rural fiction in Communist Romania can be divided into two main groups. The first group describes the grim reality of peasant existence before the Communist takeover and as such continues a literary trend that dates back to the early nineteenth century. Like Müller's writings, these were pessimistic and critical, yet their authors used such a literary strategy with a completely different purpose: to emphasize implicitly the great progress that peasant life had undergone since communism.[11] The second group can be considered pure propaganda literature since it was introduced and supported by the regime and focused on the process of collectivization. Unlike the first group of texts, which did indeed reflect upon the drama of the pre-Communist peasantry struggling with an abject poverty that had been overcome in more economically developed countries, the second group heavily distorted the subsequent drama of collectivization, in which the peasantry was forced—through the use of violence and terror—to abandon its private property, in this case its land.[12] Negative aspects were also included in the officially approved stories of collectivization, as this process implied a struggle between old and new mentalities among the peasantry. However, these negative aspects illustrated the difficulties that had been overcome and not the deplorable state of villages under the Communist regime as in Müller's writings.

The political, social, and economic changes that the Communist regime enforced upon Müller's village were the same as everywhere else in Romania, but the perception of these changes among the German rural communities in the Banat had its specificities. Above all, the decline of the villages in the Banat was more extreme than elsewhere. Until the Communist takeover, the peasants of the Banat—Romanians, Hungarians, and Germans alike—had been in fact the wealthiest of all of the peasants in Greater Romania, especially when compared to the historical regions of Wallachia and Moldavia. For the local Banat peasant this wealth was a source of pride, regardless of the ethnic group to which he belonged.[13] With the intrusion of the party-state in the village and the introduction of collective farming, the traditional way of organizing work in the countryside was fundamentally shaken. At the same time, in the Banat urban migration was the lowest in all of Communist Romania because agricultural productivity there was the highest in the country.[14] Thus most German communities isolated themselves in their rural settings and lived as if the Communist rule could not touch them, while in fact the regime profoundly affected their daily routines.[15]

Müller's writings fully capture the various faces of the decay of the German communities. Mediocrity, nepotism, poor organization, deficient sanitation, and general impoverishment characterized the social and economic state of the village in the author's view. The local village officials in Müller's writing look as if they had emerged from a Hieronymus Bosch painting. Furthermore, from those in the local administration to those in agricultural enterprises, all officials were related and all supported each other to maintain their dominance in village affairs. The farmers' markets, once full of animals to be sold, now were mostly empty. The fields, once consistently producing crops, became useless for agriculture. Schoolchildren were educated only through punishment. Needless to say, such a literary characterization heavily contrasted with the official state views, which stressed only the benefits of collectivization and the increased standard of living in rural areas. It was this derogatory view of the peasantry in a "state of workers and peasants" that provoked the Communist authorities, who in 1983 ordered the initiation of Müller's constant surveillance by the secret police.[16] After Rotbuch published Müller's uncensored version of *Niederungen* [*Nadirs*] in 1984, her visibility increased dramatically in the FRG, and as a result, the secret police sharpened their surveillance because a person conducting "hostile" actions "against the socialist order" obviously required "enhanced measures meant to annihilate her influence inside and outside the country."[17]

Müller's critical perspective on the German village went beyond displaying the dysfunctions of the Communist system in the countryside. The blend of conservatism and duplicity that marked these German peasant-dominated communities troubled Müller far more. As the regime's drive for industrialization and urbanization touched these rural minority communities only marginally, their members made a virtue out of the preservation of the premodern way of life. Most rural Germans in Romania, many of whom could not speak the language of the majority, remained connected to their traditions, their rituals and ancient customs. Far from considering this conservatism a virtue, Müller insightfully perceived her village as a world of deceit, where tradition was no longer capable of maintaining morality, while Communist ethics were corrupting everyone. Even her (fictionalized) family was depicted as deeply touched by this general loss of virtues, which led in practically every house to the birth of illegitimate children. Müller also exposed the supposedly "higher standards" of the German minority (as compared to the other ethnic communities in Romania), a source of pride among Germans, as shallow and deceptive.[18]

Once Müller was in Berlin, the Securitate successfully activated some Romanian Germans in the FRG against the author; they not only criticized Müller's books but also wrote her insulting letters, explaining that she was unwanted in West Germany.[19] The Swabians in the Banat, who gradually left Romania for West Germany during the Communist period, strived to preserve their identity in the FRG, their new "homeland," by reproducing their archaic culture and traditions at a time when these were fading away everywhere else. Their identity was not just marked by folklore, but also by a problematic relation with their recent past. During World War II the

Germans in Romania acted as part of the larger German nation, and most men in the Swabian communities fought for the Third Reich, as Müller's father had done. As Hitler's allies, the Romanians also contributed substantially to the German war effort and the Holocaust until Romania switched sides in August 1944. However, in the postwar settlement the Romanians turned, unwillingly, into allies of the Soviet Union. Thus antifascism in Communist Romania—like in the former GDR—became part of the official ideology.

However, a genuine process of *Vergangenheitsbewältigung* [coming to terms with the past], which could have adequately defined responsibilities for past crimes, never happened in Communist Romania, as it did in a democracy like the FRG.[20] Accordingly the postwar pro-Soviet regime in Bucharest collectively labeled only ethnic Germans in Romania as Nazi collaborators, while completely obliterating the contribution of ethnic Romanians to the horrors of World War II. Thus many German-Romanians ended up in the Gulag without a trial, as did the author's mother.[21] Others, however, only switched allegiance from one dictatorship to another, without ever assuming responsibility for their past. Nevertheless, members of this community managed to whitewash their doubly problematic past and reemerge in the FRG as victims of communism seeking political asylum. Moreover, some of its members assumed the role of informants for the Romanian secret police and continued to collaborate with this institution to discredit Müller's character and her writings even after immigration.[22]

This mixture of conformism and duplicity that her native community adopted in order to survive historical adversities determined Müller's distancing from her Swabian origins and the collective identity attached to it. Her early writings worked as a means of expressing this symbolic rejection, while her actual departure took place quite early in her life, once she realized that only leaving could save her from the entrapment in a rotten community that was decaying under a veneer of civility. As she put it in the Banquet Speech of December 10, 2009: "I started to read books. The village seemed more and more to me like a box in which a person was born, married and died. All people in the village . . . were born old. I thought: sooner or later you have to leave the village if you want to grow young." In Ceaușescu's Romania, urban migration was a widespread social phenomenon triggered by a Communist type of modernization, characterized by rapid industrialization and subsequent urbanization. It was a phenomenon that gave birth to the new social category of "workers with a rural background," individuals in search of a better life in an urban setting but unable to adapt to urban habits. Unlike most of these internal migrants, Müller did not move to the city of Timişoara for economic reasons but to escape the guarded conformism of her rural community. Once in the city, however, she soon discovered the supervised compliance imposed by the Communist regime. Nevertheless, with the help of books and friends, she also discovered a new identity.[23]

An Identity Assumed: The Literary Circle Aktionsgruppe Banat

Müller's testimony of the abuses of Ceauşescu's dictatorship, reiterated in all her writings after leaving Romania, turned her into an internationally acclaimed author. Her direct experience of dealing with the secret police in Timişoara made her a victim of human rights abuses. It was Müller's association with the writers' circle known since 1972 as Aktionsgruppe Banat that helped her resist the harassment of the secret police while simultaneously increasing the interest of the Securitate in her case. "These friends were essential. Had it not been for them I would not have been able to stand the repression," Müller confessed in her Nobel Prize speech (chapter 2 in this volume).

While in Romania, Müller and the German writers associated with this circle were not actual dissidents in the way Western journalists use this term to refer to individuals who openly criticized the East European dictatorships. The writers of the Aktionsgruppe Banat did not articulate an explicit criticism of the Communist regime but tried to express their own thoughts rather than simply reproducing the ideological views of the party, as many writers were willing to do in order to get published. In countries with noticeable dissident networks the writings of the Aktionsgruppe would not have attracted any attention. In Romania, where dissidents were rare, the atypical views of the literary circle drew the constant surveillance of the secret police. In its malevolent endeavors, the Securitate received the support and assistance of fellow German-Romanian writers, especially those from older and more established generations, from whom the younger Aktionsgruppe Banat had distanced itself. Actually this group stood out in the literary landscape of Romania when compared to both the earlier generations of German writers, with whom it had an antagonistic relationship, as well as to the writers of the Romanian community, with whom it scarcely interacted. Inspired by the corresponding generation of 1968 in West Germany, the Aktionsgruppe Banat criticized the older generation of writers in the German minority because none of them had ever assumed any responsibility for the fascist past.[24] This attitude also made the group different from the Romanian majority, which never revolted against the fascist past of its parents. As already mentioned, the monopoly on the relation with that most recent part of history belonged to the Communist regime, which dealt with it undemocratically—namely, by externalizing guilt and assigning responsibilities collectively: not Romanians but solely Germans were blameworthy for past crimes. It is very telling that according to such a frame of reading the past, Müller and the writers from the Aktionsgruppe Banat were identified by the Securitate as "nationalist Germans," while the Romanian writers put under surveillance were included in the category "art and culture."[25]

The contrast with the Romanian writers had another, more important dimension. Obviously the literary milieu of the Romanian ethnic majority was very diverse and included authors ranging from Ceaușescu's court poets to open dissidents. In the early 1970s, when the Aktionsgruppe Banat established itself as a circle of writers promoting greater freedom of expression, barely any Romanian was taking a critical stance against the regime. Dissent among Romanians developed only much later; after a first attempt at organizing a human rights movement was aborted in 1977,[26] it took until the 1980s for several isolated intellectuals to publicly speak out against the Communist dictatorship, while collective protests emerged only in 1989.[27] However, no collaboration in dissent was ever established between the different ethnic groups living in Romania. As already pointed out, the majority of the Romanian intellectuals, from writers to other professional categories, adopted a passive attitude toward the regime, neither openly supportive nor publicly in conflict with the official views. After 1989 these intellectuals retrospectively called this strategy "resistance through culture," which was in their view a silent but effective rejection of the party apparatchiks' guidance in literary and artistic creations.[28] This strategy emerged in reaction to the strengthening of official supervision in the field of culture initiated by Ceaușescu at the beginning of the 1970s.[29] The worst consequence of this self-assumed risk of resisting the cultural policy of the regime was professional marginalization, as upward mobility in any career was not merit-based but controlled by the party-state.[30] The secret police put many of these intellectuals reluctant to pay lip service to the party-state under surveillance but never harassed them; the apolitical "resistance through culture" was a strategy tolerated by the Communist regime.

Members of the Aktionsgruppe Banat, among them Richard Wagner and William Totok, reckoned that their circle of German-language writers also could be understood as a response to the cultural policy of Ceaușescu's regime but one that distanced itself from the type of resistance practiced by Romanian writers. It too aimed at rejecting the interference of the party in professional matters but not by carefully avoiding sensitive issues related to the current situation in the country. Its nonconformism was not skillfully disguised but rather openly manifested. The writers of the Aktionsgruppe Banat aimed at reflecting in their writings—mostly poetry, a genre that presented additional challenges to the censors—the world in which they lived, as they saw it. Their goal obviously hinted at a greater freedom of expression and as such had implicit political connotations. The use of a different language than that of the ethnic majority and the stronger influence of Marxist vocabulary—totally rejected by the Romanian "resisters through culture"—actually helped the group to maintain its radical position for a longer period of time.[31] The liberties of a writer were not broader in German, but as the Romanian-dominated Securitate had to depend on translators, its reactions to these writings were slower. Therefore, the Aktionsgruppe Banat could be officially active as the literary circle of German students in Timișoara for almost three years after its first group publication in 1972.

The activity of Aktionsgruppe Banat became a serious problem for the regime only when it emerged as a self-organized group whose visibility surpassed that of local literary circles. The 1974 publication of the group's anthology of texts (though in a censored version) in the Writers' Union journal *Neue Literatur* under the name Aktionsgruppe Banat transformed a self-reference, hitherto only informally used, into the officially recognized appellative of a coherent group.[32] After launching a series of defamatory attacks, the secret police arrested four members of the Aktionsgruppe in 1975, although Romania had signed the Final Act of the Helsinki Conference that same year. The pressure of international media and human rights organizations, however, forced the Romanian authorities to liberate them after only a relatively short detention.[33] Yet at that point the group could not resume literary activity as an independent entity but only as part of the conformist circle of the older and obedient generation of German writers known as the Adam Guttenbrunn Circle.[34] Ever after and until each of the members decided to emigrate, the literary careers of those in the Aktionsgruppe Banat were marked by restrictions on publication or travel abroad and dismissals from positions with potential ideological influence upon the public, especially those working in the educational system or in the print media.[35] At the same time, repeated searches in their domiciles, periodical interrogations, and the pressure to spy on each other were routine treatments applied by the Securitate. However, this constant harassment did not lead to the expected result, as the group did not dissolve itself but rather strengthened its solidarity and continued to defend the right to produce fiction rooted in reality.[36] Its position amounted to less than open criticism of the regime; perhaps this is why the Aktionsgruppe Banat refrained from joining the above-mentioned human rights movement initiated in 1977 by Romanian writer Paul Goma.[37] Yet its position amounted to much more than that of the largest majority of Romanian writers, who chose to resist through culture. Moreover, the members of the Aktionsgruppe Banat demonstrated a sense of solidarity in facing the secret police, a stance that Romanians writers were capable of only in 1989, when the regime was on the brink of collapse.[38] That the solidarity of the group represented a real challenge to the regime provides at least a partial explanation for the violence of the measures used against its members.

Müller was not among the founding members of the Aktionsgruppe Banat. She joined the initial group only after it had overcome its interdiction and reemerged from the ashes in the frame of the officially approved circle of German writers in Timişoara. However, she then fully assumed informal membership to this group, which sought nothing else than to enlarge the liberties of critically writing about Communist Romania instead of simply conforming to the limits of (self-)censorship. This membership represented not only the most important formative stage in her "Romanian period," but also a shared experience of testing group loyalties when dealing with the ubiquitous secret police.[39] As mentioned above, because of the members' German ethnic origins, the secret police labeled the entire group "German nationalists"; their allegiance to the Romanian Communist yet nationalist regime was by definition under suspicion. At the same time, their German origins worked for all the members of the Aktionsgruppe as a window to the outside world. While they were in Romania, their mother tongue gave them access to a literature from the other side of the Iron Curtain, banned in Ceaușescu's Romania but smuggled into the country by various travelers. This literature, radically different from the party-controlled publications available in Romanian libraries and bookshops, helped these German-language writers to emancipate their minds from the conformism enforced by the Communist regime. It taught them to think freely while living in a country that heavily restricted the freedom of thinking.[40] Finally, their German origins offered them the opportunity to reach a wider audience as testifying witnesses to the abuses in their country of birth. It was exactly this kind of knowledge dissemination that the Securitate wanted to avoid. Therefore, the secret police remained an integral part of these authors' lives even after emigration, as Müller's file, for one, clearly demonstrates.[41]

Readers can discover in Müller's file, as in those of many other enemies of the regime, the Orwellian world of dictatorships that aimed at totally controlling lives: constant surveillance that annihilated any intimacy; information gathered from friends, colleagues, and neighbors; denigrating rumors that were meant to and did produce social isolation.[42] When Müller read her file, she discovered much more though. Like many other individuals under surveillance, she also found out who had informed on her. After 1989 such disclosures destroyed families and lifelong friendships everywhere in the former Communist bloc. At a more general level such revelations illustrated, sadly enough, that the methods of the secret police were effective due only to the more or less willing collaboration of individuals around the targeted person, including those in the most intimate circles. Yet when comparing her own memories of past encounters with the secret police to those of the existing documents in her Securitate file, Müller had to conclude that her file must have been "deprived of substance" in the meantime. On the one hand, all secret police files used an institutional parlance meant either to mention only euphemistically the methods to be applied against troublesome individuals or to describe repressive actions as bureaucratic routines. On the other, the postponement of the process of transitional justice in Romania assured favorable conditions for the selective destruction of files.[43] Thus the suspicion that Müller's file, among many others, suffered alterations is strong and will never disappear.

In any case, Müller found no mention of the attempt to make her a collaborator, no records of her friendships with people who later died in suspicious circumstances, nothing about the everyday harassment that she subsequently endured.[44] The deprivation of intimacy by the everyday intrusion of the Securitate into her life represents a recurrent theme in all her novels, but neither the illegal house searches nor the periodical "appointments" with secret police officers have made their way into the documents written by the secret police.[45] It is only her testimony that conveys the complete repertoire of brutal measures taken by the Romanian Communist dictatorship against a person considered "hostile." Had these records fully preserved all her entanglements with this institution, the reconstruction of Müller's "Romanian period" based on such files would nevertheless have been a methodological fallacy. No such records could ever express the sentiment of insecurity felt by the victims of the Securitate.[46] But these records do show that in the midst of a universe of disloyalty and opportunism, of malaise and hopelessness, of violence and corruption, Müller, unlike the largest majority, did not let herself be deprived of dignity. It has been a traumatic experience that has never left her but one that makes hers a voice that should be listened to.

Conclusion

Paraphrasing a famous question of the Literaturstreit in the pre- and post-unification FRG, we might conclude that surveillance does not make one creative, but a creative person forced to undergo such extreme experiences can use his or her talent to bear witness.[47] Müller's work represents one of those fortunate cases that make the following question irrelevant: Should one evaluate a literary work that depicts the author's lived experience under a dictatorship—given the hardships endured in dignity—by different criteria than those applied to other literary works? Everyday bravery in facing the adversities of the dictatorial regime, resolute determination to bear witness for past injustice, as well as literary talent to convey this testimony, come together in Müller's work. Thus her writings are an invaluable source for those who want to understand how non-democratic regimes control individuals. She stands up against both right-wing and left-wing dictatorships: the former mutilated the lives of her parents, the latter her own. However, her autobiographically inspired works are a different kind of testimony for abuses committed against innocent individuals than those of Alexander Solzhenitsyn or Jorge Semprún, who bear witness for atrocities perpetrated in Stalinist or Nazi camps. Müller's writings describe the Communist dictatorship in its post-totalitarian phase,[48] when camps no longer existed and thus the line between victims and their perpetrators was no longer clear-cut.[49] In this phase dictatorships no longer needed to suppress physically but nevertheless profoundly affected the daily existence of individuals who lived in the midst of an atomized society where anyone could be an informant of the secret police. This strategy of control was successful only when individuals abandoned basic human values for the sake of personal benefits. Moreover, as this strategy requires no more than the perversion of institutions that exist in any democratic state, it illustrates the danger that menaces even a democratic state, which could potentially turn against its own citizens by simply and arbitrarily redefining its enemies.[50] Thus, as Müller phrased it in the Banquet Speech, her Nobel Prize has a double significance: it "helps both those who lived through this kind of repression, which aims to break human beings, and those who, thank God, did not have to: the ones to remember what they experienced, and the others to bear these things in mind."

Notes

1. "Normal exception" was first coined by Eduardo Grendi in "Microanalisi e storia sociale." This school criticized large-scale quantitative research on grounds

that it allowed generalizations that were more often than not contradicted when tested at small-scale level. Instead, microhistorians concentrate on small-scale analysis focused on individuals who did not follow average paths, on "normal exceptions" who were considered strange and dangerous in their societies, in order to draw general conclusions about what represented the accepted normality in those societies. For more on the contribution of the Italian school of microhistory to the development of historical methods and its current relevance in historical studies, see Levi.

2. Ginzburg and Poni; English version in Muir and Ruggiero.

3. To this day, the most representative work of this school remains Carlo Ginzburg's analysis, based on documents related to the investigation and trial of a humble individual by the Catholic Church during the Counterreformation.

4. This debate occurred during Müller's visit in her country of birth following her Nobel Prize, and it stirred enormous public interest. The perspective of Romanian intellectuals, expressed by philosopher Gabriel Liiceanu, maintained that one's simple refusal to put his or her writing in support of the Communist regime represented an honorable form of resisting the dictatorship. Müller explained that such an apolitical stance never disturbed the regime; as proof, none of the intellectuals who had done so had problems with the secret police, so they must have been tolerated by the dictatorship. See Müller, "Dialogul Herta Müller–Gabriel Liiceanu." In turn, Romanian intellectuals consider Herta Müller obsessed with the Securitate, a person who advocates moral regeneration in vain, a kind of female version of the Florentine preacher Girolamo Savonarola, as former dissident Mircea Dinescu put it (quoted in Mayr 131).

5. For an analysis of the difference between the methods of control used by the Romanian Communist regime after the takeover of power, which were centered on sheer repression and terror, and those applied in late communism, see Deletant.

6. According to former dissident Václav Havel, it was the complicity of the multitude of average people, who accepted the social contract offered by the Communist system without putting it into question, that in fact helped maintain these regimes in power for so long.

7. In *Der König verneigt sich und tötet* Müller confesses that she dislikes the very word "homeland." While in Romania, either her fellow Swabians in the Banat or the servants of the Romanian Communist dictatorship monopolized the meaning of the word. As for the assertion "SPRACHE IST HEIMAT" [The German (language)

is one's homeland] (28), one should remember that refugees from Hitler's dictatorship formulated it. Thus one should never forget the suffering that was associated with this phrase, coined by individuals who had no place to return to after the end of the war. Therefore, Müller agrees with Semprún: "Nicht Sprache ist Heimat, sondern das, was gesprochen wird" [Homeland is not the language but the substance of its spoken words] (30).

8. The Swabians in the Banat [Banater Schwaben] must be distinguished as a group from the earlier German settlers in the neighboring region of Transylvania called Saxons [Siebenbürger Sachsen]. The region in which they settled became part of Greater Romania (except for its westernmost part, which went to the Kingdom of Yugoslavia) only after World War I. The Banat was one of the most ethnically diverse regions of this country and one in which the Germans represented a numerically significant group. According to the census of 1930, the Banat comprised 54.3 percent Romanians, 23.8 percent Germans, and 10.4 percent Hungarians. For comparison, the Germans represented only 4.1 percent of the total population of Greater Romania and were the third largest minority (Manuilă and Georgescu 50–51).

9. Since 1989, as a reaction to the Communist regime's attempt to erase cultural differences, the memory of the Banat as a region of ethnic pluralism has become a popular research object. With the help of oral history, a group of researchers connected to Western University, Timișoara, has made efforts to preserve the richness of a society where different ethnic groups lived separately yet deeply influenced each other (Vultur).

10. Müller's "file of informative surveillance" (in Romanian *dosar de urmărire informativă*; mentioned in the Securitate parlance with the acronym DUI), registered under the code name "Cristina," opened with a report that—given the content of her debut volume—recommended the immediate initiation of her surveillance in order to better document her activities. Müller's prose was evaluated as "distorting the socioeconomic realities . . . especially in rural areas, and [misrepresenting] the party leadership." The proposal to put her under surveillance was approved on February 26, 1983 (ACNSAS, f. 1).

11. Perhaps the most relevant such example is that of the writer Marin Preda. He had established himself as a reputable author with the novel *Moromeții*, inspired by his childhood years. The novel depicts the hardships of a peasant family from an interwar village in southern Romania; the family struggles to overcome pov-

erty but manages to send the younger and more gifted child to school. To this day, the first volume of *Moromeţii* remains a point of reference in Romanian literature due to the insightful description of peasant mentalities.

12. A joke used to circulate in Romania that succinctly captures the discrepancy between the official version of collectivization and the one preserved only in the memory of the peasantry. When the party tried to collect testimonies from the few survivors of a revolt in 1907—considered the last great uprising of the peasantry in Europe, during which about eleven thousand people were killed according to most estimates—one witness of those events, an old peasant who knew very well what was expected of him, told the interviewers how he had been repeatedly beaten hard by the oppressing bourgeois authorities. His wife, less clever, interrupted him: "You are already senile; the beating happened when collectivization was enforced upon our village, not in 1907!"

13. According to a survey regarding the state of the peasantry from the late 1930s, a peasant household in the region of Banat owned more agricultural machinery than in other parts of Greater Romania, while an average land property was 8.7 hectares per household, well above the average of 4.6 hectares. The quality of the agricultural soil was also better than in most other regions, so productivity was higher (Golopenţia and Georgescu 17, 127, 250–51). These differences were actually perceived as such in Romania, and they explain the saying "Banatul este fruntea" [The Banat comes first].

14. In contrast to the situation in the German villages, which tended to isolate themselves from the overall social disruptions provoked by industrialization, the rural world all across Romania was profoundly affected by the Communist societal transformation. In addition to a large urban migration there was also a social phenomenon that led to the formation of the hybrid category of "the commuter": a worker in the city during the day and a peasant in the village in the afternoon. For more on the social transformations imposed by the Communist modernization in the Banat as compared to other regions, see Ronnås (214–18).

15. The German rural communities in Romania lived secluded from other ethnocultural groups, above all from the Romanian majority that to them represented the Communist rule. A historian originating from such a village told the author of this chapter that the Germans felt they had nothing to do with the Communist authorities, which were Romanian and belonged to a distant world that they only saw on TV.

16. A thorough review of her debut volume—made for the secret police by a native German informant—summarized several of her stories and underlined everything that conflicted with the official views of the party, as well as with "socialist ethics." The review concluded that the stories included "criticism and only criticism, so destructive that one asks oneself what are these texts good for?!" (ACNSAS, f. 5).

17. Actually the reports of the secret police illustrate that this institution was informed about the publication of the book in West Germany and even about the prize that the book was to be awarded before their actual occurrence. In view of such prospective events, the secret police planned to "attract into collaboration" more people from her entourage in order to better grasp her intentions (ACNSAS, ff. 31–33).

18. While she was in Romania, Müller's source of inspiration remained the rural German community in the Banat, and her perspective on it remained critical. After *Niederungen*, she published a second volume of prose, *Drückender Tango*, which reiterated the previous views on the misery of life in such villages but also introduced another inconvenient theme for the regime: the Swabians' exodus to West Germany. A note from a German-speaking informant signaled to the secret police what was "interesting" in her book (ACNSAS, f. 91).

19. Such letters were intercepted by the secret police; their photocopies were attached to secret police reports, while the excerpts considered most relevant were included in the Securitate officer's periodical notes of analysis concerning Müller. "In Germany you are not wanted. It is a disgrace to write such things about the Banat," mentioned a letter signed by twenty-two individuals. Another went as far as to ask for her imprisonment and for her books to be burned (ACNSAS, ff. 258–59, 267–71).

20. The way in which the Romanian Communist authorities dealt with the legacy of World War II only deepened the distance the German minority—convinced of its superiority—kept from the Romanian majority. The very use of the word "island" reminded Müller of this isolation of her childhood: "Diese deutsche Minderheit wurde als Insel der Nazifritzen gesehen und empfand sich selber als Insel der schuldlos von den Rumänen Bestraften" [This German minority was seen by the others as an island of Nazis, but it regarded itself as an island of those punished without guilt by the Romanians] (*König* 162). Her childhood was marked by the feeling of being the child of a Nazi and that Germans were superior to others (*König* 162–63).

21. This type of retribution, specific to dictatorships—which define enemies as well as responsibilities in collective terms and thus condemn without trial innocent people alongside real wrongdoers—touched the German community in Romania in a slightly different way than the rest of the population, although all ethnic groups suffered indiscriminately because of the Communist repression. After the Red Army occupied Romania, most adult Germans capable of work—that is, those between seventeen and forty-five years of age—were deported to forced labor camps in the Soviet Union. This traumatic event informs Müller's latest novel, *Atemschaukel* [*The Hunger Angel*]. Although her mother was among the deportees, Müller did not rely solely on family memories as sources for this novel. Like many individuals who experienced imprisonment, her mother remained mostly silent about her traumatic past; in the small circle of family and friends she only made allusive remarks but gave no explicit narratives. Thus the Gulag recollections of the poet Oskar Pastior served as Müller's primary source of inspiration. It is ironic that Pastior was recently shown to have provided information to the Securitate in the period following his liberation from the Gulag. In reaction to such a perturbing disclosure, Müller affirmed that she judges Pastior according to the same criteria as those applied to the informants in her file, although one must take into account that as a former political prisoner, Pastior's collaboration must have been forced upon him (Lovenberg).

22. The problematic past of the Banat-Swabians, which they never assumed or put into question in the new and democratic homeland of the FRG, constituted yet another reason for which Müller distanced herself from this community while in Romania, as well as after immigration. See comments in Müller's *Cristina und Ihre Attrappe*.

23. Müller's novel *Herztier* [*The Land of Green Plums*] describes the anxieties of a group of young people with a peasant background who came to study in the city in order to distance themselves from their rural communities. In such small, so-called face-to-face communities in rural areas, where everyone knows everyone, there was no privacy of thoughts, so one either conformed to the rules or was marginalized. However, as the group soon discovered, in the cities one simply could not hide from the ubiquitous secret police.

24. Richard Wagner, cofounding member of the Aktionsgruppe Banat, formulated the following credo during a roundtable in 1972; the group's discussions were published in the student supplement *Universitas* of the newspaper *Neue Banater*

Zeitung: "We are the first generation of writers born under the sign of socialism. ... As compared to those who are older, we could perceive the current reality in a less prejudiced and a more complex way. ... The education of our fathers had created false schemes of thinking, which hamper an objective perspective" (quoted in Totok 14).

25. Actually such categories did not originate solely in a problematic treatment of the past, but also in the overall xenophobia quietly promoted by Ceauşescu's regime. Accordingly the Hungarian writers under surveillance were labeled "Hungarian irredentists," while the writers of Jewish origin, "nationalist Jews." Some of the secret police reports on Müller mentioned, in their specific parlance, that she was "processed in a file of informative surveillance" in the so-called line of problems labeled "German nationalists" (ACNSAS, f. 58).

26. The Romanian writer Paul Goma initiated this collective protest in January 1977, immediately after Charter 77 announced its establishment. Inspired by this human rights group in the former Czechoslovakia, the Romanian movement initially gained momentum and succeeded in enlisting around two hundred signatories on a collective letter of protest, a figure comparable to the number of individuals supporting Charter 77. However, in just a few months the Romanian secret police disbanded this movement, which had lacked cohesion among its supporters. As none of the following protests against the Communist regime ever gained so many adherents, this aborted movement remains nevertheless a point of reference in Romanian recent history. For Goma's personal account on the events and excerpts from his secret police file, see Goma, *Culoarea Curcubeului '77*.

27. The former dissident Dorin Tudoran authored a seventy-page essay on the condition of the intellectual in Communist Romania that represents to this day the most concise yet comprehensive study on the causes that hampered the development of a more consistent criticism of the dictatorship. The author highlights the different political traditions in Romania as compared to Central Europe; the terror of the first fifteen years of communism that forced many to surrender morally; the complete dependence on the state for professional survival; and the skillful manipulation of vertical mobility by the Communist authorities. The essay was first published in an abridged version in French; see *L'Alternative* (Paris) 5 (September–October 1984), and 6 (November–December 1984). The unabridged version was published in Romanian as "Fear of Cold? On the Condition of the Romanian Intellectual Today" in Tudoran (31–76).

28. The Romanian philosopher Gabriel Liiceanu best summarizes this model of resisting through culture in a speech addressed to the European College of Cultural Cooperation in 1990. "This model . . . hampered the systematic and total destruction of culture, betting on the idea that only the spirit can ensure the survival of a historically menaced country. But . . . this model turned its back upon the real history, that of events. . . . [It] . . . disregarded the dissidents as victims of an illusion, caught up in an unimportant fight" (Liiceanu 13-14).

29. In 1971 Ceaușescu's so-called July Theses marked a radical nationalist turn in the cultural policy of the regime that in fact mirrored developments in its external policy as well, especially its alleged independence from the Soviet bloc. In addition to the return to such obsolete Stalinist notions as Socialist Realism and the leading role of Communist teachings, the new guide for cultural productions also included an astonishing directive: in order to express its true national spirit, Romanian culture must be kept "pure" of foreign—that is, West European—influences. The enforcement of such directives required increased control over all publications, as well as over the circulation of books and persons from and to Romania. For more on this turn, see Verdery.

30. However, many such intellectuals continued to enjoy a high professional reputation. The anthropologist Vintilă Mihăilescu expresses a self-critical and ironic view on the posteriori defined model of "resistance through culture": "It was normal to come together in the end. . . . Because we acted with professionalism. . . . We were not against the institutions . . . , but we did what we could to stay in their shadow. . . . I found out later that this was 'resistance through culture'" (Mihăilescu 18).

31. The Marxist influence actually made the Aktionsgruppe unique among intellectuals in Romania. Obviously this influence did not originate in the primitive reception of Marxism by the Romanian Communist regime but mostly in the works of the Frankfurt School of critical Marxism. Authors of this school had barely any influence upon Romanian intellectuals who resisted through culture; they rather read Hegel or Heidegger than Adorno or Marcuse. For an analysis of the writings produced by the Aktionsgruppe and their Marxist sources of inspiration, see Langer.

32. The year 1974 was the peak in the activity of the group, when it became known on the national level. Its members toured university centers to read from their works. The publication of their anthology drew the attention of the authori-

ties, and the journal issue was withdrawn from circulation (Totok, esp. 17-25).

33. In October 1975 four prominent members of the group—writers Gerhard Csejka, Gerhard Ortinau, Richard Wagner, and William Totok—were for the first time arrested under false allegations. The Communist authorities released them after several days; only Totok spent several months in prison. Ernest Wichner, another member of the group who had immigrated to West Germany at the beginning of the year, was instrumental in attracting the attention of the Western media to the group. Ever after, the support of the members who decided one by one to emigrate furthered the resistance of those who remained behind. For more on intra-group relations, see Archive of Oral History of CNSAS (AIOCNSAS), Common interview with William Totok and Ernest Wichner, February 16, 2006.

34. Adam Müller-Guttenbrunn (1852-1923) was a writer of Banat-Swabian origins who made a successful career in Vienna at the end of the nineteenth century as the first director of the Kaiser-Jubiläums-Stadttheater (today the Volksoper). Some of his writings evoke the rural Banat and the German traditions preserved in villages like his hometown, Guttenbrunn (Romanian Zăbrani). The cultural center of the Banat Germans still bears his name.

35. A typical example is the trajectory of Richard Wagner, Müller's former husband. After working as a German teacher in the city of Hunedoara, he found a position as editor of the weekly *Karpaten Rundschau* in Brașov, a job that did not require his daily presence at work and thus allowed him to return to Timișoara. As the literary activity of the Aktionsgruppe Banat could be continued only as part of the literary circle Adam Müller-Guttenbrunn, Wagner managed to take over the coordination of this circle in order to increase the influence of his own group's radical views among the others. He held this position from 1981 to 1982; after his public declarations again started to annoy the Communist authorities, he lost not only his leading position in the literary circle, but also that at the newspaper.

36. It was again Wagner who best articulated the refined credo in 1982 in the German-language daily newspaper *Neuer Weg*: "We are connected by a minimal program. . . . Beyond difference, our aim is to promote a critical literature in the German language that would surpass the traditional quest for confirmation by the literature in minority languages and cope with the current stage of the social dialogue. We want to test the capabilities of such a literature" (quoted in Totok 109).

37. Paul Goma was a former political prisoner, arrested as one of the organizers of the student protests that emerged at the University of Bucharest after the outbreak of the Hungarian Revolution of 1956. After his release in 1964, he managed to publish, with various Western publishing houses, two books rejected by censorship, as well as a testimony of his prison experience (Goma, *Gherla*). Because of his attempt to initiate a human rights movement inspired by Charter 77, Goma was again arrested but released shortly after and pushed to emigrate. To this day Goma is bitter because only two writers in Romania joined his human rights movement. For more on his activity, see OSA/RFE Archives, Romanian Fond, 300/60/5/Box 6, File Dissidents: Paul Goma. For Goma's highly critical position with regard to the position adopted by the Aktionsgruppe Banat in relation to the Communist regime, expressed after Herta Müller's Nobel Prize, see the entry for October 9, 2009, in Goma, "Jurnal 2009 întreg" 502-05.

38. It was the so-called Letter of the Seven of April 1989—eventually endorsed by nine intellectuals—that marked the first moment of solidarity against the Communist regime among Romanian writers. The letter stood in defense of freedom of speech when two Romanian poets were banned from publication. Given the prestige of the signatories, this letter had a significant impact on Romanians prior to the collapse of the regime. For the text of the letter, see Domestic Bloc No. 560, April 21, 1989, OSA/RFE Archives, Romanian Fond, 300/60/3/Box 18, File Open Letters: The Group of Seven.

39. The Securitate tested the solidarity of the group in 1984, when a young member, Helmut Frauendorfer, was harassed into collaborating with the secret police. In his defense seven writers from the group, including Müller, sent a letter of protest to the president of the Writers' Union and the local party leadership. Their letter argued that the measures taken against several German writers were violations of their freedom of speech and serious abuses against the German minority. The letter is reproduced in Totok (111-12). See also AIOCNSAS, Interview with Helmut Frauendorfer, November 12, 2008.

40. It is interesting to note that Müller connects immigration to West Germany to the German books smuggled into Communist Romania, an activity that allowed her and her friends to surpass the cultural isolation imposed by the regime. While for most people the FDR was the country of welfare, for her group it was a country where one could think freely, like the authors of those German books. "The books ... had been smuggled into the country.... They were in our mother tongue, but

the silence of the villages, which forbids thought, wasn't in them. We imagined the land where the books came from as a land of thinkers. . . . All the people . . . wanted to go there. In the land those books came from, there were blue jeans and oranges, soft toys for children and portable TVs for fathers and whisper-thin nylons and real mascara for mothers" (*The Land of Green Plums* 47).

41. Müller's file includes a plan of measures of March 31, 1988, when she was already in West Germany; it envisaged her denigration and isolation in order to annihilate her constant criticism of the Romanian Communist regime in the German media (ACNSAS, ff. 295–97).

42. The documents in Müller's Securitate file indicate, as mentioned above, that her surveillance was not triggered solely by her association with Aktionsgruppe, but also by her own fiction. At the same time, it also seems clear from this file that her identification with the group and her solidarity in defending its members against the abuses of the authorities added new grounds for strengthening the surveillance. The repeated measures to be taken against her included the following: the installation of microphones; the interception of her telephone calls and letters; the constant surveillance of her every move; and the gathering of information about her whereabouts, attitudes, and intentions with the help of various informants. In Müller's case, though, the secret police also devised more perverse measures, such as allowing her to travel to the West—at a time when such travel represented a privilege for most Romanians—in the hope of substantiating the rumors that she worked for the Securitate. For the Romanian secret police, the rather natural connections that writers of this minority group established with the Embassy of West Germany or the German cultural center counted as evidence of their collaboration with foreign intelligence services against the Communist state. A telling example in this respect is a plan of measures of July 1, 1985, that entailed the surveillance of all foreign diplomats and journalists with whom Müller or her husband had entered into contact. The aim was to gather evidence to open a criminal file for her alleged collaboration with the West German secret services (ACNSAS, ff. 153, 156–60).

43. Indeed, for instance, in 1990 journalists from the daily newspaper *România Liberă* discovered that important documents related to the activity of the former secret police had been destroyed. A large quantity of partially burned Securitate documents was found in the mountain area of Argeș County (around two hundred kilometers north of Bucharest). The so-called Berevoiești Case, named

after the village nearby which the half-burned documents were discovered, enhanced the heated debates on the necessity to preserve all the documents related to the Communist past. Due to the fact that former party apparatchiks dominated Romanian post-Communist politics, it was only in 1999 that an institution designed to deal with the files of the former secret police—the National Council for the Study of the Securitate (Romanian acronym CNSAS)—was established by law. However, the bulk of the files of the Securitate were transferred into its custody only in December 2005. For more on the avatars of transitional justice in post-Communist Romania and their influence upon the process of dealing with the past, see Petrescu and Petrescu.

44. The betrayal of her closest friend, as well as the inconsistencies between her memory and her file, could constitute the subject of an entire book. Reading these documents, Müller discovered two different persons: the bearer of her code name, "Cristina," an enemy of the Communist state kept under surveillance, and her dummy, as an alleged agent of this institution, fabricated by the Securitate in order to discredit her (*Cristina und ihre Attrappe*).

45. In particular her novel *The Appointment* conveys to the readers the sense of anxiety and the struggle for maintaining a mental balance as experienced by a young girl who is periodically summoned to the secret police. Encounters with Securitate officers became an intrinsic part of everyday routines in a decaying world dominated by treason, violence, and corruption. The novel *Der Fuchs war damals schon der Jäger* captures perfectly the distress, angst, and humiliation caused by the continuous invasion into one's private life: the main character is reminded of the vigilant eye of the Securitate that watches her because a piece from a fox fur is cut every time the house is searched. The novel also refers to the status Securitate people enjoyed in Romania; they had special privileges at a time when the rest of the population was enduring severe shortages.

46. In this respect, Müller compares her circle of friends to a circle of young writers in Bucharest that in the 1980s had among its members the currently internationally best-known Romanian writer, Mircea Cărtărescu. The latter confessed in an interview with the *Frankfurter Allgemeine Zeitung* that under communism, in spite of certain hardships, writers had more stability than they have today since they could anticipate what to expect the next day. In her reply, given in an interview with the Romanian daily *România Liberă*, Müller underlined that such stability, which she and her friends had never enjoyed, was assured only when taking

an apolitical stance. "Not one day did I know what to expect the next day. Every day I was afraid that in the evening I would no longer be alive" (Müller, "Scriitorii români erau prea încurcați cu dictatura").

47. See Marcel Reich-Ranicki's question "Macht Verfolgung kreativ?" [Does surveillance produce creativity?] in an article that heavily criticized the writings of the GDR author Christa Wolf and was published in the *Frankfurter Allgemeine Zeitung* in 1987. This article initiated the famous Literaturstreit [Dispute on Literature], a debate about the literary standards to be applied when judging the works of authors who had to endure the adversities of dictatorships. For more on this, see Garbe.

48. For a typology of non-democratic regimes and the meaning of post-totalitarianism, see Linz (esp. 30–31).

49. The case of poet Oskar Pastior perfectly exemplifies the strategy of control applied by Communist regimes in their post-totalitarian phase. Many former political prisoners turned into more or less zealous collaborators of the secret police in order to whitewash their pasts as enemies of the regime or for other reasons. Obviously these individuals can no longer be considered pure victims of the dictatorship, yet they deserve to be treated differently from those who never went through extreme experiences as imprisonment and collaborated only for the sake of financial or other types of benefits.

50. After reading his Stasi file the Oxford-based historian Timothy Garton Ash, who had visited the GDR numerous times before 1989, reflected upon the thin line that separates the methods and scope of the secret police in a dictatorship from those of the intelligence services in a democratic country and wondered whether a citizen of a democracy could have any guarantees that in particular circumstances this line would not be crossed. However, he ended his book by expressing his gratitude that his children would never have a file of their own (Ash, *The File*, esp. 236–56).

Works Cited

ACNSAS (Archive of the National Council for the Study of the Securitate). File 1233477, vol. 1.

Ash, Timothy Garton. *The File: A Personal History*. New York: Random House, 1997.

Deletant, Dennis. *Communist Terror in Romania: Gheorghiu-Dej and the Police State, 1948–1965*. London: Hurst, 1999.

Garbe, Joachim. *Deutsche Geschichte in deutschen Geschichten der neunziger Jahre.* Würzburg: Königshausen and Neumann, 2002.

Ginzburg, Carlo. *The Cheese and the Worms: The Cosmos of a Sixteenth-Century Miller.* Trans. John and Anne Tedeschi. Baltimore: Johns Hopkins University Press, 1980.

Ginzburg, Carlo, and Carlo Poni. "Il nome e il come: Scambio ineguale e mercato storiografico" [The name and the game: Unequal exchange and the historical marketplace]. *Quaderni Storici* 40 (1979): 181–90.

Golopenția, Anton, and D. C. Georgescu. *60 sate românești* [60 Romanian villages]. Bucharest: Institutul de Științe Sociale al României, 1941.

Goma, Paul. *Culoarea curcubeului '77: Cod "Bărbosul"* [The color of the rainbow 1977: Code name "Bearded Man"]. Iași: Polirom, 2005.

——. *Gherla.* Paris: Éditions Gallimard, 1976.

——. "Jurnal 2009 întreg" [Unabridged diary 2009]. Web. February 6, 2011. http://www.paulgoma.com/17-jurnal-2009-intreg.

Grendi, Eduardo. "Microanalisi e storia sociale" [Microanalysis and social history]. *Quaderni Storici* 35 (1977): 506–20.

Havel, Václav. *The Power of the Powerless.* New York: M. E. Sharpe, 1985.

Langer, Sarah. "Zwischen Bohème und Dissidenz: Die Aktionsgruppe Banat und ihre Autoren in der rumänischen Diktatur." BA thesis. Abschlußarbeiten am Institut für Europäische Studien (AIES-online). December 8, 2010. Web. January 15, 2010. http://www.tu-chemnitz.de/phil/europastudien/aktivitaeten/aies/veroeffentlichungen/LangerBA-Arbeit8.pdf.

Levi, Giovanni. "On Microhistory." *New Perspectives on Historical Writing.* Ed. Peter Burke. University Park: Pennsylvania State University Press, 1998. 93–113.

Liiceanu, Gabriel. *Jurnalul de la Păltiniș: Un model paideic în cultura umanistă* [The Păltiniș diary: A Paideia-like model in the humanistic culture]. Bucharest: Humanitas, 1991.

Linz, Juan J. *Totalitarian and Authoritarian Regimes.* Boulder and London: Lynne Rienner, 2000.

Lovenberg, Felicitas von. "Nobelpreisträgerin Herta Müller im Interview: Die Akte zeigt Oskar Pastior umzingelt." *Frankfurter Allgemeine Zeitung*, September 17, 2010. Web. November 17, 2011.

Manuilă, Sabin, and D. C. Georgescu. *Populația României* [The population of Romania]. Bucharest: Imprimeria Națională, 1937.

Mayr, Walter. "Gift im Gepäck." *Der Spiegel* 3 (January 2011): 131. Web. January 20, 2011.

Mihăilescu, Vintilă. "Ăştia eram noi" [So we were]. *Cum era? Cam aşa: Amintiri din anii comunismului (românesc)* [How was it? Something like this: Remembering (Romanian) Communism]. Ed. Călin-Andrei Mihăilescu. Bucharest: Curtea Veche, 2006.

Muir, Edward, and Guido Ruggiero, eds. *Microhistory and the Lost People of Europe.* Baltimore: Johns Hopkins University Press, 1991.

Müller, Herta. *The Appointment.* Trans. Michael Hulse and Philip Boehm. New York: Metropolitan Books, 2001.

———. *Atemschaukel.* Munich: Carl Hanser, 2009.

———. *Cristina und ihre Attrappe oder Was (nicht) in den Akten der Securitate steht.* Göttingen: Wallstein, 2009.

———. *Der Fuchs war damals schon der Jäger.* Reinbek: Rowohlt, 1992.

———. *Der König verneigt sich und tötet.* Munich: Hanser, 2003.

———. "Dialogul Herta Müller–Gabriel Liiceanu, moment istoric pentru cultura română" [The Herta Müller–Gabriel Liiceanu dialogue, a historical moment in the Romanian culture]. *România Liberă*, September 29, 2010. Web. September 29, 2010. http://www.romanialibera.ro/arte/oameni/dialogul-herta-muller-gabriel-liiceanu-moment-istoric-pentru-cultura-romana-200986.html.

———. *Drückender Tango.* Bucharest: Kriterion, 1984.

———. *Herztier.* Reinbek: Rowohlt, 1996.

———. *The Hunger Angel.* Trans. Philip Boehm. New York: Metropolitan Books, 2012.

———. *The Land of Green Plums.* Trans. Michael Hofmann. New York: Metropolitan Books, 1996.

———. *Niederungen.* Bucharest: Kriterion, 1982.

———. "Scriitorii români erau prea încurcaţi cu dictatura: Interviu cu Sabina Fati" [Romanian writers were too entangled with the dictatorship: Interview with Sabina Fati]. *România Liberă*, September 16, 2010. Web. September 16, 2010. http://www.romanialibera.ro/opinii/interviuri/scriitorii-romani-erau-prea-incurcati-cu-dictatura-199678.html.

Petrescu, Cristina, and Dragoş Petrescu. "The Piteşti Syndrome: A Romanian *Vergangenheitsbewältigung?*" *Postdiktatorische Geschichtskulturen im Süden und Osten Europas: Bestandsaufnahme und Forschungsperspektiven.* Ed. Stefan Troebst. Göttingen: Wallstein, 2010. 502–618.

Preda, Marin. *Moromeții* [The Moromete family]. Bucharest: ESPLA, 1955.

Ronnås, Per. *Urbanization in Romania: A Geography of Social and Economic Change since Independence*. Stockholm: Stockholm School of Economics, 1984.

Totok, William. *Constrîngerea memoriei: Însemnări, documente, amintiri* [The constraint of memory: Notes, documents, recollections]. Iași: Polirom, 2001.

Tudoran, Dorin. *Kakistocrația* [Kakistocracy]. Kishinev: Arc, 1998. 31–76.

Verdery, Katherine. *National Ideology under Socialism: Identity and Cultural Politics in Ceausescu's Romania*. Berkeley: University of California Press, 1991.

Vultur, Smaranda, ed. *Memoria Banatului* [Memory of the Banat]. Web. September 14, 2010. http://www.memoriabanatului.ro/index.php?page=e-books.

6 "Die akute Einsamkeit des Menschen"

Herta Müller's *Herztier*

Brigid Haines

Totalitarian government, like all tyrannies, certainly could not exist without destroying the public realm of life, that is, without destroying, by isolating men, their political capacities. But totalitarian domination as a form of government is new in that it is not content with this isolation and destroys private life as well. It bases itself on loneliness, on the experience of not belonging to the world at all, which is among the most radical and desperate experiences of man.

(Arendt 475)

Loneliness is an unnatural and unwanted state of isolation in which the individual cannot thrive.[1] It is not to be confused with solitude, which may be sought and savored. Loneliness is often seen as a feature of modernity, associated with the breakdown of traditional communities and extended family structures. In the second half of the twentieth century it was identified more as a product of Western capitalist societies, which tend to atomize individuals, than of Eastern bloc societies. The latter attempted to unite their citizens through socialist values and central planning, while in practice often uniting them in disaffection. Many retreated from the public sphere into a *Nischengesellschaft* [niche society], attempting to lead "perfectly normal lives" (Fulbrook 129–50) and mocking authority in private through jokes. Indeed there is currently a wave of nostalgia for the community values lost after the fall of communism in such countries as Hungary, Poland, Russia, the Czech Republic, and the German Democratic Republic, whose citizens are now prey to the insecurities resulting from the introduction of market forces (Boym).

The works of Herta Müller, however, repeatedly make the case that no such retreat was possible in Ceaușescu's Romania because the penetration of the private sphere, even of the bodies and minds of its citizens by intrusive power, was so complete. This resulted in "die akute Einsamkeit des Menschen" (Müller, "Jedes Wort"). The phrase comes from Müller's 2009 Nobel Prize speech, in which she thematizes how totalitarian power thwarts the desire for intimacy and isolates individuals. The examples she gives come from various times and places, including the Banat-Swabian village in which she was born, where her mother could only express tenderness indirectly through a gesture; the Romanian factory from whose employ Müller was sacked for refusing to collaborate with the Securitate; the Ukrainian village where, in the late 1940s, her friend, the poet Oskar Pastior, half starved from incarceration in the Gulag, found soup and a surprise gift; and the 1980s Securitate interrogation cell. In linking these scenes, a move repeated in many of her works, Müller links the experience of life in Ceaușescu's Romania, not so much to other contemporaneous Eastern bloc regimes during the Cold War, but to Nazi-controlled Europe and to Stalin's Soviet Union. In other words, Müller repeatedly connects the dictatorships of the twentieth century by highlighting the loneliness and the cost of survival of their victims. She is not the first to do this: in *The Origins of Totalitarianism* Hanna Arendt argued that while tyranny, which had always existed, isolates individuals, totalitarian rule also invades private life, producing loneliness, which is a far more desperate condition: "What makes loneliness so unbearable is the loss of one's own self which can be realized in solitude, but confirmed in its identity only by the trusting and trustworthy company of my equals. In this situation, man loses trust in himself as the partner of his thoughts and that elementary confidence in the world which is necessary to make experiences at all. Self and world, capacity for thought and experience are lost at the same time" (Arendt 477). Those familiar with Müller's works will find this description of disorientation entirely apposite.

But both Müller and Arendt also locate the limits of totalitarian power in the paradox of loneliness. Loneliness is, for Arendt, "contrary to the basic requirements of the human condition" but also, because of the fact of mortality, "one of the fundamental experiences of every human life" (Arendt 475). Mortality is, for Arendt, linked to natality, which mounts a daily challenge to the master narratives of totalitarianism: totalitarian rule claims its legitimacy from ideology based on history or nature; however, while subordinating the individual to the point of rendering him or her dispensable, it cannot master the awkward fact that with each new birth, newness enters the world (Arendt 466). Particularity is also integral to Müller's unique aesthetic and her individualistic response to power. She downplays overarching narratives in favor of a collage technique that brings together isolated details to create intensely poetic effects. Similarly it is through focusing on their atomization and the peeling back of existence to its bare necessities that Müller's disorientated protagonists discover unexpected strength to muster the only agency left to them under totalitarianism. Like Arendt, Müller locates the possibility of agency in material, unexpected, living detail.

No text exemplifies the centrality for Müller of loneliness as theme and as structuring principle more than her best-known work to date, the novel *Herztier* (1994), the autobiographically inspired story of a group of friends subjected to persecution by the Securitate in 1980s Romania.[2] This dark novel conjures up an unremittingly bleak picture of a society that is both materially impoverished and ruled by a fear that borders on paranoia. The looming figure of Ceaușescu, sinister as a latter-day vampire, and the high death toll, together with the sometimes abstract-sounding, almost obscure use of language—for example, the neologisms *Holzmelonen* and *Blechschafe*—can strain the credulity and patience of Western readers. Drawing on recent research into the period and its aftermath and on Müller's subsequent publications—in particular her autobiographical and poetological essay volume *Der König verneigt sich und tötet* (2003) and *Cristina und ihre Attrappe* (2009), an account of her dealings with the Securitate—I will argue that the extreme content and unusual style of the novel are not willful or fanciful. Rather, Müller was one of the first to represent in literature, albeit obliquely, "the soul-corroding, the unctuous brutalisation of public and private life . . . in Ceaușescu's Romania" (Steiner), a regime in which the loneliness that Arendt identified as the hallmark of totalitarian societies was relentlessly pursued as a matter of state policy. Furthermore, her representation is not simply synchronic but also diachronic; she shows how present identity is conditioned by more than one imposition of totalitarian rule. Her unique aesthetic of atomization and collage makes her work profoundly political, a defiant and appropriate response to specific social and historical repression, against which her protagonists too fight back.

"Organized Loneliness"

The plot of *Herztier* shows how the regime persecutes and intimidates a group of young people and their families by isolating them, driving several of them to their deaths, and threatening to undermine the sanity of the others, a persecution both autobiographically based and of a type well attested.[3] The regime effectively creates dissidents through direct targeting and harassment. The young friends—an unnamed female narrator, Georg, Edgar, and Kurt, all ethnic Germans—are students whose only crime is to read imported German books and discuss literature. They do not organize politically or plan to flee, although like many in the country, they entertain fantasies of flight. But their friendship is enough to draw them to the attention of the authorities, who subject them to interrogations, house searches, and psychological intimidation and then, as was the normal fate of all but a few privileged young people, disperse them to a variety of soul-destroying jobs around the country. Still to some extent sustained by their friendship even as the regime drives a wedge between them and their families, they attempt to evade the censors by adopting a secret code in their letters.

But friendship is severely tested in *Herztier* and its limits exposed. Müller writes: "Ich habe zeigen wollen, wie Freundschaft aussieht, wenn es nicht selbstverständlich ist, daß man heute abend, morgen früh, nächste Woche noch lebt" [I wanted to show what friendship looks like when you can't take for granted that you will still be alive tonight, tomorrow morning, next week] (*König* 52). The action of the novel is framed by two acts of betrayal, in which the narrator is first a *Mitläufer* [fellow traveler] and then the victim. Both undermine the principle of friendship as an inviolable space. Early on she joins in the public vote for her friend Lola to be posthumously expelled from the Party after Lola's suicide; disappointed by her own behavior, she becomes the custodian of Lola's diary, and it is the circumstances surrounding Lola's death that bring her into contact with Kurt, Georg, and Edgar. Later she is devastated to discover that her Romanian friend Tereza, who visits her in Germany, where she has begun her new life, has been sent to spy on her by the Securitate. This loss of an intimate friendship—"du und ich [war] vernichtet" [you and I were finished] (*Herztier* 158)—haunts the novel. Friendship is thus revealed to be an insubstantial thing; it cannot protect individuals from state terror. Lola hangs herself—or is hanged; it is not clear—as a result of an affair with a Party official; Tereza dies prematurely of cancer; Georg, the first of the friends to cede to the pressure and leave for West Germany, is found dead there in suspicious circumstances; Kurt, who stays behind, commits suicide. All of this tests the validity of the statement in the poem that precedes the text that in times when the world is full of fear—and much of the novel evokes a society permeated by fear—"Freunde kommen nicht in Frage" [friends are out of the question] (5). Though the narrator and her friend Edgar succeed in reaching the West, they look back with no sense of closure, intactness, safety, or relief. Overwhelmed with survivor guilt, they remain traumatized, isolated in their grief, unable to rest or to thrive. Nor can they escape their loneliness by talking to others about what has happened, for they have lost Arendt's "elementary confidence in the world."[4]

The persecution depicted in the novel—the atomization and dispersal, the breaking up of family trust, the invasion of the self through mind games and the threat of violence, plus physical and sexual intimidation—is based on the experience of Müller and her friends and former husband Richard Wagner in the Temeswarer Schriftsteller Vereinigung, a successor to the

Aktionsgruppe Banat, a group of ethnic German writers in Timișoara in the 1980s. The memory of these writer friends continues to inspire her; in her Nobel dinner speech in Stockholm she paid tribute to them in a way that again evoked the distress of their enforced isolation: "Glücklich sein ist vielleicht teilbar, Glück haben leider nicht" [Happiness can maybe be shared, but not being lucky].[5] Behind the five main characters can clearly be seen Müller herself, Wagner, and three of their identifiable friends, none of whom survived the Ceaușescu regime.[6] Georg and Kurt are based on the poets Rolf Bossert and Roland Kirsch respectively, and Tereza, on Müller's Romanian friend Jenny. Müller's recent writings and a major exhibition devoted to her containing photographs and artifacts worked into the novel—for example, Bossert's last postcard to Müller and Wagner, as well as the *Hühnerqual*, a toy that makes the friends laugh[7]—make clear how close the depiction is to life, as does the true story of Tereza, the last poignant detail of which was revealed to Müller only when she was finally able to read her Securitate file, or what was left of it after much material had been removed, in 2008. Jenny's betrayal became a recurrent scene in Müller's fictional and essayistic writings; Müller's haunting fear that the relationship with Jenny had been engineered from the start by the Securitate—that there never had been a friendship—was dispelled when she read that Jenny was approached to spy on her because of the "großes Vertrauen zwischen ihnen" [great trust between them] (*Cristina* 31), an unexpectedly comforting revelation.

The persecution described is entirely consonant with the methods of the Securitate, an organization that has been described as "as much a state of mind as the instrument of state terror" (Deletant 393). The Securitate's program of action, finally published in 1993, makes clear its direct line of command from the dictator. It was charged with "acting consistently to carry out to the letter the orders and indications of the Supreme Commander of the Armed Forces, Comrade Nicolae Ceaușescu." Deletant explains that its objectives were to discover, anticipate, and act to prevent and vigorously combat any deed likely to affect state security and national integrity, independence, and security; to ensure the safety of the Supreme Commander and to carry out to the full all missions of an exceptional importance"; and "to prevent, counter and neutralize actions perpetrated by reactionary circles and nationalist, irredentist and Fascist groups abroad, by hostile *émigré* groups and by hostile elements in the country" (Deletant 337). The reach of the Securitate abroad (alleged in the novel through the suspicious death of Georg and the death threats received by the narrator) is well attested (Deletant 328; and Smith), as is its practice of pressuring those leaving to spy from abroad, as happens to Georg (Müller, *Herztier* 233).

"This Suffocating Regime"

The central action concerning the friends in *Herztier* is set among an evocation of 1980s Romania pervaded by an overwhelming sense of desperation and alienation; Müller depicts a totalitarian regime that actively poisons the physical and mental health and well-being of its citizens. The various settings—the German villages, the girls' dormitory, the streets and bodegas of Timişoara, the desolate towns where the friends are exiled, the beckoning border—are all equally injurious. This is a world of extreme poverty and deprivation, where every aspect of the population's existence is subject to control, and where people are reduced to animal-like subservience: hungry, afraid, and abject. Children are indoctrinated and aspire to be guards; workers are brutalized; women are subjected to domestic violence; many of those who do not conform escape into madness or become prisoners; most dream constantly of flight. There appears to be no organized resistance, for spies are everywhere: "Man spürte den Diktator und seine Wächter über allen Geheimnissen der Fluchtpläne stehen, man spürte sie lauern und Angst austeilen" [You could feel the dictator and his guards hovering over all the secret escape plans, you could feel them lurking and doling out fear] (*Herztier* 56). There is little human solidarity, even within families—the protagonist's mother does not even stand by her when the persecution starts. The ubiquity and centrality of the dictator, metaphorically sucking the lifeblood of his people in a sick echo of Count Dracula, determines everything: "Edgar sagte: Wenn der Richtige gehen müßte, könnten alle anderen im Land bleiben" [If only the right person would leave, everyone else would be able to stay in the county] (69). The protagonist senses a contemporary uniqueness to Romania: "Ich spürte den Unterschied zwischen dem Land und der Welt. . . . Ich dachte damals noch, man könne in einer Welt ohne Wächter anders gehen als in diesem Land. Wo man anders denken und schreiben kann, dachte ich mir, kann man auch anders gehen" [I felt the difference between this country and the world. . . . At the time I still believed that in a world without guards people would walk differently from the way we do in our country. Where people are allowed to think and write differently, I thought, they will also walk differently] (128). What she senses is the extraordinary power of Romania to mutilate its citizens, both physically (as witnessed, for example, by Georg when he notes the many missing fingers of the men in the sawmill town) and mentally.

Once again, this extraordinary novelistic account of extreme atomization and abjection, inspired by autobiographical experience, is backed up by historical record. The regime of Nicolae Ceaușescu, who ruled Romania with his wife Elena from 1967 until the pair were toppled at Christmas 1989, was unlike the regimes of the other Eastern bloc states in four significant ways: first, in the degree of economic crisis to which it had reduced the country by the late 1980s; second, in the centralization of power in the person of the dictator; third, in the relative absence of organized opposition; and fourth, in the extraordinary degree to which all aspects of human life were subject to control. Ceaușescu was courted by the West in the early years of his rule for charting a course independent from Moscow, for trading with the West, and for refusing to support the Soviet clampdown in Czechoslovakia in 1968. Indeed he was also something of a hero at home due to his populist nationalism and semi-independent foreign policy. But by the 1980s the country was in economic ruin and was internationally isolated, and Ceaușescu himself was internally loathed and internationally reviled. He had borrowed heavily from the West to fund development programs and made it a policy to repay these crippling debts in full, whatever the cost to his country and people (something he had accomplished at the time of his death in 1989). As a result, industrial and agricultural products were exported, leading to extraordinary levels of hunger and hardship for the population. Food was rationed, energy supplies were often cut off, medical supplies were extremely scarce, and the environmental degradation was extreme. No other Eastern bloc regime inflicted such deprivation that denied the basic living needs of its people.[8]

Power was centralized to an unprecedented degree. The cult of personality around Ceaușescu resulted in his increasing ignorance of his people and the truth about their plight. He wanted to be remembered as the leader who modernized Romania; his maniacal schemes included the razing of large parts of Bucharest, including many churches of huge historical importance; the creation of his vanity project, the Casa Poporului [House of the People], still one of the largest buildings on earth; and in the last years of his rule, the systematization of the country's villages, with the intention of "break[ing] the spirit of peasant enterprise and individualism" (Rady 70) and producing an industrial working class.[9] The historian Martin Rady confirms that the view of Ceaușescu as ghoul and vampire, which might strike Western and Eastern readers as clichéd, was common (Rady 116), and he adds a blood-related detail to Müller's account of slaughterhouse workers drinking fresh blood: hungry adults were known to volunteer for blood transfusions in their search for sustenance (Rady 81).

There was opposition to Ceaușescu, but it was sporadic rather than systematic: a miners' strike in the Jiu Valley in 1977, an uprising in Brașov in 1987, and a courageous stand taken by a few individuals such as Paul Goma, who publicly declared support for Charta 77; Silviu Brucan, who spoke to the Western media about conditions in Romania in 1987; and the human rights activist Doina Cornea, who released many texts and protests against the regime during the 1980s and was persecuted for it. The defection of Ion Mihai Pacepa, a high-ranking intelligence officer, in 1978 and subsequent revelations about the Securitate in his book *Red Horizons* also damaged Ceaușescu's reputation (Deletant 235–93). There was nothing equivalent to the Solidarity movement in Poland or the principled opposition of some of the churches in the GDR. The reasons for such a lack have to do with the nature of Ceaușescu's hold on power. Communism did not have a historical tradition or a large base but was an artificially grafted and forcefully imposed phenomenon. Romania was, until the latter half of the twentieth century, largely a peasant population, lacking an urban working class, which might have produced a Communist movement, and a large middle class, which might have produced a democratic tradition. Historically, therefore, there was a tradition of political conformity. So when Müller wrote in 1991 that she sometimes wanted sympathy from the landscape "weils Solidarität zwischen Menschen in diesem Land nicht gibt" [because there is no solidarity among people in this country] (*Teufel* 131), she was not exaggerating.

While the period of Ceaușescu's rule was not marked by terror in the same way as that of his predecessor, Gheorghe Gheorgiu-Dej—there were no more mass arrests or "wholesale deportations" (Deletant 64)—the regime ruled through the institutionalization of fear, as what Denis Deletant calls a "labour-saving device" (Deletant xiii). The regime fostered "a corrosive atmosphere of deceit and distrust which made personal acts of resistance seem both futile and self-defeating" (Rady 57). There was nothing here of the perestroika and glasnost infiltrating other Eastern bloc regimes, just hard-line Stalinism. The film *4 Months, 3 Weeks and 2 Days* (Mungiu 2007), an account of a backstreet abortion under Ceaușescu and a chilling disection of total power, demonstrates that Müller is not alone in her depiction of the penetration and violation of the individual in *Herztier*. But her protagonist's despairing cry, "Wie müßte man leben, dachte ich mir, um zu dem, was man gerade denkt, zu passen" [How do you have to live, I wondered, to be in harmony with what you honestly think?] (71), sums up the desperation of a people denied the dignity of being able to think and act for themselves.

All of these aspects are eloquently summed up in the following letter to Ceaușescu from the dissident Doina Cornea and six others on April 9, 1989; the letter shows Müller's grim evocation of life in Romania to be not a result of her fevered imagination but a representation of the historical truth:

> This suffocating regime which you imposed against our very being, moral and biological, has become ever more difficult to bear. You have razed to the ground our oldest and most beloved churches. You have dug up the graves of our past rulers. You have started to destroy the country's villages, some of them hundreds of years old, in order to destroy their natural life. You have crushed the inner souls of people, humiliating them in their hopes and legitimate aspirations, humbling their consciences, forcing them, through pressure and terror, to accept lies as truth and truth as lies, and thus to acquiesce in their own moral crippling. . . . Put an end to this repressive

policy which is even more destructive than the economic disaster you have caused. (Deletant 270)

Thus many strange details in *Herztier* are historically grounded. The interrogator Pjele's suspicion of the folk song the friends like is, for example, evidence of the regime's suspicion of the potential collective power of the proletariat, which it tries to destroy:

> Der Hauptmann Pjele sagte zu Edgar, Kurt und Georg, das Gedicht fordere zur Flucht auf. Sie sagten: Es ist ein altes Volkslied. Der Hauptmann Pjele sagte: Es wäre besser, einer von euch hätte das selber geschrieben. Das wäre schlimm genug, aber so ist es noch schlimmer. Diese Lieder waren vielleicht einmal Volkslieder, das waren jedoch andere Zeiten. Das bürgerlich-gutsherrliche Regime ist längst überwunden. Heute singt unser Volk andere Lieder.
>
> [Captain Pjele said to Edgar, Kurt, and Georg that the poem was an incitement to flee the country. They said: It's an old folk song. Captain Pjele said: It would be better for your sake if one of you had written it. That would be bad enough, but not as bad as this. Maybe it was a folk song once, but those were different times. The rule of the bourgeoisie and the landowning class is long gone. Today our people sing different songs.] (*Herztier* 89)

Similarly Müller's phrase "Das Proletariat der Blechschafe und Holzmelonen" [the proletariat of tin sheep and wooden melons] (*Herztier* 37) encapsulates the specific alienation of uprooted Romanian villagers forced to move to towns and engaged in senseless and poorly planned industrial production, and Georg's observation that "Alle bleiben hier Dörfler.... In einer Diktatur kann es keine Städte geben, weil alles klein ist, wenn es bewacht wird" [Everyone's a villager here.... No cities can grow in a dictatorship, because everything stays small when it's being watched] (52) expresses the frustration of a population whose infiltration by informers was proportionately four times that of the GDR (Deletant xiv).

"Everyone Was an Island, and the Whole Country Too"

Müller locates power in forced isolation, not just on a synchronic but also on a diachronic plane, something shown in *Herztier* and theorized in her later work. *Herztier* depicts loneliness being bred in the separation between, and the silences within, ethnic groups in Romania, and these have historical causes. The majority Romanian population and the minority German and Hungarian populations are separated by mutual suspicion and memories of conflict. The narrator's loneliness is not simply the result of persecution by the Securitate but has been with her since childhood, inherited from the previous generation and learned through the touchy silences of the family and the village. The friendship of the literary group, the collective *wir* [we], is new and most welcome to her when she first meets Georg, Kurt, and Edgar after the death of Lola and they start to spend time together, for she has never experienced it before (43). Intercut into the present-time narrative are scenes from her childhood, narrated in a distancing third person, all of which reveal not only her loneliness, but also the loneliness of those around her in the Swabian village in the Romanian Banat where she grew up. These memories are triggered by events in the narrative present. For example, when the adult friends have fun with a wooden toy she covets, she is reminded of her inability as a child to share her toys and her consequent loneliness and sense of abjection: "Dann das Alleinsein. Das Kind ist häßlich und so verlassen wie sonst nichts auf der Welt" [And then alone again. The child is ugly and more forlorn than anything in the whole world] (166). The pervasive loneliness is not just that of the only child but was learned from the unspoken traumas of the previous generations, in whom a sense of victimhood and guilt often intermingle. The dominant figure in her childhood was her father, an ex-Waffen-ss soldier and unreconstructed Nazi who sought solace from his bad conscience in drink and in slashing weeds. Returning from the war, he was driven by loneliness into the arms of a woman he did not love; this is the story of the narrator's conception and of her parents' unhappy marriage (21). The traumatic memories of the grandparents' generation—of World War I, of denunciations during the Nazi period, and of *Enteignung* [expropriation] and forced collectivization after it—also infused the atmosphere in which the narrator grew up. That these wounds are still open is shown, for example, by the grandfather's pain when the Securitate steals a piece of his precious chess set, which survived World War I (51, 77).

Müller later used the metaphor of the island to theorize the pervasive isolation in this "nach außen abgeschottetes, nach innen überwachtes Land" [a country sealed off from the outside and subject to surveillance within] (*König* 160).[10] Reversing the travel industry's promotion of *Inselglück*, which equates happiness with the apartness of a holiday island, she describes Romania as an archipelago of isolated groups and individuals, from the nomenklatura, a state within the state, constantly shoring up its power and afraid of the masses; to the villages in her area, two Romanian, one Slovak, and one Hungarian—"Jedes für sich mit seiner anderen Sprache, seinen Feiertagen, seiner Religion, seiner Kleidung" [each independent with its different language, its feast days, its religion, its costumes] (*König* 161); to the members of the German minority, seen from the outside as an island of *Nazifritzen* but seeing themselves as "Insel der schuldlos von den Rumänen Bestraften" [an island of innocents, punished by the Romanians] (*König* 162); to her own mother and father, locked in their own silent misery.

Another abstracting phrase—*Friedhöfe machen* [making cemeteries] (*Herztier* 21)—is used to link the unspoken crimes of the narrator's father and those of Edgar's Nazi uncles with the present-day crimes of Hauptmann Pjele and Ceaușescu: "Wenn einer, nur weil er geht, ißt, schläft und jemanden liebt, Friedhöfe macht, sagte Edgar, dann ist er ein größerer Fehler als wir. Ein Fehler für alle, ein beherrschender Fehler ist er" [Anyone who makes graveyards just because he walks, eats, sleeps, and loves, said Edgar, is a bigger mistake than we are. A mistake of the first order. A master mistake] (8). This use of language deliberately suggests a continuity of crimes among totalitarian regimes. Müller's musings on the workings of power under dictatorships are contained in the title essay of the volume *Der König verneigt sich und tötet*. She uses the term *König* to describe the different manifestations of power within the village and the state, all of which serve to isolate. The choice of the word is, as so often in Müller, overdetermined. It refers to Ceaușescu's literal power but also the way power held sway at all levels of society and through the lasting effects of terror—and it is here that she talks of her mother's deportation after the war (*König* 71-72), a topic she pursues later in *Atemschaukel* (2009). But she came upon the word through serendipity, through what she perceives as the separate life of words that she exploits in her collages: because *Kenig* [king] rhymes with *alleenig* [alone] in her village dialect. One of Müller's most abiding memories is of guarding the cows in the wide open fields near her village of Nitzkydorf in the Romanian Banat, feeling utterly alone, vulnerable and insignificant. The word *einsam* [solitary] did not exist in her dialect, she writes, "nur das Wort 'allein.' Und dieses hieß 'alleenig,' und das klingt wie 'wenig'—und so war es auch" [just the word "alone." And this was "alleenig," and that sounds like "little" and that's how it was] (*König* 12). From this rhyme followed another: "alleenig—wenig—Kenig" [alone—little—king] (55), with the result that "Der König war von Kind an in meinem Kopf" [The king was in my head from childhood] (*König* 57).

"Differentiating and Seeing Reality Anew"

As I have been arguing and others have shown, notably Valentina Glajar, the state of affairs of which Müller writes in *Herztier* was horribly real.[11] Yet she writes obliquely in ways that assume a lot of background knowledge on the part of the reader—John White describes her works as not mimetic but "palimpsests of the political" (White 76)—and that also allow for connections to be made with other examples of dictatorships. Fellow Romanian writer Mircea Cărtărescu described Müller's style as the pearl resulting from the irritation of a grain of sand. The disparity between poetic result and the brutal spur to her writing has often been commented on. The formal complexity and densely, almost willfully poetic, effects of the text arise from its composition out of details extracted from their diegetic contexts and linked together associatively to form what Beverley Eddy calls "an elaborate grid of imagery" (Eddy 67). Her literary technique thus echoes the technique she uses to create her pictorial poetry collages: cutting individual words and syllables from newspapers and magazines, she recombines them into rhyming poems. Each collage is accompanied by a surreal image that reinforces the poem. The creation of collages reenacts the isolating violence of the political system to which she was subject until she left Romania. The finished results are reminiscent of blackmail notices yet are not anonymous or threatening but instantly recognizable and richly evocative.

Herztier, and indeed most of her other literary texts, work in the same way. An early example is the recollecting narrator's comment in that crucial first scene—"Ich kann mir heute noch kein Grab vorstellen. Nur einen Gürtel, ein Fenster, eine Nuß und einen Strick" [To this day, I can't really picture a grave. Only a belt, a window, a nut, and a rope] (*Herztier* 7)—a statement that only gradually reveals its meaning: each of these overdetermined objects represents a mode of death: the belt, the window, and the cord, suicide (of Lola, Georg, and Kurt respectively), and the nut, Tereza's cancerous growth, which it resembles. Nuts, mulberry trees, green plums, weeds, hair, and grass, extracted from their natural environments and recombined in the text take on an intensification of meaning. Müller employs this technique in order to overcome the credibility gap; she was warned when she came West with her then husband Richard Wagner in 1987 that people would not believe her accounts of what she had left behind: "Schon die harmlosen Beispiele galten hierzulande als übertrieben" [Even the harmless examples were considered exaggerated in these parts] (*König* 104). In the opening scene of *Herztier*, the narrator and her friend Edgar, who have escaped Romania for the relative safety of the West, reflect on the necessity yet impossibility of giving adequate witness to what they have experienced: "Wenn wir schweigen, werden wir unangenehm ... wenn wir reden, werden wir lächerlich" [When we don't speak, we become unbearable, and when we do, we make fools of ourselves] (7). Yet *Herztier*, through its patterning, does give voice to that experience.

Müller's aesthetic of fragmentation and poetic intensity is also born of loneliness and impoverishment. She came to write because of the silences in which she grew up and describes writing itself as a lonely activity, "eine Sache des Alleinseins" [a question of being alone] (*König* 85). She has always reacted against Socialist Realism, with its positive heroes and overarching narratives, and even against other potentially liberating movements such as feminism if they have a totalizing tendency. Her fiction focuses on details as an aesthetic and a political choice, pitching itself against ideology, which "hat das Ganze im Auge" [has the totality in its gaze] (*König* 87). She rejects the concept of languages as *Heimat*, something one can inhabit as a close fit, for to her the use of language is always particular.

Sie lebt immer im Einzelfall, man muß ihr jedesmal aufs neue ablauschen, was sie im Sinn hat. In dieser Unzertrennlichkeit vom Tun wird sie legitim oder inakzeptabel, schön oder häßlich, man kann auch sagen: gut oder böse. In jeder Sprache, das heißt in jeder Art des Sprechens sitzen andere Augen.

[It lives always in the particular case; you have to learn what it has in mind by listening to it anew each time. In this inseparability from action it becomes legitimate or unacceptable, lovely or ugly; you could also say: good or evil. Different eyes inhabit each language, that is, each kind of speaking.]

(*König* 39)

The dynamic interplay between languages—for example, the fact that "lily" is masculine in Romanian and feminine in German—creates two realities and "ein rätselhaftes, niemals endendes Geschehen" [a puzzling, never-ending happening] (*König* 25). Müller's texts create an Arendtian newness out of a reconfiguration of the gaps between languages and words.

"Beginning ... Is the Supreme Capacity of Man"

The characters in *Herztier* find themselves reduced by trauma and persecution to a state of isolation and bare existence: "Sie wissen doch, dachte ich mir, daß uns gleich nichts mehr bleibt, als wer und wo wir sind" [Surely they must know, I thought, that we soon won't have anything left except who and where we are] (167). In the interrogation cell each of the friends is utterly alone. But in this unlikely place, both the protagonist and her mother resist the paralyzing effects of fear, the mother by cleaning her oppressor's office in a familiar bodily gesture using the only object she has, a handkerchief, and the narrator by mentally rehearsing a body-parts list to match her interrogator Pjele's inventory of her possessions:

Mich selber schrieb der Hauptmann Pjele nicht auf. . . . Es wird auf keine Liste stehen, daß ich 1 Stirn, 2 Augen, 2 Ohren, 1 Nase, 2 Lippen, 1 Hals hatte, als ich hierher kam. . . . Ich wollte im Kopf die Liste meines Körpers machen gegen seine Liste.

[Everything except me, whom Captain Pjele failed to write down. There won't be any list saying that I had in my possession when I arrived here 1 forehead, 1 pr. eyes, 1 pr. ears, 1 nose, 1 pr. lips, 1 neck. . . . I wanted to take a mental inventory of my body to counter Captain Pjele's list.] (*Herztier* 145)

Though the narrator had not managed to carry through what might seem to readers an infantile prank (daubing Pjele's house with excrement, the nearest she comes to an act of resistance in this country characterized by the absence of such acts), nevertheless, reduced to standing naked in the corner, singing to order for her interrogator, she finds that "es kränkte mich nichts mehr, ich hatte auf einmal fingerdicke Haut" [nothing hurt me anymore, suddenly my skin was an inch thick] (*Herztier* 145). Just as she refused to commit suicide on the grounds that it would be doing the regime's work for it, so here her itemized bodily existence—in Arendt's terms, her natality—enables her to resist.[12]

The name given by Müller to individual bodily existence, the only locus of resistance because irreducible even if not inviolable, is one of her most difficult-to-decode neologisms, in *Herztier*. Used differently on a number of occasions in the novel, in connection with the friends but also the narrator's unsympathetic grandmother and the "Conducător" himself, the term seems neither consistently positive nor negative but neutral and dynamic. Müller later theorized it thus:

> Das "Herztier" ist im Unterschied zum gelebten "König" ein geschriebenes Wort. Es hat sich auf dem Papier ergeben, beim Schreiben als Ersatz für den König, weil ich für die Lebensgier in der Todesangst ein Wort suchen mußte, eins, das ich damals, als ich in Angst lebte, nicht hatte. Ich wollte ein zweischneidiges Wort, so zweischneidig wie der König sollte es sein. Sowohl Scheu also auch Willkür sollten drin sitzen. Und es mußte in den Körper hinein, ein besonderes Eingeweide, ein inneres Organ, das mit dem ganzen äußeren rundherum befrachtet werden kann. Ich wollte das Unberechenbare ansprechen, das in jedem einzelnen Menschen sitzt, gleicherweise in mir und in den Mächtigen.

> [In contrast to the lived "king," the "heart-beast" is a written word. It arose on the page, a substitute for the king when writing, because I had to find a word for passion for life in the middle of deadly fear, a word that I didn't

have back then when I was living in fear. I wanted a word which cut both ways, which cut both ways as much as the king did. It should contain shyness but also arbitrary power. And it had to be bodily, a particular innard, an inner organ which can be loaded with the total outer one. I wanted to address the unpredictable that inhabits each person, whether in me or in the powerful.] (*König* 57–58)

Thus it is the possibility latent in each individual bodily existence, even that of a dictator—Arendt's "natality" providing an inexhaustible supply of new lives—that is Müller's antidote to monumental power. And it is gestures, objects, and the free life of words that, for Müller, lend some temporary stability to Arendt's subject in crisis. She addresses this in the Nobel Prize speech with which I began. The handkerchief, which represents her mother's unarticulatable tenderness, briefly becomes Müller's office: she sits on it on the staircase in the machine tools factory when she is thrown out of her actual office for refusing to work with the Securitate. And the "Pantomime der Wörter" [pantomime of words] ("Jedes Wort" 18) offers comfort when she, forced into the role of a *Treppenwitz*, reflects on the anthropomorphic associations of technical building terms such as *Treppenwangen* [stair-cheeks] and *Treppenaugen* [stair-eyes]: "also hat die Treppe ein Gesicht" [so the stair has a face] ("Jedes Wort" 11). The pantomime of words, which is inextricably linked to the omnipresence of dictatorship, takes on a life of its own, for as Arendt recognized, "Selbstverständlichkeit nie mehr wiederkehrt, wenn sie einem fast komplett geraubt worden ist.... Nichts mehr stimmt und alles ist wahr" [Nothing can ever be matter of course again when you have been almost completely robbed of the matter of course.... Nothing is right anymore and everything is true] ("Jedes Wort" 18). Müller's apparently surreal but deeply materialist aesthetic is inspired, as the Nobel committee recognized, by compassion for the disposessed;[13] it gestures to overcome "die akute Einsamkeit des Menschen."

Conclusion: "Ein Überlebensbuch" [A Book of Survival]

One of the anthropomorphic words that fascinates the narrator of *Herztier* is *überendlich* [transfinite], which she comes across in her work as a translator in relation to a hydraulic machine.[14] The word, which she cannot find in a dictionary, stays with her, for it seems to her, like *Herztier*, to connote something of the human; furthermore, it helps her to evade the power of Hauptmann Pjele, who, like her father and Ceaușescu, has deaths on his conscience, and to memorialize her lost friends (*Herztier* 140, 248). The word, which had always seemed to her to describe the human rather than the machine world, occurs to her again at Georg's grave.

Herztier thematizes the loneliness resulting from the dictatorships and upheavals of Europe's twentieth century. If the young friends are forcibly isolated through political persecution, the older generations are isolated in their traumatic memories, about which they cannot speak. The identities of the older generations are formed in the silences following the great catastrophes of World War I, the Nazi project, and the Stalinist terror of the postwar period. The suffering of those generations tends now to be well documented and memorialized, though this was not always the case, and Müller's novel *Atemschaukel* does important memory work by giving voice to the suffering of German deportees to the Soviet Union after World War II. What is less well known than the crimes against humanity of the Nazi and Soviet dictatorships are the barbarous and comparatively recent crimes of the Ceaușescu regime to which *Herztier* testifies. *Herztier*, with its relentless claustrophobia, omnipresent *Angst*, and poetic effects, can appear to Western readers paranoid and surreal, but it is actually a more literal representation of the peculiarities of Romania in the 1980s than many without direct experience of the regime might assume; it bridges the credibility gap, not through realism, which for Müller would be inappropriate—"Man kann kein holzig realistisches Buch über eine Diktatur schreiben" [You can't write a woodenly realistic book about a dictatorship] (Haines and Littler 19)—but through its collage form and intense images. Müller writes that she has moved on from Romania but not from "der gesteuerten Verwahrlosung der Menschen in der Diktatur" [the regulated neglect of people under dictatorship] (*König* 185). Like all of Müller's works, *Herztier* fictionalizes with enormous precision a unique set of historical circumstances that resonate with some of the darkest moments of twentieth-century European history.

Notes

1. The title of this chapter (in English "The Acute Loneliness of the Individual") is taken from Herta Müller's Nobel Prize speech ("Jedes Wort weiß etwas vom Teufelskreis. Nobelvorlesung," *Immer derselbe Schnee und immer derselbe Onkel* 21).

2. In English *The Land of Green Plums*. This prizewinning translation by Michael Hofmann won Müller the Dublin Impac Prize in 1998.

3. The term "organized loneliness" is from Arendt (478).

4. For readings of *Herztier* in the light of trauma theory, see both Eddy and Marven.

5. http://nobelprize.org/mediaplayer/index.php?id=1312.

6. For details of the surveillance of Müller, see Glajar, "The Presence of the Unresolved Past."

7. Both items formed part of the exhibition Der kalte Schmuck des Lebens, showed in the Literaturhaus in Munich, Berlin, and Stuttgart in 2010 and in the Buddenbrookhaus in Lübeck in 2011.

8. The account of Romania under Ceaușescu and before is indebted to Deletant and Rady.

9. Begun in 1988, this program meant reducing the country's villages by more than half, razing the newly vacant ones, and moving the displaced villagers to "agro-industrial complexes." See Rady (68).

10. The heading above (in the original, "Jeder für sich war eine Insel und das ganze Land noch einmal") is also from *König* (160).

11. See Glajar, "Banat-Swabian, Romanian and German" and "The Discourse of Discontent." The section heading is from Apel, "Unterscheiden und Neusehen der Wirklichkeit."

12. The quote in the heading is from Arendt (479).

13. The Nobel citation describes Müller as a writer "who, with the concentration of poetry and the frankness of prose, depicts the landscape of the dispossessed"; http://nobelprize.org/nobel_prizes/literature/laureates/2009/.

14. The heading is from Michaelis, "In der Angst zu Haus."

Works Cited

Apel, Friedmar. "Kirschkern Wahrheit. Inmitten beschädigter Paradiese: Herta Müllers *Herztier*." FAZ, October 4, 1994. Web. March 18, 2011.

Arendt, Hanna. "Ideology and Terror: A Novel Form of Government." *The Origins of Totalitarianism*. San Diego, New York, and London: Harvest, 1966. 460–79.

Boym, Svetlana. *The Future of Nostalgia*. New York: Basic, 2001.

Cărtărescu, Mircea. "Das Schwert im Innern." Web. March 7, 2011. http://www.fr-online.de/kultur/debatte/das-schwert-im-innern/-/1473340/2843756/-/index.html.

Deletant, Dennis. *Ceaușescu and the Securitate: Coercion and Dissent in Romania, 1965–1989*. London: Hurst, 1995.

Eddy, Beverley Driver. "Testimony and Trauma in Herta Müller's *Herztier*." *German Life and Letters* 53.1 (2000): 56–72.

Fulbrook, Mary. *Anatomy of a Dictatorship: Inside the GDR 1949–1989*. Oxford: Oxford University Press, 1997.

Glajar, Valentina. "Banat-Swabian, Romanian, and German: Conflicting Identities in Herta Müller's *Herztier*." *Monatshefte* 89.4 (1997): 521–40.

———. "The Discourse of Discontent: Politics and Dictatorship in Herta Müller's *Herztier* (1994)." *The German Legacy in East Central Europe, as Recorded in Recent German-Language Literature*. New York: Camden House, 2004. 115–60.

———. "The Presence of the Unresolved Recent Past: Herta Müller and the Securitate." *Herta Müller*. Ed. Brigid Haines and Lyn Marven. Oxford: Oxford University Press, 2013. 49–63.

Haines, Brigid, and Margaret Littler. "Gespräch mit Herta Müller." *Herta Müller*. Ed. Brigid Haines. Cardiff: University of Wales Press, 1998. 14–25.

Marven, Lyn. *Body and Narrative in Contemporary Literatures in German: Herta Müller, Libuše Moníková, Kerstin Hensel*. Oxford: Oxford University Press, 2005.

———. "*Herztier*." *The Novel in German since 1990*. Ed. Stuart Taberner. Cambridge: Cambridge University Press, 2011. 180–94.

Michaelis, Rolf. "In der Angst zu Haus. Ein Überlebensbuch: Herta Müllers Roman *Herztier*." *Die Zeit*, October 7, 1994. Web. February 18, 2011.

Müller, Herta. *Cristina und ihre Attrappe, oder, Was (nicht) in den Akten der Securitate steht*. Göttingen: Wallstein, 2009.

———. *Der König verneigt sich und tötet*. Munich: Hanser, 2003.

———. *Der Teufel sitzt im Spiegel. Wie Wahrnehmung sich erfindet*. Berlin: Rotbuch, 1991.

———. *Herztier*. Reinbek bei Hamburg: Rowohlt, 1994.

———. *Immer derselbe Schnee und immer derselbe Onkel*. Munich: Hanser, 2011.

———. "Jedes Wort weiß etwas vom Teufelskreis. Nobelvorlesung." December 7, 2009. Web. December 7, 2009. http://nobelprize.org/nobel_prizes/literature/laureates/2009/.

———. *The Land of Green Plums*. Trans. Michael Hofmann. New York: Metropolitan Books, 1996.

Mungiu, Christian, dir. *4 Months, 3 Weeks and 2 Days*. Romania, 2007.

Pacepa, Ion Mihai. *Red Horizons*. Washington DC: Regnery Gateway, 1987.

Rady, Martin. *Romania in Turmoil: A Contemporary History*. London and New York: Tauris, 1992.

Smith, Craig S. "Eastern Europe Struggles to Purge Security Services." *New York Times*, December 12, 2006. Web. February 15, 2011.

Steiner, George. "You're Ruled by Hooligans. Your Friends Spy on You. Hellish, Isn't It?" *The Observer*, August 30, 1998. Web. March 15, 2011.

White, John J. "'Die Einzelheiten und das Ganze.' Herta Müller and Totalitarianism." *Herta Müller*. Ed. Brigid Haines. Cardiff: University of Wales Press, 1998. 75–95.

7 Facts, Fiction, Autofiction, and Surfiction in Herta Müller's Work

Paola Bozzi

Over the last fifteen years the emergence of groundbreaking work on trauma in literature and critical theory has made a profound impact both within and beyond the field of literature. This cutting-edge research has been applied to Herta Müller's work by scholars such as Beverley Driver Eddy, Brigid Haines, and Lyn Marven, who have connected images and strategies of fragmentation and disruption with trauma theory. Müller surely represents and reflects upon the traumatic events of twentieth-century Europe, as well as the cultural diversity of East Central Europe; she feels compelled to write about them (Glajar 2) and to show her aversion to all forms of authoritarian rule. There is no doubt that Müller's commitment to uncover political and cultural "truths" distinguishes her as an author for whom personal integrity is everything (*In der Falle* 6, 27–28). In her fiction, this voice is at all times apparent, laying the ground for a very uncomfortable moral challenge to her reader. Müller's installation of a resolute and absolute moral position actually runs the risk of alienating her readership—but does not.

In fact, Müller's work is structured not only by a narrative of trauma, articulated with increasing directness, but also by a remarkable lyrical intensity that manages to preserve a substantial, enriching imaginative space for the reader within such unremitting anger. I argue that this characteristic feature is not only a mark of her aesthetic achievement or her consummate artistry, but also the key to her convincing critical voice. The author makes powerful use of the literary imagination, which requires a response on behalf of the reader, grounded as much in poetic, imaginative sensibility as in sociopolitical (self-)criticism. Free play of imagining is indeed indispensable not only for poetics but also, curiously, for ethics itself. If ethics is left entirely to itself or allowed to dictate poetics at every turn, it risks degenerating into cheerless moralism. Poetics without ethics leads to dangerous play; ethics without poetics leads to the self-censuring of the imagination. In this sense, Müller's concern for a particular, imaginative reality has an inherently ethical and political dimension, one that has not "remained 'in der Falle'—totalitarianism's trap" (White 93).

Müller describes her original writing style, following Georges-Arthur Goldschmidt, as "autofictional" (*In der Falle* 21). Coined by Serge Doubrovsky in 1977 with reference to his novel *Fils*, the term "autofiction" points to Müller's creative reworking of her own biographical experiences, to the fictionalization of (parts of) her life.[1] Indeed in most of Müller's literary work the central character is either a girl or a young woman who bears a close relationship to the author at various ages: the child's perspective of the first-person narrator in *Niederungen* [*Nadirs*]; the teacher Adine in *Der Fuchs war damals schon der Jäger* and the first-person narrator in *Herztier* [*The Land of Green Plums*], both subjected to systematic psychological terror by the Securitate; the first-person narrator in *Heute wäre ich mir lieber nicht begegnet* [*The Appointment*], who wants to leave the country and is therefore summoned for daily interrogations as punishment; and finally, Irene in *Reisende auf einem Bein* [*Traveling on One Leg*], who most faithfully mirrors Müller's own position at the time of writing. Still, fiction is often autobiographical, while autobiography, despite its extraliterary truth value, is fictional because autobiography, no less than fiction, is the art of fabrication:

> So kommt es, daß selbst Autobiographisches, Eigenes im engsten Sinne des Wortes, nur noch vermittelt, nur noch im weitesten Sinne des Wortes mit meiner Autobiographie zu tun hat. Schon aus dem einfachen Grund, daß ich selber nur noch vermittelt mit mir zu tun habe, wenn ich über mich schreibe.
>
> [Therefore, even the autobiographical, the self in the strictest sense of the term, has to do with my autobiography only in a mediated form, and only in the broadest sense of the term. Simply because when I am writing about myself, I, too, only relate to myself in a mediated manner.] (*Teufel* 43)[2]

The fact of telling or writing a story, the fact of relating an event, always distorts that story or that event—fictionalizes it in the sense that it displaces the story or the event from reality into the realm of the imaginary.

Müller's writings as a whole perform processes of memory work, reconstructing and confronting the past, yet the vital imagination of her texts, its creative process, operates as more than a simple reflection of facts and life because Müller symbolically projects in her writings an as of yet unnoticed, neglected constellation of existence waiting to be discovered by the reader: "Das Gedärm unter der Oberfläche ist überall" [The entrails under the surface are everywhere] (*Teufel* 18).[3]

Thus the reader is not only confronted with "autofiction," as Müller herself suggests, but also with something akin to "surfiction," a term coined by American author and critic Raymond Federman in a manifesto titled "Surfiction: Four Propositions in Form of an Introduction," where Federman attempts to set new conditions for modern narrative practices. He calls the kind of writing that thematizes the constructedness of reality "surfiction," not because it imitates reality but because this kind of writing exposes the fictional nature of reality (7). In analogy to the surrealists, who were keen on calling the locus of man's subconscious experience "surreality," Federman focuses his attention on the kind of experience that levels the difference between life and fiction (7). For Federman fiction is thus not a representation of reality but creates its own autonomous reality instead. Surfiction does not draw a distinction between memory and imagination, between what really happened in the world and what it imagines happened. As such "surfiction" erases the lines among past, present, and future and liberates itself from the conventions of realism.

Müller's much-used and much-cited expression "die erfundene Wahrnehmung" [the invented perception] is closely related to Federman's notion of "surfiction." Perceptions are normally experienced as passively received, as standing in contrast to our voluntary control over images. This contrast should not be overstated, however, because there are limits to how imagining is subject to willing (Brann 159): in some cases images don't come to us; in other cases they come to us against our will or refuse to recede once imaged. While reproductive imagination is largely limited to calling up the images of phenomena from past perception, productive imagination, on the other hand, has the power to reinterpret things through the layering of images over perceptions and plays a range of roles crucial to cognition, aesthetic appreciation, and artistic creation. In Kant's *Critique of the Power of Judgement* (1790) the imagination is essential to the play of mental powers in which the philosopher thinks we feel the pleasure of finding something beautiful. Moreover, productive imagination is the guiding power of artistic genius; its "aesthetic ideas" (for Kant the expressed content of works of art) create "another nature, out of the material which the real one gives" (192). In artistic genius, imagination "steps beyond nature" (192) by producing a perspective on or an interpretation of things that supplements perception with fresh possibilities of significance. In turn, Wittgenstein observes in *Philosophical Investigations* that we can see something "in various aspects according to the fiction [we] surround it with" (sec. 234). To see imaginatively is to clothe something in a fiction that transforms its meaning and may take the simple form of an image, a system of images, or a fiction proper evoked by the language.

In her poetologic rejection of the "myth of the Given" (Sellars), Herta Müller, too, regards perception as an *active* process, defining here on the one hand the transgressive imagination of the child in the village of a totalitarian state and, on the other, the methodological tools for the author's representation of a certain authentic experience dependent on the senses and therefore radically individual. The voluntarism of imagining is, of course, what allows it to serve as a ready alternative to the annoying, threatening persistence of the perceived: "der den 'normalen' Dingen zugestandene Wahn" [the delusion granted to "normal" things] (*Teufel* 13). At the same time there is no discursive rehabilitation of the writing self in recollection because the textual fixing of memory cannot ensure any sort of domestication of that undisciplined memory:

> Die Wahrnehmung, die sich erfindet, steht nicht still. Sie überschreitet ihre Grenzen, da, wo sie sich festhält. Sie ist unabsichtlich, sie meint nichts Bestimmtes. Sie wird vom Zufall geschaukelt. Ihre Unberechenbarkeit trifft jedoch die einzige mögliche Auswahl, wenn sie sich wählt. Der Zeigefinger im Kopf bricht ständig ein.
>
> [The perception that invents itself does not stand still. It transgresses its boundaries precisely at the point where it grabs hold. It is without intentions, it does not mean anything specific. It is swayed by chance. Its unpredictability makes the only possible choice when it chooses itself. The mind's pointing finger always interrupts.] (*Teufel* 19)

Müller insists also on the tragic ambivalence of writing, on what in De Man's words "can be considered both an act and an interpretive process that follows after an act with which it cannot coincide. As such, it both affirms and denies its own nature" (152). She writes: "Doch bevor ich den Satz schreibe, beobachtet mich der Satz. Ich fange an, ihn zu schreiben, wenn ich zu wissen glaube, wie er aussieht. Doch jedesmal stellt sich heraus, daß ich noch lange nicht weiß, wie er aussieht, wenn ich es zu wissen glaub" [Before I start writing the sentence, the sentence observes me in fact. I start writing the sentence when I think I know what it looks like. But every time it turns out that I am far from knowing what it looks like when I think I know] (*Teufel* 35).

Further: "Oft, wenn ich im nachhinein einen Text lese, den ich selbst geschrieben hab, kann ich, daß ich ihn geschrieben hab, nicht mehr nachvollziehen" [Often, when I reread a text that I wrote myself, I can no longer imagine that I actually wrote it] (*Teufel* 45). A truly fictional discourse can only be self-reflexive; genuine fiction constructs itself through self-deconstruction and constant suspicion of its fictiousness. Thus Müller explores the relationship between fiction and autobiography, as well as between critical commentary and interpretation "in an act of *disruptive complicity*" (Federman, "Self-Reflexive" 33): "Autobiographisches, selbst Erlebtes. Ja, es ist wichtig. Aus dem, was man erlebt hat, sucht sich der Zeigefinger im Kopf auch beim Schreiben die Wahrnehmung aus, die sich erfindet" [The autobiographical, one's own experiences. Yes, that is important. From one's own experiences the mind's pointing finger selects, also while writing, the perception that invents itself] (*Teufel* 20).

Müller tries to explore the possibilities of fiction in order to challenge the tradition that governs it and to develop a strong poetics of imagination. Her works are exemplifications of possible meanings on the term "imagination": the ability to evoke absent objects with things present here and now; the construction and use of forms and figures to represent real things in some "unreal" way; the fictional projection of non-existent things as in dreams (*Teufel* 63-65); the capacity of human consciousness to become fascinated by illusions, confusing what is real with what is unreal. At the same time, the fictionalization and the transfiguration of her lived experience through writing ("autofiction") both allow and facilitate access to a certain "truth." For Müller truth reached through creative imagination is "truer" than truth constructed mimetically in reference to facts (representation): "Da er aus der lückenlosen Unwirklichkeit hervorgegangen ist, ist der Text, wenn er mal geschrieben ist, lückenlos wirklich. Er ist Wahrnehmung, erfundene Wahrnehmung, die sich im Rückblick wahr nimmt" [Because it emerged from seamless irreality, the text, once written, is seamlessly true. It is the invented perception that looks at itself retrospectively] (*Teufel* 38).

Imagination is thus an attempt to release one's true self, to discover a mode of experience that under the great pressures to conform to all of society's socializing and repressive forces—family, group, community, and nation or state—had been surrendered. A literary text gains the power to affect reality through this interaction of self and world:

> Nicht nur aus den eigenen Texten gehen die Sätze hinaus, in die Dinge. Auch aus den Texten anderer Autoren. Aus Büchern, die man gelesen hat, die einem was bedeuten. Und meist stellt sich dieses Bild der konkreten Wahrnehmung als Kopie der gelesenen, erfundenen Wahrnehmung im Kopf

dar. Das Konkrete hat selbst im Fall dieses zufälligen Nebeneinanderstehns keine Priorität. Der Hinweis darauf kommt aus dem Kopf. Die erfundene Wahrnehmung, die man gelesen hat, verlängert sich. Sie ist stärker. Sie besetzt. Nicht die Bilder im Kopf werden wie der Ort, sondern der Ort wird wie die Bilder im Kopf.

[Sentences don't just emerge, enter into things, from the texts you wrote. No, also from books that others have written. From books that you read and that were meaningful to you. And often this image of concrete perception takes shape in my mind as a duplicate of an invented perception that I once read somewhere. Even in the case of this coincidental parallel the concrete does not have priority. The sign comes from the mind. The invented perception, which one has read, is drawn out. It is stronger. It takes over. The images in our mind do not become like the places; the places become like the images in the mind.] (*Teufel* 53)[4]

This phenomenon leads to a conception of the relation between fiction and reality that is the exact opposite of what informs realism: in Müller reality reflects fiction and not vice versa. In her account of literature as a means to overcome corrupt consciousness, Müller describes it as rooted in the childish experience of the incommensurability of seeing and perceiving and in the recognition that "[d]as, was wir sehen, überschreitet seine Grenzen" [what we see oversteps its boundaries] (*Teufel* 15). In fact, Müller's texts focus on a constant critical dialogue between the literal and the metaphorical, even in short sentences such as: "Das Abteil fuhr. Die Scheibe hetzte Bilder" [The compartment moved. The windowpane hurried images along] (*Barfüßiger Februar* 5).

Taking up Roman Jakobson's notion of "split reference," or *référence dédoublée*, Paul Ricoeur shows that the reference of language is not confined to "descriptive reference" and that fictional and literary texts point to reality with their own metaphorical reference (*La Métaphore* 11, 282, 289, and passim). The imaginative layering of image over perceptions inspires the metaphorical cognition of one thing as another.[5] In the case of the metaphor, the dissolution of descriptive reference, which in a first step results in language pointing to itself, becomes, in a second step, the negative condition for consulting a more radical reference to the world

Facts, Fiction, Autofiction, and Surfiction

on the ruins of the literal meaning of the expression. Just as a metaphor thus acquires meaning by displacing the literal denotation, Müller's writings gain their virtual signification and reference (or the "meaning of a second order") through the suspension of any literal meaning. It is this secondary sense, which is capable of describing reality and referring to it in a new way, that is not available to descriptive, denotative language. Müller insists that language always expresses more than any plastic representation can suggest; she resists the idolatry of total meaning and concedes to the other the time of the other.

At the same time, her narrative fiction is autofictionally linked with reality in that every refiguration has to be prefigured in the pre-narrative structure of human experience. According to Ricoeur, "La littérature serait à jamais incompréhensible si elle ne venait configurer ce qui, dans l'action humaine, fait déjà figure" [Literature would forever be incomprehensible if it did not configure that which already figures in human action] (*La Métaphore* 100). A metaphor is indeed essentially the linguistic expression of "seeing-as"; imaginative seeing pursued in words rather than images in Müller's writings appears in expressions such as "das Gehirn der Nüsse" [the brain of the nuts] (*Barfüßiger Februar* 24); "das Blut der Melonen" [the blood of the melons] (*Der Fuchs* 77); "Proletariat der Blechschafe und Holzmelonen" [the proletariat of the tin sheep and the wooden melons] (*Herztier* 37); or titles like *Niederungen, Barfüßiger Februar, Herztier, Reisende auf einem Bein,* and *Atemschaukel*. A metaphor distills the seeing of one thing in another into language so that, when this is successfully achieved, it inspires creative "seeing-as" on the part of its reader.

Experimental postmodernists were already in the sixties and seventies enabling their readers to get involved as creative "co-conspirators" with more process-oriented texts asking them to help invent the story along with the writer. As Federman says in "Surfiction," "All the rules of and principles of printing and bookmaking must be forced to change as a result of the changes in the writing (or the telling) of a story in order to give the reader a sense of free participation in the writing/reading process, in order to give the reader an element of choice (active choice) in the ordering of the discourse and the discovery of its meaning" (9). Surfiction, as a writerly practice focused on revolutionizing narrative experience, was an attack on the false consciousness with which most modern fiction associated itself. Modernist writing throughout the twentieth century has been interested in presenting a "fragmentary narrative composition" that would give the reader an opportunity to "create a whole" reading experience. For modernist writers, the notion of interactivity was tied to the reader's desire for wholeness, but for the Surfictionists, the components and the details were always greater than the wholes, and besides, for the Surfictionists the wholes do not exist, or if they do, they exist as holes, black holes, for readers to get sucked into, at which point Surfiction writers try, perhaps, to help them get out.

In Müller's works too, images do not come together to produce a whole picture; in fact, the perception of reality is made of a series of individual and discrete images (*Hunger und Seide* 59). In her poetological and "critifictional" (Federman, "Critifiction" 49) essays, Müller describes her view of literature by highlighting simultaneity and the suppression of connections as well as the value of what is left unsaid, of interstices, and of breaches within the text. As a matter of fact, the power of her narrative to evoke images and emotions comes as much from what is to be found between the lines as from what was actually written down. The creative, imaginative act of "reading between the lines" is then constitutive of the reading process as such. In her poetological essay "Wie Wahrnehmung sich erfindet," the author claims that "[d]as, was fällt und aufschlägt oder kein Geräusch macht, daß was man nicht aufschreibt, spürt man in dem, was man aufschreibt" [what falls and hits the ground or makes no sound, what you don't write down, you intuit in what you do write down] (*Teufel* 19); "Der verschwiegene (ausgelassene) Satz muß mit der gleichen Lautstärke sprechen wie der geschriebene Satz" [The unwritten (omitted) sentence has to speak with the same volume as the written sentence] (*Teufel* 36). From this viewpoint she goes on describing herself as reader: "Das, was mich einkreist, seine Wege geht, beim Lesen, ist das, was zwischen den Sätzen fällt und aufschlägt, oder kein Geräusch macht. Es ist das Ausgelassene" [What surrounds me also goes its own way, while reading is what falls between the sentences and hits the ground, or makes no sound. It is that which was omitted] (*Teufel* 36).[6] As a consequence, the narrative is supported by a well-defined interplay of real and imagined, the image itself and its associations, the represented text and the signified "extra-text," in which the reader is implicated as an active force, as the following two examples from Müller's *Nadirs* illustrate:

> Mutter schneidet mir die Nägel so kurz, daß mir die Fingerspitzen wehtun. Ich fühle mit den frischgeschnittenen Fingernägeln, daß ich nicht richtig gehen kann. Ich gehe immerzu auf den Händen. Ich fühle auch, daß ich mit diesen kurzen Nägeln nicht richtig reden und nicht richtig denken kann. Und der Tag ist nichts als eine riesengroße Anstrengung. (*Niederungen* 43)

> [Mother cuts my nails so short that my fingertips are hurting. With those newly cut fingernails, I feel I can't walk well. I constantly walk on my hands. I also feel that I can't really talk or think well with those short nails. And the day is nothing but a huge exertion.] (*Nadirs* 32)

> Die Straßenkehrer haben Dienst. Sie kehren die Glühbirnen weg, kehren die Straßen aus der Stadt, kehren das Wohnen aus den Häusern, kehren mir die Gedanken aus dem Kopf, kehren mich von einem Bein aufs andere, kehren mir die Schritte aus dem Gehen. (*Niederungen* 138)

> [The street sweepers are at work. They sweep out the light bulbs, they sweep the streets out of the town, they sweep the living out of the houses, they sweep thoughts out of my head, they sweep me from one leg to the other, they sweep the steps out of my walk.] (*Nadirs* 115)

In fact her texts operate with principles of fragmentation and omission that are expressed on the level of syntax and in their narrative structure. The logical, semantic progression of ideas, the progression of the texts themselves, is disrupted by frequent shifts in narrative chronology as well; the sentences, as well as the individual chapters or incidents, are not linked; the verbs point both to timelessness and a lack of movement; blank spaces and silences often occur in the text; the description degenerates into a series of images or a list of nouns: "Amalie spürt die Absätze der weißen Sandalen im Bauch. Die Glut aus der Stirn brennt in den Augen. Amalies Zunge drückt im Mund. Das silberne Kreuz glänzt in der Fensterscheibe. Im Apfelbaum hängt ein Schatten. Er ist schwarz und aufgewühlt. Der Schatten ist ein Grab" (*Der Mensch* 104) [Amalie feels the heels of the white sandals in her stomach. The fire from her forehead is burning in her eyes. Amalie's tongue presses down in her mouth. The silver cross gleams in the window pane. A shadow in the apple tree. It's black and disturbed. The shadow is a grave] (*Passport* 86). Within the text, individual words, innocuous at first, gradually become weighted with significance through a process of juxtaposition, in a way that renders any explicit narrative stance unnecessary. Sensory perceptions are privileged over reflection, with the result that the text is no more than the impression of the world—in a strong sense—upon a (mostly absent) narrator; the lack of subordinating conjunctions and relative clauses suppresses causality.

Müller's conception of the poetic is also based on the *Riß* [gap] in language, on the break of its normal flow, which gives special importance to the poetic function of the text over the referential, emphasizing stasis, freezing a moment of perception in time and refusing its incorporation into narrative memory (Bozzi 164–71). Connections do gradually become apparent; otherwise unimportant descriptions come to be significant, by emphasizing individual elements or by focusing on specific moments, until the minute detail develops into the grotesque, into the overwhelming, and "exposes the fixation of desire in language" (Federman, "Self-Reflexive" 33). Grotesquely literal details work to produce non-literal associations and modulate effortlessly into the surreal: "Der Agronom hatte einen hellgrauen Anzug mit dunkelgrauem Muster an. Es war ein Fischgrätmuster, und es war hell an den Schultern und dunkel am Rückgrat. Der Agronom ging mit schwarzen Wirbeln in seinen Fischgräten hinter der Kantorin her" [The agronomist wore a light grey suit with a dark grey pattern. It was a herring-bone pattern, light at the shoulders and dark at the spine. The agronomist walked behind the cantor's wife in his herring bones with his black vertebrae] (*Barfüßiger Februar* 14).

Haines defines the "micro-politics of resistance" ("Leben wir im Detail" 109) as an aesthetic strategy and as a reaction against totalizing systems, whether political or literary. Organized in superimposed aesthetic patterns, the particular attention to an observed, remembered, or imagined detail rather than to plots and meanings is central to both the content and the form of Müller's work, thus eschewing the building of narratives to make sense of the world and the individual:

Tausend Details ergeben etwas, aber keinen gespannten Faden vom Leben, keine allgemeine Übereinkunft, keine Utopie. Details sind nicht in Kette und Glied zu stellen, in keiner geradlinigen Logik der Welt. Ich habe mich nie für das Ganze geeignet. Ich sorgte mit aller Verzweiflung, die Kleinigkeiten, die meinen Weg streiften, nachzuvollziehen.

[A thousand details do yield something but not a thread of life, no general understanding, no utopia. Details cannot be placed together in a chain, or in a linear logic of the world. I was never interested in the whole. Filled with despair, I tried to understand the smallest details that crossed my path.] (*Hunger und Seide* 60–61)

Thus the author issued the directive, borrowed from Eugène Ionesco, her fellow Romanian exile, to live in the detail (*Hunger und Seide* 61): "Der literarische Text läuft nicht neben der Nachweisbarkeit geschichtlicher Realität her. Er allein schafft es, durch das Detail der Sinne, die Vorstellbarkeit der Sinne zu erzwingen" [The literary text does not run parallel to the demonstrability of historical reality. By focusing on sensual details the literary text alone manages to capture what the senses can conceive] (*In der Falle* 5).

Müller is a master of producing this sort of experience of self-intensification and self-extension via the rendering of the visual, auditory, tactile, and olfactory detail. Her novelistic prose works on difference, allowing the reader's creative space to grow.[7] Whereas self-intensification occurs via the focusing of attention and emotion on familiar details that may otherwise have drifted away from us, self-extension expands one's range of noticing and feeling to attentively take in aspects of a larger world. In Müller's works thematic (often symbolic) associations operate in place of an explicit syntactic or narrative link. Linguistically the text derives its nourishment from the accumulation of internal patterns that follow a principle of contiguity and contextuality. While this procedure allows the reader to substantially exert his or her own imagination, it also produces a specific aesthetics grounded in the incommensurability of what can be defined as "pure," literal, and descriptive language (rooted in the reference to a familiar world) and its (intentionally over-)loaded metaphorical and conceptual use. In this way language maintains an equivocal position, makes the reader uneasy by allowing him or her to reflect on the proximity of familiarity to uncanniness (*Heimlichkeit* to *Unheimlichkeit*): "Den fremden Blick als Folge einer fremden Umgebung zu sehen, ist deshalb so absurd, weil das Gegenteil wahr ist: Er kommt aus den vertrauten Dingen" [To interpret the unfamiliar, foreign gaze as the consequence of a strange or foreign environment is precisely so absurd because the opposite is true: it arises from the familiar objects] (*Der fremde Blick* 26).

The quality of much of Müller's writings is thus unequivocally surreal (Tudorică 92–98); her combination of estranging focalizers, associative thought, and grotesque imagery is deliberate. In fact the author investigates another possible sense of things in relation to human experience and emotional involvement. The truth of Müller's narration as fiction provides a true account of the complexity of the human subject in relation to time and suffering through a strong use of imagination. Her writing finds a path toward the neglected other and entails a body of poetry that opens up an alterity exceeding the imagination of the author herself. Such a poetic language functions to fill the gap between the world of the text and the world of the reader (Ricoeur, *Temps et récit* 1, 117–21) and gives him or her the possibility to see the world from a different perspective or, better yet, an "unfamiliar or strange view" (*Der fremde Blick*). This offers both an escape from the daily externally imposed "normal" and a threat to the normative (*Teufel* 13; *Hunger und Seide* 91–92). Indeed "imagination is an inescapable and essential element in cultural critique" (Whale 196), and a tradition made gospel by Sartre identifies its power as a principal source of human freedom: a creature devoid of freedom would be one completely obliged to the determinacy of the present, unable in any way to escape its clutches.

Müller's work shows that imagination regularly enacts our free transcendence of our actual situation toward something else. "To posit an image," writes Sartre, "is to construct an object on the fringe of the whole reality, which therefore means to hold the real at a distance, to free oneself from it, in a word, to deny it" (266). Sartre understands the voluntarism earlier attributed to imagining, the fact that the calling up of images is largely subject to the will, as a hallmark of human consciousness and as an experience of freedom from present situations. "For a consciousness to be able to imagine," he writes, "it must be able to escape from the world by its very nature, it must be able by its own efforts to withdraw from the world. In a word it must be free" (267). Sartre underlines that however much awareness negates the present world in apprehending it as not-itself, imagination's freeing production of images always occurs from a certain perspective on that world: "[E]very apprehension of the real as a world tends of its own accord to end up with the production of unreal objects because it is always, in one sense, a free negation of the world and that always *from a particular point of view*.... [An] image, being a negation of the world from a particular point of view, can never appear excepting *on the foundation of the world* and in connection with the foundation" (Sartre 269). In this manner both Müller and her reader have to detach themselves from the world so as to rethink the definite objects in the world anew, as signifying something else. Comprehending Müller's work, then, requires setting aside current reality in order to envision another one from a certain "foreign" point of view.

There is hardly a more pervasive feature of mental existence than imagining. Nevertheless, one of the greatest paradoxes of contemporary culture is that at a time when image reigns supreme, the very notion of a creative human imagination seems under mounting threat. The imminent demise of imagination is clearly a postmodern obsession: postmodernism undermines the modernist belief in image as an authentic expression, and one is tempted to say that we are lacking passionate commitment to imagining. We live in a "civilization of images" (Richard Kearny) where human beings are deemed less and less responsible for the working of their own imagination. The individual subject is no longer considered the maker or communicator of his own images and increasingly finds himself or herself surrounded by simulated images, produced, or reproduced, by mass-media technologies operating outside his or her control. In our "Society of the Spectacle" (Guy Debord), where the imaginary circulates in an endless play of imitation, where each image becomes a replay of another that precedes it, the idea of an *authentic* or *unique* imagination becomes redundant. In his 1972 essay "Idéologie et idéalisme," Lévinas offers an apocalyptic account of our society of simulation, where sameness reigns supreme: "The contemporary world—of science, technology, leisure—sees itself as trapped . . . not because everything is now permitted, and thanks to technology possible, but because everything is the same. The unknown immediately becomes familiar, the new normal" (245).

Therefore we nowadays rely more than ever on the power of imagining to find other ways of being in the world and to recast other possibilities of existence: "To grasp this new role, we need to bring together: the old idea of images ... ; the idea of the imagined community (in Anderson's sense); and the French idea of the imaginary, as a constructed landscape of collective aspirations.... The image, the imagined and the imaginary—these are all terms which direct us to something critical and new in global cultural processes: the imagination as a social practice" (Appadurai 31). Structuralist and post-structuralist criticism often carry the suspicion that narrative has a totalizing function that suppresses difference, desire, and otherness. Müller's work shows how such ethical responsibility can resist the ideology of the simulacrum pervading our social imaginary, how we can retrieve some ethical dimension of *poiesis* from the faceless civilization of images that informs our experience. She responds to the fetishizing power of images by producing counter-images, word-images, which disclose how being for the other, in and through language, is the first event of existence.

Müller's lyrical prose is an act of creative imagination that stimulates the production of images. It accomplishes this intensively through the evocation of dense imagery via the most economical use of language, thus avoiding hermeneutic closure. Far from being a shortcoming, the incompleteness inherent in her texts invites the imaginative interpretations through which the reader fills out fictional worlds and, more important, through which the reader uses fiction to reinterpret and reach a new understanding of his or her own world. As readers, we are invited to *see* things not present and to understand or value what is present before us by complementing and extending our imaginative vision. Müller's imaginative literary texts pose outright challenges to our conventional understanding of the *given* world before us. "Seeing-as" layers images onto the perceived world and provides it with new meanings; it transforms worldly things at the level of their significance for us readers, and it does so not merely in our heads, but also in the world (*Teufel* 52).[8]

Furthermore, as readers we can see the world under the light of unrealized possibility: "Überall, wo Menschen sich befinden, oder hinsehen, werden sie selbst, wird das, was sie sehen, eine Möglichkeit für das Unvorhersehbare" [Everywhere where people are, or where people look, they become, or what they see becomes, an opening for the unforeseeable] (*Teufel* 18). To do so is not merely to fantazize some other world but to see *this* world's other potentials. "Seeing-as" is a freeing critical distance from the pressing present before us. In this sense the role of the imagination in Müller's literary production and its reception makes her work a powerful source of pressure placed upon the real to be different. Imagination in her literary texts is a transgressive expression of freedom, regarding the ethical imperatives of imagining and regarding imagining as the cultivation of a "double vision" (Brann 774) that not merely shapes her fictional worlds but also creatively—*poietically*—reshapes our own.

Seeing double can be a dizzying experience, but works of literature at their most powerful create dizzying imaginative possibilities. *Der fremde Blick*, the particular or subjective foreign point of view of reality, does "elicit a second appearance from the visible world" (Brann 774) that "sticks out" as a surplus knowledge. That is, therefore, a form of suspense—it suspends the ostensible meaning of a thing or situation—and, what is more, the representation of subjectivity itself (*Teufel* 25). Discovering what we are more or less able to imagine can teach us much about ourselves because subjectivity is precisely such a surplus knowledge. It is that which cannot remain neutral or objective but which looks at the world from a particular, "foreign" point of view. Indeed what Müller makes clear in her works is that without our own specific imagination and fantasy we would be left not with a sober, "objective" version of reality but with no access to reality at all. In fact, "With regard to the basic opposition between reality and imagination, fantasy is not simply on the idle side of imagination; fantasy is, rather, the little piece of imagination by which we gain access to reality—the frame that guarantees our access to reality, our 'sense of reality' (when our fundamental fantasy is shattered, we experience the 'loss of reality')" (Žižek 122). There is not only in all human beings a capacity to go beyond what is immediately in front of them, but also an absolute necessity for them to do so. By confronting the unreality of reality, they can come closer to the truth of the world today.

Thus Müller shows that despite its everyday connotations, fantasy is not just a flight of fancy or an imaginative indulgence. On the contrary, it is the vista from which we see the world—and can survive, neutralizing the fiasco of reality and the imposture of history (*Teufel* 29). Furthermore, the slant of our most fundamental fantasy is what objectively makes us subjective. Our roles in the Lacanian symbolic order can be filled by anyone, but what is irreplaceable about a person, what remains objectively unique is his or her imagination and fantasy. The imaginative and fantasmatic core, the *Herztier*, that makes a person an individual is not reproducible. As individual imagination is the support of being, it is little wonder that it is extremely precious and therefore sensitive to the intrusion of others. Fantasy is, as it were, the tender nerve of the subject's psyche and can cause serious distress if we treat it with insufficient care.

The threats of dullness, inattentiveness, and the mere suffering of feeling persist within modernity and postmodernity, now accompanied by a perhaps sharper sense of felt isolation, within an occupational, social, or familial circle that is marked off from others by violence rather than articulated with others in clear relations of mutual interest and support. Müller's lyrical prose of individual consciousness, which seeks and achieves exemplariness in attention and feeling, remains a central way of responding to these threats, even if it does not point toward solutions to sociopolitical problems. Learning to see and feel right is also perspicuously modeled for us in Müller's work. By participating imaginatively in these explorations, Müller's readers, too, enter into finding another emotional sense of things, attention to life, and freedom in feeling.

"Seeing-as" is a worldly act of free and creative interpretation, but it does not free us of being in the world. Thus the exercise of imaginative seeing, in both the production and appreciation of Müller's literary work, entails ethical obligations that raise imagining above escapist play. It requires describing the consequences of traumatic experiences; the effects of violence, cruelty, and terror; and at the same time, it requires the courage to achieve a fresh imaginative vision. Ethics needs poetics to be reminded that its responsibility toward the other includes the possibility of play, liberty, and pleasure, just as poetics needs ethics to be reminded that play, liberty, and pleasure are never self-sufficient but originate in, and aim toward, an experience of the other-than-self. That is where ethics and poetics meet in Müller's texts—in those words that the self receives from the other and returns to the other.

Notes

1. For a broad definition of "autofiction" as "self-fabulation," see Colonna, who speaks not only of a "biographical autofiction," but also of different aspects of the issue (75, 119, 135).

2. Translated from the German by Bettina Brandt unless otherwise noted.

3. Müller writes on this issue: "Ich merke an mir, daß nicht das am stärksten im Gedächtnis bleibt, was außen war, was man Fakten nennt. Stärker, weil wieder erlebbar im Gedächtnis, ist das, was auch damals im Kopf stand, das, was von innen kam, angesichts des Äußeren, der Fakten" [I notice in myself that what sticks most strongly in my mind is not that what was outside, what one calls the facts. What is stronger, because it can be recalled by memory, is what at the time was going on in my head as well, what came from the inside in response to what was going on in the outside, in response to the facts] (*Teufel* 10). Furthermore: "Als ich noch in Rumänien lebte, kamen oft Freunde, aber auch Fremde zu Besuch. Ich lebte in einem schiefen, grauen Wohnblock aus Betonfertigteilen, am Rand der Stadt. Sie aber wollten das Dorf sehen, aus dem ich kam. . . . Das Dorf gibt es nur in den 'Niederungen,' hab ich gesagt" [When I was still living in Romania friends but also strangers would regularly come to visit me. I was living in a lopsided, grey apartment building made of prefabricated slabs of concrete at the edge of the city. But they wanted to see the village where I came from. . . . The village only exists in *Nadirs*, I told them] (*Teufel* 16).

4. Eke talks of Müller's "Versuch einer Aneignung der Wirklichkeit durch das gemachte Bild" [attempt to appropriate reality through the constructed image] (90).

5. Following Lakoff, "The locus of metaphor is not in language at all, but in the way we conceptualize one mental domain in terms of another" (203).

6. This appears to be in contradiction with Müller's disingenuous statement that she doesn't worry about the reader: "Ich mache mir über den Leser gar keine Gedanken!" ("Gespräch" 18).

7. In this sense Müller's work creates an opportunity and a challenge for the reader that is more than a simple "active, constructive response" and more than a participation "in the construction of the text" (Midgley 35).

8. Warnock conveys this eloquently: "Imagination is our means of interpreting the world, and it is also our means of forming images in the world; they are our way of thinking of the objects in the world" (194).

Works Cited

Appadurai, Arjun. "Disjuncture and Difference in the Global Cultural Economy." *Colonial Discourse and Postcolonial Theory: A Reader*. Ed. Patrick Williams and Laura Christman. New York: Columbia University Press, 1994.

Bozzi, Paola. *Der fremde Blick. Zum Werk Herta Müllers*. Würzburg: Königshausen and Neumann, 2005.

Brann, Eva T. H. *The World of Imagination*. Savage MD: Rowan and Littlefield, 1991.

Colonna, Vincent. *Autofiction et autres mythomanies littéraires*. Paris: Tristram, 2004.

Debord, Guy. *The Society of the Spectacle*. Cambridge MA: MIT Press, 1995.

De Man, Paul. *Blindness and Insight*. 2nd rev. ed. London: Routledge, 1989.

Doubrovsky, Serge. *Fils*. Paris: Galilée, 1977.

Eddy, Beverley Driver. "Testimony and Trauma in Herta Müller's *Herztier*." *German Life and Letters* 53 (2000): 56-72.

Eke, Norbert Otto. "'Überall, wo man den Tod gesehen hat.' Zeitlichkeit und Tod in der Prosa Herta Müllers. Anmerkungen zu einem Motivzusammenhang." *Die erfundene Wahrnehmung. Annäherung an Herta Müller*. Ed. Norbert Otto Eke. Paderborn: Igel, 1991. 74-94.

Federman, Raymond. "Critifiction: Imagination as Plagiarism." *Critifiction: Postmodern Essays*. Albany NY: SUNY Press, 1993. 48-64.

———. "Self-Reflexive Fiction or How to Get Rid of It." *Critifiction: Postmodern Essays*. Albany NY: SUNY Press, 1993. 17-34.

———. "Surfiction: Four Propositions in Form of an Introduction." *Surfiction: Fiction Now and Tomorrow*. Ed. Raymond Federman. Chicago: Swallow Press, 1975. 5-15.

Glajar, Valentina. *The German Legacy in East Central Europe as Recorded in Recent German-Language Literature*. Rochester: Camden House, 2004.

Haines, Brigid, ed. *Herta Müller*. Cardiff: University of Wales Press, 1998.

———. "'Leben wir im Detail': Herta Müller's Micro-Politics of Resistance." *Herta Müller*. Ed. Brigid Haines. Cardiff: University of Wales Press, 1998. 109-25.

———. "'The Unforgettable Forgotten': The Traces of Trauma in Herta Müller's *Reisende auf einem Bein*." *German Life and Letters* 55 (2002): 266-81.

Kant, Immanuel. *Critique of the Power of Judgment*. Ed. Paul Guyer. Trans. Paul Guyer and Eric Matthews. Cambridge: Cambridge University Press, 2000.

Lakoff, George. "The Contemporary Theory of Metaphor." *Metaphor and Thought*. 2nd ed. Ed. Andrew Ortony. Cambridge: Cambridge University Press, 1995. 202–51.

Lévinas, Emmanuel. "Idéologie et idéalisme." *De Dieu qui vient à l'idée*. Paris: Vrin, 1982. *The Levinas Reader*. Ed. Seán Hand. Oxford: Blackwell, 1989. 235–48.

Marven, Lyn. *Body and Narrative in Contemporary Literatures in German: Herta Müller, Libuše Moníková, and Kerstin Hensel*. Oxford: Clarendon, 2005.

———. "'In allem ist der Riß': Trauma, Fragmentation, and the Body in Herta Müller's Prose and Collages." *Modern Language Review* 100.2 (2005): 396–411.

Midgley, David. "Remembered Things: The Representation of Memory and Separation in *Der Mensch ist ein großer Fasan auf der Welt*." *Herta Müller*. Ed. Brigid Haines. Cardiff: University of Wales Press, 1998. 24–35.

Müller, Herta. *The Appointment*. Trans. Michael Hulse and Philip Boehm. New York: Metropolitan Books, 2001.

———. *Atemschaukel*. Munich: Hanser, 2009.

———. *Barfüßiger Februar*. Berlin: Rotbuch, 1987.

———. *Der fremde Blick oder Das Leben ist ein Furz in der Laterne*. Göttingen: Wallstein, 1999.

———. *Der Fuchs war damals schon der Jäger*. Reinbek: Rowohlt, 1992.

———. *Der Mensch ist ein großer Fasan auf dear Welt*. Reinbek: Rowohlt, 1989.

———. *Der Teufel sitzt im Spiegel. Wie Wahrnehmung sich erfindet*. Berlin: Rotbuch, 1991.

———. "Gespräch mit Herta Müller." *Herta Müller*. Ed. Brigid Haines. Cardiff: University of Wales Press, 1998. 14–24.

———. *Herztier*. Reinbek: Rowohlt, 1994.

———. *Heute wäre ich mir lieber nicht begegnet*. Reinbek: Rowohlt, 1997.

———. *Hunger und Seide*. Reinbek: Rowohlt, 1995.

———. *In der Falle. Bonner Poetik-Vorlesungen*. Ed. Karin Hempel-Soos. Göttingen: Wallstein, 1996.

———. *The Land of Green Plums*. Trans. Michael Hofmann. New York: Metropolitan Books, 1996.

———. *Nadirs*. Trans. Sieglinde Lug. Lincoln: University of Nebraska Press, 1999.

———. *Niederungen*. Berlin: Rotbuch, 1984.

———. *The Passport*. Trans. Martin Chalmers. London: Serpent's Tail, 1989.

———. *Reisende auf einem Bein*. Berlin: Rotbuch, 1989.

———. *Traveling on One Leg*. Trans. Valentina Glajar and André Lefevere. Evanston: Northwestern University Press, 1998.

Ricoeur, Paul. *La Métaphore vive*. Paris: Seuil, 1975.

———. *Temps et récit*. Vol. 1. Paris: Seuil, 1983-85.

Sartre, Jean-Paul. *The Psychology of Imagination*. New York: Carol, 1991.

Sellars, Wilfried. *Empiricism and the Philosophy of Mind*. Cambridge MA: Harvard University Press, 1997.

Tudorică, Cristina. *Rumäniendeutsche Literatur (1970-1990): Die letzte Epoche einer Minderheitenliteratur*. Tübingen and Basel: Francke, 1997.

Warnock, Mary. *Imagination*. Berkeley: University of California Press, 1976.

Whale, John. *Imagination under Pressure, 1789-1832: Aesthetics, Politics and Utility*. Cambridge: Cambridge University Press, 2000.

White, John J. "Herta Müller and Totalitarianism." *Herta Müller*. Ed. Brigid Haines. Cardiff: University of Wales Press, 1998. 75-95.

Wittgenstein, Ludwig. *Philosophical Investigation*. Trans. Gertrude Elizabeth Margaret Anscombe. New York: Macmillan, 1953.

Žižek, Slavoj. "Is It Possible to Traverse the Fantasy in Cyberspace?" *The Žižek Reader*. Ed. Elizabeth Wright and Edmond Leo Wright. Oxford and Cambridge MA: Blackwell, 1999. 102-24.

8 From Fact to Fiction

Herta Müller's *Atemschaukel*

Olivia Spiridon

The novel *Atemschaukel* [*The Hunger Angel*] marks an important turning point in the career of Herta Müller—an author who fought her way from writing literary texts with the regional touch of a small minority into the center of German mainstream literature. In 2009, the year of its publication, *Atemschaukel* became the focus of attention for the most prestigious German-language newspapers: *Die Zeit, Süddeutsche Zeitung, Neue Zürcher Zeitung, Frankfurter Rundschau,* and *taz*. Its reception intensified further when Müller received the Nobel Prize for literature in the same year. In this chapter I will discuss the novel's success in connection with Müller's treatment of the deportation of ethnic Germans from Southeastern Europe to the Soviet Union at the end of World War II and examine to what extent the particularity of the process of transformation of a historical fact, the *res gestae*, into fictional/narrative text, a *historia rerum gestarum*, has facilitated the novel's extraordinary reception. By discussing the genesis of this novel, its poetic achievement, and the debates it has generated, I will investigate the particular function of *Atemschaukel* to "enlarge experience" (Wild) in relation to the historical deportation to Russia.[1]

"The deportation to Russia" is a historical term to describe the transportation of hundreds of thousands of ethnic Germans from Central and Southeastern Europe to forced labor camps in the USSR during the last months of World War II. Affected by these measures were civilians of German nationality from the regions east of the rivers Oder and Neisse, the Baltic states, Romania, Hungary, Yugoslavia, Czechoslovakia, and Bulgaria. It is difficult to offer exact figures. Because of the paucity of historical sources, the estimates oscillate between 270,000 and well over 360,000, with an average mortality rate of 20 percent (Beer 465). It is estimated that 70,000–80,000 were from Romania (Gündisch and Beer 221). The road to the collective denunciation of the Germans had already been paved years before. On the one hand, Nazi Germany found fertile ground for ideological penetration in the Banat and Transylvania as only very few German-Romanian politicians and intellectuals resisted the Nazi ideology.[2] On the other hand, the German minority in Romania got caught in the millstones of international agreements. The treaties between the Third Reich and Romania, a consequence of their political alliance during the 1930s, serve as an illustrative example. Through the economic conventions of March 23, 1939, and May 29, 1940, and finally through Romania's accession to the Axis pact (Germany, Italy, and Japan) on November 23, 1940, the country became an integral part of Germany's economic and war plans. On May 12, 1943, Germany and Romania signed a fatal treaty for German-Romanians; it stipulated the legal possibility for the recruitment of ethnic Germans from Romania into the infamous Waffen-SS (Gündisch and Beer 205–10).[3] On August 23, 1944, Romania switched sides and became Russia's ally. About sixty thousand Germans from Romania were still serving in the Waffen-SS and the German Wehrmacht at that time.[4] January 1945 saw the sudden deportation of Romania's German minority to the USSR for the purpose of reconstruction "on the basis of the Soviet demands, based on the truce of September 12, 1944, and the Soviet-Romanian economic convention of January 1945" (Gündisch and Beer 214, 219).[5]

Women between the ages of nineteen and thirty, as well as men between seventeen and forty-five years of age, were abruptly recruited on the basis of so-called national registers, which had been updated in the autumn of 1944 (Gündisch and Beer 219). Inquiries in the Soviet archives make it clear that the Soviet plans for the postwar period, in which reparations were to play a significant role, date back to the defeat of the German troops in the battle of Stalingrad, the turning point on the eastern front (Beer 465). Because of their ethnic affiliation, German-Romanians, regardless of their political affiliation or individual responsibility, were collectively held responsible for the destruction inflicted by the German troops during their war of aggression against the USSR. The Romanian authorities actively took part in the implementation of the Soviet order of deportation. The theory of collective guilt, the official political position of Romania at that time, provided the Romanian government with the legal basis for the measures implemented against the Germans—especially after August 1944, when expropriations, the deprivation of rights, arrests, and widespread legal uncertainty began.[6]

The deportation experiences of the German-Romanian minority are recorded in oral testimonies as well as in a multitude of written records. In literary texts written in Romania before 1989 there are only veiled allusions to these traumatic postwar events.[7] In Western Europe, however, several memoirs about the deportations to Russia were published during the first postwar years.[8] The citation of facts and sometimes even complete documents are part of these chronologically narrated stories; law texts, regulations, secret service reports, photos, and notes support and complement the personal memories of the deportees.

Two publications are exemplary for the strategies used to organize the narrative material. The first, Matthias Kandler's *Nr. 657. Im Donbass deportiert, 1945–1949. Russlanderinnerungen* [Nr. 657. Deported to Donbass, 1945–1949. Memories of Russia] is a highly informative yet intensely emotional personal memoir that also includes a series of documents.[9] The second, Hedwig Stieber-Ackermann's *Allein die Hoffnung hielt uns am Leben* [Only hope kept us alive], also juxtaposes subjective recollections with official documents, images, and photographs in an attempt to represent the events more appropriately.[10] Stieber-Ackermann calls her volume "a milestone against oblivion": "This book is dedicated to all those women and girls who rest somewhere in Russia, buried without a coffin and without a cross. No gravestone and no monument bear their names. They are forgotten, or they live only in the memories of their relatives or their fellow-sufferers" (5). Kandler describes his experience as follows:

The deportation to Russia in 1945 was sadder and more brutal than many people could imagine. Who can comprehend the pain of separation from the family, often leaving behind a small child, the humiliations and the hunger behind the barbed wire? Death was our constant companion.... The memories of the time in Russia, which portray our period of suffering, are based on real experiences, without resentment and without hate.... The memories of the time in Russia are my farewell to my friends and my fellow compatriots from the Banat and Transylvania. It is a remembrance of all who suffered with us and especially of those who were not so lucky to return home. (5–6)

The texts of Kandler and Stieber-Ackermann can be read as both fact and fiction. On the one hand, they represent a medium of factual memory since their sources are in the reservoir of history and collective memory. But on the other hand, they are stories due to their narrative structure, the presentation of the protagonists, and the dramatization of the action.

Atemschaukel does not document, in contrast to the previously discussed documentary memoirs, a first-hand experience of deportation. Some reviewers, most harshly perhaps Iris Radisch in *Die Zeit*, have criticized Müller's novel and expressed doubts about the value of fictional memoirs that address historical events through "secondhand" experiences.[11] Indeed Müller's project began in 2001 as an intergenerational effort, as teamwork between generations (Müller, "Nullpunkt" 73). The memories of her family, especially those of her mother, served as a basis for the documentation, in addition to discussions Müller had with former deportees from her native village, Nitzkydorf.[12] The detailed conversations with Oskar Pastior, who was deported to a labor camp in Ukraine at the age of seventeen, helped her to grasp the difficulties associated with the linguistic and stylistic concept of survival. In an interview with Nicole Henneberg, Müller described her collaboration with Pastior as follows:

> Oskar Pastior hat erzählt, ich habe aufgeschrieben. Ich wollte wissen, was ein Mensch in so einer Situation fühlt und habe nach den winzigsten Kleinigkeiten gefragt. Oskar Pastior hat das Lager und das Kokswerk auch aufgezeichnet. Er hat sich an alle Details erinnert. [...] Seine detaillierten Erinnerungen waren ein Glücksfall, denn die anderen Überlebenden, die ich

befragt habe, konnten nicht über sich reden, sie hatten keine Sprache für ihre Gefühle. Es kamen immer nur Klischees: Man hatte gelitten, was haben wir durchgemacht ... Klischees, mit denen man nichts anfangen kann.

[Oskar Pastior talked about his experiences and I wrote them down. I wanted to know about a man's feelings in such a situation and therefore asked him to elaborate even about the tiniest details. Oskar Pastior even made drawings of the labor camp and the coke factory. He remembered all the details. ... His detailed memories were a real stroke of luck, because the other survivors I interviewed were not able to talk about their experiences in this way; they had no language for their feelings and emotions. They only came up with stereotypes: we have suffered, we have suffered so much ... clichés with which you cannot work at all.] (Henneberg 23)

Pastior's memory of exact details offered Müller access to the experience of the labor camps in a way that the "geraffte Sprache" [shortened language] (Henneberg 23) of the other deportees had not.

A ten-day trip to Ukraine in June 2004, which Müller took with Pastior and Ernest Wichner, represents a further stage in the preparation of the writing of the novel.[13] Müller explains: "Only because I had seen this landscape was I able to invent the situation. Oskar had no inner relationship with the plants; he always talked about lavender, but it was tufted vetch. He also had a mountain vocabulary when describing landscapes. But there are no mountains there; there are only slag-heaps" (Henneberg 23). In search of the once familiar landscape, Pastior behaved like a *Heimgekehrter* [homecomer]. "Aber alles war wieder kaputt—meine Arbeit war hier umsonst, sagte Oskar Pastior traurig" [But here everything was in ruins—my work here was in vain, Oskar Pastior said sorrowfully] (Henneberg 23).

Müller's direct experience of and acquired familiarity with the landscape constituted the last stage in her preparation for writing *Atemschaukel*. During the journey Müller added Pastior's accounts: "Herta hatte große Kladden, in denen sie alles aufschrieb, was Oskar erzählte. Sie hat mit ihm über jeden zweiten Grashalm diskutiert, vom Lagergelände hat sie Kräuter gerupft" [Herta had taken big notebooks with her, where she wrote down everything Oskar told her. She discussed with him every blade of grass. In the area of the labor camp, she picked up herbs] (Sander 9). During his narration of events, Pastior imbued a lot of his experiences with *Sprachbilder* [word images], thus "making his experiences more endurable, even beautiful" (Sander 9).

References to the extra-textual reality turned out to be more complex than was the case with personal memories. *Atemschaukel* is a fictional text, a retrospective construct in which Müller incorporated the recorded experiences of deportation, as well as fictional elements, paradigms of literary traditions, and esthetic principles of organization. In the configuration stage of the text, the Müller-Pastior team revised the text several times. "Wir begannen bald, im Aufschreiben zu erfinden, zu 'flunkern,' wie Oskar Pastior es nannte" [We began already to invent situations, to fib, as Oskar called it] (Müller, "Nullpunkt" 73). Being unaccustomed to prose, Pastior evidently delivered lyrical fragments, admitting not to have known "that prose was so difficult" (Henneberg 23). Müller and Pastior presented the first completed chapter of the novel *Hungerengel* (*Hunger Angel*) on March 13, 2005, in the Literaturhaus in Stuttgart.[14] One year after Pastior's death in 2006, Müller began revising the notes she had taken during her conversations with him. This move implied a transition from the impossibility of a collective "We" to the creation of the narrator's harmonizing "I."

After Pastior's death Müller had to work with fragments, partially with transcribed oral reports and partially with *Fertigteilen* [prefabricated components], with short and revised written parts, to which she had to add only a few phrases (Henneberg 23). An exhibition titled Minze Minze flaumiran Schpektrum presented several photocopied pages of Müller's notebooks. They comprise drawings of the camp barracks, sketches of "the work in the basement," comments grouped around central terms—for example, "the organizing of shiftwork as work of art"—and also drawings of French spinach, accompanied by synonymous terms like *Gartenmelde* [mountain spinach] or *Wildspinat* [sea purslane] and the Romanian term for it, *lobodă*, as well as a Romanian saying comprising this term. The narrative web had to be spun further. The revision of the longer chapters and the "invention" of characters turned out to be rather difficult, as Müller explains to Henneberg: "Oft wusste ich über eine Figur oder eine Situation nur einen Satz. Ich habe dann versucht, zwischen den Personen eine Beziehung herzustellen, Spannung aufzubauen" [On many occasions, I knew only a single phrase about a certain character or situation. In that case I tried to establish a relationship between the characters to produce a certain tension] (23). In the process Müller also had to treat Pastior's homosexuality with utmost discretion. But it was clear that Leo Auberg, *Atemschaukel*'s main protagonist, had to be a homosexual. "Oskar Pastior hat nur gesagt: nicht zu viel. Ich hoffe, das habe ich eingelöst" [Oskar Pastior had only said: "Not too much!" I hope I was able to keep this promise] (Henneberg 23).

Documentation played a crucial role in the genesis of *Atemschaukel* even though Müller did not intend to give a realistic depiction of the deportation and experience in the Russian labor camps. But the thorough documentation set up the basis for the fictional reality created in *Atemschaukel* through the organization of material and the poetical transformation of the deportees' narrated memories. Müller's text is fictional, but it simultaneously offers documentary material and para-texts that ensure historical reliability and referentiality. As such, *Atemschaukel* creates an indelible impression of the experience of deportation.

To what extent does *Atemschaukel* affect the contemporary view on the historical deportation of Germans at the end of World War II as compared, for example, with the documentary memoirs mentioned above? Which literary methods and poetic means did Müller employ to render a feeling of authenticity and intensity of the experience?

To gauge the effectiveness of *Atemschaukel* I will take a closer look at selective communicative memory aspects of the German-Romanian minority as represented in the novel. Leo Auberg, the main protagonist, is an outsider who does not identify with the German-Romanian community. His story can be summarized in a few sentences: Leo Auberg, an ethnic German from Romania who happens to be homosexual, is deported to a Soviet labor camp at the age of seventeen; he spends five years there, returns to his native city, gets married, moves to Bucharest, and finally divorces his wife and emigrates to Austria. Because of his incompatibility with the petty bourgeois and authoritarian core values of the ethnic German society of Transylvania, the seventeen-year-old teenager ekes out an outsider's existence and longs feverishly and somewhat surprisingly for the big trip to the east: "Ich wollte weg aus der Familie und sei es ins

Lager" (*Atemschaukel* 11); [I wanted to escape from my family; to a camp if need be] (*The Hunger Angel* 2).

The Leo figure represents the intersection of several processes of semantification. As Pastior's alter ego, Leo ensures the documentary character of *Atemschaukel*, which is based on Pastior's autobiographical report. In addition, Leo, much like Pastior, moves from one prison to another and represents the eternal prisoner: in his native city, in the labor camp, after his return home. The fact that Leo wishes to be deported and looks forward to leaving his intolerant community behind also emphasizes the striking difference between the first prison (the city) and the second one (the labor camp). The labor camp represents for him the experience of an existentially extreme situation where his sexuality is erased by hunger— a space where inmates lose any sense of individuality or sexuality.

The mixing of documentary details and poetically revised perceptions causes a permanent shift between the portrayals of the outside world and the characters' inner world. The text astonishes due to the extensive details it provides while simultaneously addressing the emotional and cognitive mechanisms that were a strategy of survival for the deportees. Hunger and homesickness, toil and extreme temperatures, for example, represent important elements both in *Atemschaukel* and in the autobiographical reports of other deportees. In Müller's novel these elements structure and illustrate the five-year duration of the imprisonment in the labor camp.

> Aber mein Ein und Alles, meine Jeden-Tag-Schlacke und Tag-und-Nachtschichtschlacke war die Dampfkesselschlacke aus den Kohleöfen, die heiße und die kalte Kellerschlacke. Die Öfen standen in der Oberwelt, fünf hintereinander, hoch wie Etagenhäuser. Die Öfen heizten fünf Kessel, produzierten Dampf für das ganze Werk und für uns im Keller die heiße und kalte Schlacke. Und die ganze Arbeit, die heiße und die kalte Phase jeder Schicht.
>
> Die kalte Schlacke entsteht nur durch die heiße, sie ist nur der kalte Staub der heißen Schlacke. Die kalte Schlacke muss nur einmal pro Schicht entleert werden, die heiße Schlacke jedoch ständig. Sie muss im Takt der Öfen in unzählige Wägelchen geschaufelt, den Berg hinaufgestoßen und am Schienenende des Berges ausgekippt werden. [*Atemschaukel* 173)

> [But my one-and-only slag, my daily slag, the slag of my day and night shift was the clinker-slag from the boilers at the coal furnaces, the hot and cold cellar slag. The furnaces stood above us, in the world of the living, five to a row, each several stories tall. They provided heat to the boilers, producing steam for the entire plant and hot and cold slag for us in the cellar. They also provided all our work, the hot phase and the cold phase of every shift.
>
> Cold slag can only come from hot slag, it's nothing more than the dusty residue left when hot slag cools. Cold slag only has to be emptied once per shift, but the hot clinker-slag requires constant removal, following the rhythms of the furnaces. It has to be shoveled onto countless little rail-carts, then pushed to the top of the mountain of slag at the end of the tracks and dumped.] (*The Hunger Angel* 164)

The narrator recounts not only the exhaustion and the hunger he experienced but portrays also, by providing detailed information about his psychological condition and word associations, his inner sensitivities. He unveils his personal mechanisms of survival: he experiences the mobility of his thought association as an enormous relief, as if the free arrangement of his thoughts could be a substitute for freedom. Things in the labor camp that put less of a strain on the prisoners are reinterpreted as being beautiful; even the dangerous ones are helpful for spiritual liberation. Leo starts to love the poisonous *kalte Schlacke* [cold slag] (173) in fact. The narrator enters more and more into his imaginary world by stringing together thoughts that allow him to escape the reality of the labor camp, if only for a few brief moments:

> Sogar nach ziviler Welt roch sie und machte mich übermütig. Ich stellte mir vor, ich gehe nicht im Watteanzug aus dem Keller in die Baracke, sondern feingemacht mit Borsalino, Kamelhaarmantel und weinrotem Seidenschal in Bukarest oder in Wien ins Kaffeehaus und setze mich dort an ein Marmortischchen. So freilebig war die kalte Schlacke, die schenkte einem den Selbstbetrug, durch den man sich ins Leben zurückstehlen konnte. Besoffen vom Gift, konnte man sich mit der kalten Schlacke glücklich machen, todsicher glücklich. (*Atemschaukel* 175)
>
> [It even smelled of civilian life, and that made me cocky. I imagined that I wasn't going from the cellar to the barrack in a padded suit, but that I was

all decked out in a Borsalino, a camel-hair coat, and a burgundy silk scarf, on my way to a café in Bucharest or Vienna where I was about to sit down at a little marbled-top table. So easygoing was the cold slag that it helped feed the delusions you needed in order to steal your way back into life drunk on poison, you could find true happiness with the cold slag, dead-sure happiness.] (*The Hunger Angel* 166)

The illustration of life in the labor camp begins at the vocabulary level, with the use of compounds that include real facts but at the same time challenge the reader's imagination. A few examples from the semantic field of "hunger" are the following: *Hungerengel* [hunger angel], to whom Müller dedicates two entire chapters (*Atemschaukel* 86-91, 144; *The Hunger Angel* 76-81, 133-34); *Hautundknochenzeit* (157) [skinandbones time, 150]; *Hungerwörter* (157) [hunger words, 149]; *Brotfalle* (120) [bread trap, 110]; *Eigenbrot* (120) [one's own bread, 111]; *Wangenbrot* (121) [cheek-bread, 111]; and *Kartoffelmensch* (192) [potato man, 182]. Many of these words were Pastior's own creations; "word images," as Pastior explained in his interview with Sander, "die ihm das Erlebte erträglicher, ja schön machten" [which made his experiences more endurable, even beautiful].[15] The unloading of coal he called a *vollendetes Kunstwerk* [perfect work of art], for example; the shovel, a *Herzblatt* [heart leaf], and he talked of *Schätzen* [treasures] as a symbol of his inner life.[16] Entire chapters circle around these terms and the above-mentioned neologisms, playing on possible comparisons and associations that allow Müller to reproduce the intensity of the camp experience as described by Pastior and other former deportees.

In one of Müller's notebooks, which documents the reconfiguration of the text, there is a drawing of a man whose clothing—trousers, jacket, scarf, and cap—is filled with potatoes. Above the drawing the heading reads: "273 potatoes." The finished novel reads as follows:

Ich stopfte mich bis unter die Mütze mit Kartoffeln aller Größe aus. Ich zählte 273 Kartoffeln. Der Hungerengel half mir, er war ja ein notorischer Dieb. Doch nachdem er mir geholfen hatte, war er wieder ein notorischer Peiniger und ließ mich mit dem langen Heimweg allein. (*Atemschaukel* 197)

[I stuffed my clothes with potatoes of all sizes, all the way up to my cap. I counted 273. The hunger angel helped me—he was, after all, a notorious thief. But after he'd helped me, he was once again a notorious tormentor, and left me to fend for myself on the long way home.] (*The Hunger Angel* 187)

The novel's story of the stolen potatoes goes back to this drawing, whose margins are covered with comments and partial phrases or dialogue fragments. Under the drawing there are, for example, fragments of dialogues, versions of bits which reappear in the chapter "Kartoffelmensch" [Potato man]. Müller develops an analogy between the 273 potatoes and the absolute freezing point: "Weil minus 273 Grad Celsius der absolute Nullpunkt ist" (199) [Because minus 273 degree Celsius is absolute zero] (*The Hunger Angel* 187). This particular temperature, at which metals and gases radically change their state of aggregation, corresponds to the extremely desperate situation of the starving man, who survives thanks to his 273 potatoes.

Müller's selection of the various figures and facts in this novel is not based, as in the memoirs, on the validity of the narration; she understands them as representative of the deportees' experience and their regions of origin.

> Die Trudi Pelikan und ich, Leopold Auberg, waren aus Hermannstadt.... Arthur Prikulitsch und Beatrice Zakel, also Tur und Bea... kamen aus dem Gebirgsdorf Lugi aus dem Dreiländereck der Karpato-Urkaine. Aus derselben Gegend, aus Rakhiv, kam auch der Rasierer Oswald Enyeter.... Mein Lastautokompagnon Karli Halmen kam aus Kleinbeschkerek, und Albert Gion, mit dem ich später im Schlackekeller war, kam aus Arad. Die eine Sarah Kaunz... kam aus Wurmloch, die andere Sarah Wandschneider ... aus Kastenholz.... Irma Pfeifer kam aus der Kleinstadt Deta, die taube Mitzi, also Annamarie Berg, aus Mediasch. Der Advokat Paul Gast und seine Frau Heidrun Gast waren aus Oberwischau. Der Trommler Kowatsch Anton kam aus dem Banater Bergland, aus dem Städtchen Karansebesch. Katharina Seidel, die wir Planton-Kati nannten, kam aus Bakowa.... Der am Steinkohleschnaps gestorbene Maschinist Peter Schiel war aus Bogarosch. Die singende Loni, Ilona Mich aus Lugosch. Der Schneider Herr Reusch aus Guttenbrunn. (*Atemschaukel* 43)

> [Trudi Pelikan and I, Leopold Auberg, came from Hermannstadt.... Arthur Prikulitsch and Beatrice Zakel—Tur and Bea—... came from the village of

Lugi in the mountains, in the the Carpatho-Ukraine, where three lands meet. Oswald Enyeter came from the same region, from Rachiv. . . . My truck companion Karli Halmen came from Kleinbetschkerek, and Albert Gion, with whom I was later in the slag-cellar, came from Arad. Sarah Kaunz . . . came from Wurmloch, and Sarah Wandschneider . . . came from Kastenholz. . . . Irma Pfeifer came from the small town of Deta, and deaf Mitzi—Annamarie Berg—from Mediasch. Paul Gast the lawyer and his wife Heidrun Gast were from Oberwischau. Anton Kowatsch the drummer came from the Banat mountain region, from Karansebesch. Katharina Seidel, whom we called Kati Sentry, came from Bakowa. . . . The mechanic Peter Schiel, who died from drinking coal alcohol, came from Bogarosch. Ilona Mich, Singing Loni, came from Lugoj. Herr Reusch, the tailor, from Guttenbrunn.] (*The Hunger Angel* 43)

Yet the added physical and psychological details or character traits allow the representative figures to become distinctive individuals. One of the two Sarahs, for example, has "silky hairs on her hands," the other one a "wart on her ring finger" (*The Hunger Angel* 35), and with their childlike reports about their Transylvanian homes, they try to hold on to their individual traits in the midst of the surreal revocation of the reality of the labor camp. Heidrun Gast, with her "Totenäffchengesicht" (221) [dead monkey face, 210] and "das Schlitzmaul von einem Ohr zum andern" (221) [the slit mouth running from one ear to the other, 210] is unable to survive the chronic hunger because her own husband regularly steals her bread portion.

The narrator's lens sways from his private inner world to specific individuals and groups, thus creating sociograms—documents of social life under extreme conditions. The prisoners' behavior is scrutinized from the first years of hunger until the times of relative economic relaxation, which caused a collective bloom in the labor camps, transforming the hungry asexual "We" into individuals in need of communication and human contact. The accurate details are captivating to the reader as they depict the collective behavioral patterns of a ravaged community. Some women began to crochet hairbands and brooches. Trudi Pelikan could walk only on her heels because her frozen toes had fallen off of her feet.

Trudi Pelikan trug eine gehäkelte Seerosenbrosche wie eine an die Brust gehängte Mokkatasse. Die eine Ziri trug eine Maiglöckchenbrosche mit weißen Fingerhüten am Draht, die Loni Mich eine mit rotem Ziegelstaub gefärbte Dahlie.... Zur gehäkelten Lagermode der Frauen gab es im Laden des Russendorfs Toilettenseife, Puder und Rouge. Alles die gleiche Marke KRASNYI MAK, roter Mohn. Die Schminksachen waren rosa und hatten einen schneidigsüßen Duft. Der Hungerengel staunte. (*Atemschaukel* 251)

[Trudi Pelikan wore a crocheted water-lily brooch like a demitasse pinned to her breast. One of the Zirris wore a lily-of-the-valley brooch with white thimbles affixed with wire, Loni Mich wore a dahlia dyed with red brick dust.... A store in the Russian village enhanced the women's crocheted camp fashion with toilet soap, powder, and rouge. All were the same brand: KRASNYI MAK—Red Poppy. The hunger angel was amazed.] (*The Hunger Angel* 251)

It is precisely these expressive details—a gait, the shape of a brooch, a brand name—that allow the reader access into the labor camp experience.

The "hunger angel," as a terrorizing hallucination, threatens the labor camp inmates even after the acute danger of starvation has passed. He remains a constant companion of the deportees. Once liberated from the claws of hunger, only distorted figures remain, which, after their basic needs have been met, instinctually develop a social life and rediscover sexual tensions. These labor camp inmates seem to be simultaneously ridiculous, pitiable, and remarkable, like dented, wound-up puppets that move according to an outside preestablished plan.

The novel avoids, however, the question of any official responsibility for the deportation and for the brutal conditions in the forced labor camps. Hunger is as present in the camps as it is in the nearby Ukrainian villages in the immediate postwar period. The labor camp commander is not a person of interest in the novel either. In addition, Tur Prikulitsch, a deportee who rises to become a prison guard due to his knowledge of Russian, is a profiteer, but he scarcely personifies evil. He steals food and doesn't work, but he renders crucial assistance to Leo in the chapter "Der gutgläubige und der skeptische Flacon" (*Atemschaukel* 157–62) [The gullible bottle and the skeptical one] (*The Hunger Angel* 148–54). Prikulitsch is portrayed as an insignificant opportunist who nonetheless is killed by another labor camp inmate who takes the law into his own hands years later, after the camp's liberation.

Two geographic and generational spaces emerge in *Atemschaukel* that speak of guilt and victimhood. The first is Leo's hometown of Hermannstadt (Romanian: Sibiu) and its inhabitants, who go about their daily lives avoiding any reflection about a possible guilt of their own. Leo remembers the Transylvanian Saxons' involvement with Nazi ideology (*Atemschaukel* 55), as well as his own father's enthusiasm for the war. During the war, his father hunted rabbits and was completely uninterested in the disappearance of the Jews (56); he is not interested in Leo's story after his return home from the camp either (270). The second space is the labor camp, which is peopled with victims tortured by homesickness and hunger, trying desperately to survive. In the labor camp every single deportee feels abandoned and devoid of his or her own personality.

> Nach dem Duschen standen wir nackt im Vorraum und warteten. Verbogene räudige Gestalten, nackt sahen wir aus wie ausgemustertes Arbeitsvieh. Geschämt hat sich keiner. Wovor soll man sich schämen, wenn man keinen Körper mehr hat. Aber seinetwegen waren wir im Lager, für körperliche Arbeit. Je weniger Körper man hatte, desto mehr war man durch ihn gestraft. Diese Hülle gehörte den Russen. (*Atemschaukel* 235)
>
> [So we stood in the entrance area and waited. Bent, mangy figures, in our nakedness we looked like worn-out draft animals. What is there to be ashamed of when you no longer have a body. Yet our bodies were the reason we were in the camp, to perform bodily labor. The less of a body we had, the more it punished us.] (*The Hunger Angel* 224)

Furthermore, a focus on the young people in the camp, people like Leo or Trudi Pelikan, constitutes a crucial element of the accusation against the adults, the generation of parents and grandparents who embraced the ideology of National Socialism. First, the parents allowed the childhood of their offspring to be politicized, and then they simply looked away as their children were deported. While parents continue their lives in their own homes and bear "substitute-children," their sons and daughters swing between life and death in their *Atemschaukel* [breath-swing].[17] The young seem to be the ones paying reparations for errors and mistakes that were committed within and outside the boundaries of their region. After their children's return from the USSR, the parents appear indifferent to the young deportees' experiences at the labor camps, simply watching as their sons and daughters struggle to come to terms with the experience.

Finally, I will address *Atemschaukel*'s potential to intervene in the debate on the suffering of German-Romanians at the end of World War II. In contrast to other texts about the deportation Müller's novel reveals only a handful of historical facts, yet these are crucial for the way in which the author organized the historical and fictional material in the novel. For example, in the first pages of *Atemschaukel* Leo's story is framed by two specific and fateful dates: January 1945, the date of the deportation of the German population from Romania, and the year 1968, in which Pastior himself left Romania, where he had been living in constant fear of being arrested once more, this time because of his sexual orientation. Furthermore, Müller uses the epilogue of the novel to specifically address the absence of the historical deportation of the German minority in Romania in Romania's official memory culture:

> Weil es an die faschistische Vergangenheit Rumäniens erinnerte, war das Thema Deportation tabu. Nur in der Familie und mit engen Vertrauten, die selbst deportiert waren, wurde über die Lagerjahre gesprochen. Und auch dann nur in Andeutungen. Diese verstohlenen Gespräche haben meine Kindheit begleitet. Ihre Inhalte habe ich nicht verstanden, die Angst aber gespürt. (*Atemschaukel* 299)

> [The deportations were a taboo subject because they recalled Romania's Fascist past. Those who had been in the camp never spoke of their experiences except at home or with close acquaintances who had also been deported, and then only indirectly. My childhood was accompanied by such stealthy conversations; at the time I didn't understand their content, but I did sense the fear.] (*The Hunger Angel* 287)

The novel, however, does not throw light on collective fates but rather focuses on the complex portrayal of one individual whose life and freedom were significantly affected by the intrusion of the government into his private life. Despite scarce references to the extra-textual reality, *Atemschaukel* conveys nonetheless a sense of authenticity. The personal experience of the deportation consists, on the one hand, of extant narrative components in the communicative memory, like hunger, extreme climatic conditions, exhaustion, and death. On the other hand, there is the revision, combination, and organization of even the "smallest details" of life in the labor camp provided by Pastior since Müller's accurate and painstakingly detailed notes of Pastior's remembered emotions, perceptions, and experiences are all part of *Atemschaukel*. Müller thus creates authenticity through poetic images of camp details, literary connotations, metaphorical constructs, and chains of motifs that run through the entire novel and, last but not least, through the fictional insights in the deportees' internalized experiences.

Leo Auberg's fate represents an unsuccessful story of liberation. Being an outsider even before the deportation, he fled from the narrow moral concepts and values of his own community during his entire life. But he cannot escape his own memories:

> Seit meiner Heimkehr steht auf meinen Schätzen nicht mehr DA BIN ICH, aber auch nicht DA WAR ICH. Auf meinen Schätzen steht DA KOMM ICH NICHT WEG. Immer streckt sich das Lager vom Schläfenareal links zum Schläfenareal rechts. So muss ich von meinem ganzen Schädel wie von einem Gelände sprechen, von einem Lagergelände. (294)
>
> [Since I came back, my treasures no longer have a sign that says HERE I AM or one that says I WAS THERE. What's actually written on my treasure is: THERE I'M STUCK. The camp stretches on and on, bigger and bigger, from my left temple to my right. So when I talk about what's inside my skull I have to talk about an entire camp.] (*The Hunger Angel* 282)

Even to the community of deportees Leo Auberg remains an outsider who experiences his suffering "allein im Rudel" [alone inside the pack] (*The Hunger Angel* 121).[18]

Although *Atemschaukel* is based on a local, particular historical event, the reception of Müller's novel certainly transgresses any regional or national limitations. Even though critical voices in Germany expressed doubts about the possibility of portraying the labor camp experiences in a poetical way, the reviewers honored the novel's general stance against political terror, as well as the impressive stylistic quality of the text. In Michael Naumann's words Müller enunciates a form of "poetical indignation" that is "concerned with big matters like legality and justice, the endangering of human dignity and freedom" (Naumann 43). Andrea Köhler remarks that Müller "has found words to describe the terror of hunger, which saws the flesh off from the bones. These are as detailed and as accurate as the one hundred different types of ashes, slag, and dust of the labor camp" (Köhler 21). Karl-Markus Gauss reads *Atemschaukel* as "a disturbing masterpiece, courageous and linguistically innovative, an attempt to speak from the inside of hell in a completely particular and illustrative language." In Müller's word compounds—*Eigenbrot* [own bread], *Herzschaufel* [heart-shovel], and *Atemschaukel* [breath-swing]—Ina Hartwig recognizes similarities with Paul Celan's early poetry (Hartwig 22-23). In his laudatory speech, Anders Olsson, a member of the Nobel Prize committee, praises Müller for her courage to oppose "the backward oppression and the political terror" and thinks she deserves the Nobel Prize "for the artistic meaning of this resistance."[19] Müller's poetics are "as political as her impetus to write," writes Naumann, Müller's publisher from 1985 to 1998, and he adds, "Herta Müller's language is the microscope, which makes visible the realities of political dictatorships for everyone who has been taught to read and write."[20]

In contrast, the German media of the emigrated Germans from Romania, as well as the media of displaced persons (i.e., the Germans from Eastern and Southeastern Europe), have discussed the novel only in relation to the actual historical facts and have appropriated Müller's successful novel as a means to once again draw attention to the plight of former deportees. Wilhelm Roth, for example, pledges that "We will remember—as will the Nobel Prize laureate Müller with her book *Atemschaukel*—the destinies of these persons, who had to suffer and to die because of Germany's war guilt." Rose Schmidt, a contemporary witness, calls upon former deportees "to write down, keep and pass on reports, diaries, letters, poems, and memoirs in order to make sure that the life of the deportees, sentenced to hard labor during and after World War II, will be preserved for their children, grandchildren, and posterity, that the injustice committed against the deportees will be reappraised in terms of international law, thus finally becoming 'history.'"

Müller's *Atemschaukel* indeed represents a historical event, deeply rooted in the communicative memory of the Germans from Romania, but it transgresses any narrow spaces of regional memory. Müller takes on a complex historical subject and creates a fictional narrative based on both factual documentation (interviews, notes, and a journey to the camp sites) and her (and in part Pastior's) poetic reflection on the deportation experience. The text's main appeal does not lie in the "reality" of the personal experience but in the access it provides to (fictionalized) spaces of remembrance. *Atemschaukel* illustrates the experience-enlarging function of literature: without losing its factuality, the text, as a historical novel, remains suspended between fact and fiction as it speaks of emotions and motivations under extreme situations as well as of the long-term consequences of traumatic experiences.[21]

Translated from the German by Adrian Teleaba

Notes

1. I would like to refer in this context to Reiner Wild's explanations of the "functions" of literature, to the role of literature in view of the increasing intertwining of the social agents in the process of civilization and, as a result of this process, to the emerging necessity of an increased knowledge of other human beings and their behavior (110–17).

2. Persons who opposed the ideology of National Socialism and who also warned their compatriots about their ideological errors were swiftly eliminated: Hans Otto Roth was deprived of his political possibilities of influence; the priest Wilhelm Staedel replaced Bishop Glondys (Gündisch and Beer 206).

3. Early on, the Germans tried to make use of the war potential of the Germans in Eastern Europe for the Waffen-ss troops. Volunteers entered the Waffen-ss, disguised as agricultural laborers, as early as 1940 (Gündisch and Beer 207).

4. At the end of 1943 there were some fifty-four thousand men who were serving in the Waffen-ss, plus fifteen thousand who were in the Wehrmacht, the Organisation Todt, and the armaments companies (Gündisch and Beer 211).

5. Elena Zamfirescu gives a detailed report, supported by data from archives and British documents, about the futile protests of the Romanian government vis-à-vis the British and Americans. In a letter to the Foreign Office dated January 19, 1945, Winston Churchill asked "not to make a big fuss about the deportation of Austrians, Saxons and other Germans from Romania" since it had been promised "to leave the plight of Romania in the hands of the Russians." The Romanian government had protested on January 3, 1945, against the demand of the Soviet representatives in the Allied Commission to transfer Romanian citizens of German ethnicity to the USSR. But Churchill's point of view prevailed, and the Americans intervened only on behalf of the Germans who were American citizens (Zamfirescu 21–29, 21–23).

6. Decree 187, passed on March 23, 1945, which served as a legal basis for the implementation of a land reform, defined the expropriation of "areas of land" and "every kind of agrarian possessions" owned by "German citizens or Romanian citizens, physical and legal persons with German background who collaborated with Hitler's Germany." It affected every German in Romania who worked in agriculture (70 percent of them worked as farmers); only those who fought in the Romanian Army after August 1944 were exempted. Through this measure, the farmers lost not only their land but also their houses. One year later an electoral law passed on July 4, 1946, excluded all members of the then German ethnic minority from the elections, although the nationality status, passed on March 6, 1945, granted all Romanian citizens equal rights (Gündisch and Beer 223–26).

7. See, for example, the chapter "Die literarische Thematisierung der stalinistischen Repressionen" (Spiridon 94–112). The following are just a few names of German-language writers from Transylvania and Banat whose works held only veiled allusions: Anton Breitenhofer, Wolfgang Koch, Ernst Kulcsar, Arnold Hauser, Horst Samson, Ludwig Schwarz, Richard Wagner, Erwin Wittstock, and Joachim Wittstock. An exception is Johann Lippet's remarkable book *biografie. ein muster*, whose poeticism manages to convey in an expressive manner the experience of the deportation.

8. Some of the early, most well-known texts published in Western Europe are Bernhard Ohsam's description of his experiences during the deportation in *Eine Handvoll Machorka* (1958) and Rainer Biemel's memories from Russia in *Mein Freund Wassja* (1949). The latter was republished several times and translated into several languages; among others, it was published by Böhlau in 1995. In France this

early report on the realities of the Soviet labor camps at the end of the 1950s, appearing as *Mon ami Vassia* (published under the pseudonym Jean Rounault), caused polemics and even legal disputes with the intellectual left. Biemel even won a trial verdict against the Communist newspaper *Les Lettres Françaises* (Bruss 10).

9. In order to emphasize the validity of the narration, Matthias Kandler includes a chapter titled "Die Verschleppung aus sowjetischer Sicht" [The deportation from the Soviet perspective], in which several documents are cited in their entirety: a report of the commissar of internal affairs, Beria, to Stalin and Molotov, dated December 15, 1944 (39-41); decision 7252ss of the State Committee of Defense regarding the employment of German internees (41-42); as well as an order regarding the reception, subsistence, and employment of the mobilized and interned Germans, dated December 29, 1944 (42-43).

10. The book consists of two parts. Part 1: Hedwig Stieber-Ackermann, "Vom Überlebenskampf eines 17-jährigen Mädchens, das nach Russland verschleppt wurde" (9-187); Part 2: "Deportation in die Sowjetunion und Lagerleben von 1945 bis 1949." The appendix includes some poems written during the deportation, as well as a general map of the labor camp sites in present-day Ukraine.

11. See, for example, Radisch (43).

12. Müller incorporated some of her mother's memories in earlier texts as well: *Niederungen* [*Nadirs*] (9) and *Der Mensch ist ein großer Fasan auf der Welt* [*The Passport*] (46-47).

13. The journey was financed by the Grenzgänger program of the Robert Bosch Foundation. This program sponsors authors who write about Central, Eastern, and Southeastern Europe and about China. See Sander (9).

14. As could be seen in the exhibition Minze Minze flaumiran Schpektrum. Herta Müller und Oskar Pastior. Literaturhaus Stuttgart, December 9, 2010–March 31, 2011, under the trusteeship of Ernest Wichner and Lutz Dittrich, in collaboration with the Robert Bosch Foundation.

15. "Images of the language make the reality endurable." Matthias Sander dialogued with Oskar Pastior.

16. Selected pages from Oskar Pastior's notebooks were on display at the exhibition Minze Minze flaumiran Schpektrum in Stuttgart.

17. After his return, Leo has a chance to observe how his family stubbornly goes about its everyday life: his father paints the Carpathian Mountains, "every few days a new watercolor" (*The Hunger Angel* 252); his grandmother solves a cross-

word puzzle; and his mother knits socks for "her ersatz-child Robert" (*The Hunger Angel* 252).

18. In his novel *Januar '45 oder die höhere Pflicht* (January 45 or the higher duty) Erwin Wittstock argues, reminiscent of the Nazi ideology, that the collective values of a people have to stand above those of an individual. According to him, the individual has to do penance in solidarity with his people: "The magnificence that our homeland has given to us and which you carry with you stays invisible, like breath, although it fills your life. Be yourself, in perennial excellence, a shield that protects the legacy of your ancestors" (251).

19. Can/AP/AFP/dpa: "Herta Müller nimmt den Nobelpreis entgegen"; in *Spiegel Online*, December 10, 2009.

20. The text, slightly abridged, corresponds to Naumann's lecture on the occasion of the award of the Heinrich-Heine Prize to Herta Müller on September 27, 2009, in Düsseldorf.

21. Pastior's exposure as a Securitate informant in September 2010 (Sienerth) somehow undermined Müller's uncompromising attitude toward former collaborators. Müller admitted that Pastior "was traumatized by his detention in the labor camp and, as a homosexual in Romania, was subject to blackmail" (Mayr 129). But Richard Wagner, Müller's long-standing companion and ex-husband, persists in his unshakable opinion: "Herta's position toward Pastior has become fragile. Her work is based on the fundamental concept that literature is supposed to deal with society." Thus in Wagner's opinion the Oskar Pastior Foundation and the prize that bears Pastior's name cannot be maintained (Mayr 129). The knowledge that Pastior collaborated with the Communist Romanian secret service doesn't diminish the value and success of the novel. But one cannot help but wonder how Müller would have reacted had she known earlier of his collaboration.

Works Cited

Beer, Mathias. "Deutsche Deportierte aus Ostmittel-und Südosteuropa in der UdSSR" [German deportees from East Central Europe and Southeastern Europe to the USSR]. *Enzyklopädie Migration in Europa. Vom 17. Jahrhundert bis zur Gegenwart*. Ed. Klaus Bade et al. Paderborn: Ferdinand Schöningh, 2007. 465–70.

Bruss, Siegbert. "Brillante Persönlichkeiten der französischen und siebenbürgischen Literatur. Rainer Biemel schrieb das erste Meisterwerk über die Deportation der Siebenbürger Sachsen in die Sowjetunion." *Siebenbürgische Zeitung,* June 30, 2010:10.

Gauss, Karl-Markus. "Das Lager ist eine praktische Welt. Ein europäisches Ereignis: Herta Müllers Roman *Atemschaukel* über die Deportation der Rumäniendeutschen in die Sowjetunion nach 1945." *Süddeutsche Zeitung,* August 20, 2009.

Gündisch, Konrad, and Mathias Beer. *Siebenbürgen und die Siebenbürger Sachsen.* Vol. 8. Munich: Studienbuchreihe der Stiftung Ostdeutscher Kulturrat, 1998.

Hartwig, Ina. "Der Held heißt Hungerengel. Herta Müllers neuer, wagemutiger Roman *Atemschaukel* begibt sich in die Innenwelt eines sowjetischen Arbeitslagers." *Frankfurter Rundschau,* August 21, 2009:22–23.

Henneberg, Nicole. "'Die Zumutung des Lagers sollte in der Sprache spürbar werden': Herta Müller about Her Novel and Her Work with Oskar Pastior." *Frankfurter Rundschau,* August 21, 2009:23.

Kandler, Matthias J. *Nr. 657. Im Donbass deportiert. 1945-1949. Russlanderinnerungen.* Villingen-Schweningen: Farca, 2009.

Köhler, Andrea. "Das Buch vom Hunger. Herta Müllers ungeheurer Roman *Atemschaukel.*" *Neue Zürcher Zeitung,* August 25, 2009. Web. August 27, 2009.

Lippet, Johann. *biografie. ein muster.* Bucharest: Kriterion, 1980.

Mayr, Walter. "Gift im Gepäck. Die Enthüllungen über Spitzeleien des Dichters Oskar Pastior haben Streit ausgelöst unter rumäniendeutschen Schriftstellern. Im Zentrum der Debatte um Schuld, Verrat und den aufrechten Gang in totalitärer Zeit steht die Nobelpreisträgerin Herta Müller." *Der Spiegel,* January 17, 2011:128–31.

Müller, Herta. *Atemschaukel.* Munich: Hanser, 2009.

———. *Der Mensch ist ein großer Fasan auf der Welt.* Berlin: Rotbuch, 1986.

———. *The Hunger Angel.* Trans. Philip Boehm. New York: Metropolitan Books, 2012.

———. *Nadirs.* Trans. Sieglinde Lug. Lincoln: University of Nebraska Press, 1999.

———. *Niederungen.* Berlin: Rotbuch, 1984.

———. "Nullpunkt der Existenz. Mit Oskar Pastior in der Ukraine." *Neue Zürcher Zeitung,* October 21–22, 2006:73.

———. *The Passport.* Trans. Martin Chalmers. London: Serpent's Tail, 1989.

Naumann, Michael. "Sie kann nicht vergessen." *Zeit Online,* October 9, 2009. Web. May 31, 2010.

Radisch, Iris. "Gulag-Romane lassen sich nicht aus zweiter Hand schreiben. Herta Müllers Buch ist parfümiert und kulissenhaft." *Die Zeit*, August 20, 2009:43.

Roth, Wilhelm. "In Augsburg: Ökumenischer Gottesdienst zum Gedenken an die Russlanddeportation." *Siebenbürgische Zeitung*, March 13, 2010.

Sander, Matthias. "Sprachbilder machen die Wirklichkeit erträglich. Interview. Ernst Wichner hat 2004 mit Herta Müller und Oskar Pastior die Schauplätze des Romans *Atemschaukel* besichtigt." *Stuttgarter Zeitung*, December 9, 2009:9.

Schmidt, Rose. "Deportation vor 65 Jahren: Zeitzeugin erinnert an schweres Leid und ruft zur Versöhnung auf." *Siebenbürgische Zeitung*, February 28, 2010. Web. March 18, 2010.

Sienerth, Stefan. "Ich habe Angst vor unerfundenen Geschichten. Zur Securitate-Akte Oskar Pastiors." *Spiegelungen. Zeitschrift für deutsche Kultur und Geschichte Südosteuropas* 3 (2010): 236–71.

Spiridon, Olivia. *Untersuchungen zur rumäniendeutschen Erzählliteratur der Nachkriegszeit*. Oldenburg: Igel, 2002.

Stieber-Ackermann, Hedwig, and Olga Katharina Farca. *Allein die Hoffnung hielt uns am Leben*. Villingen-Schweningen: Farca, 1999.

Wild, Reiner. *Literatur im Prozess der Zivilisation. Entwurf einer theoretischen Grundlegung der Literaturwissenschaft*. Stuttgart: Metzler, 1982.

Wittstock, Erwin. *Januar '45 oder Die höhere Pflicht*. Bucharest: ADZ-Verlag, 1998.

Zamfirescu, Elena. "Die Deportation und die Haltung Rumäniens—damals und heute." *Deportation der Südostdeutschen in die Sowjetunion 1945-1949*. Ed. Hans-Werner Schuster and Walther Konschitzky. Munich: Haus des Deutschen Ostens, 1999.

Part 3 Müller's Aesthetics of Experimentation

8. "In meinen Schläfen." (Copyright Herta Müller.)

9 "Wir können höchstens mit dem, was wir sehen, etwas zusammenstellen"

Herta Müller's Collages

Beverley Driver Eddy

In his critique of Herta Müller's *Die blassen Herren mit den Mokkatassen*, Anton G. Leitner has remarked that he considered the form of her collage poems, which he refers to as *Schnipsellyrik*, or cut-out poetry, trite and outdated; their genius lies "in the concurrence of fortuitous and calculated word deployment by a writer who can wield not just a pair of scissors."[1]

There have been many attempts to decipher Müller's collages; many of them, like Leitner's, concentrating on the texts and largely ignoring the artworks that accompany them.[2] Some note the similarities in appearance between her collage texts and those of blackmail letters and address such questions as, Does the form demonstrate a de-personalization of the process of writing? or Is it an attempt to maintain anonymity? Others note that Müller cuts her words out from magazines and newspapers, much as repressive state censors do, and maintain that her collages therefore visibly reflect the restoration and triumph of free speech. Leitner is correct in his critique in seeing a bond between Müller's work and the techniques of the Dadaists/surrealists; he oversimplifies the issue, however, when he appears to fault Müller for blindly adopting a trite methodology. In this chapter I will examine Müller's collages as total art works of picture and text, first by tracing their origin and development as a favored literary/artistic genre; then by showing their development through the three published collections of collages—*Der Wächter nimmt seinen Kamm* (1993), *Im Haarknoten wohnt eine Dame* (2000), and *Die blassen Herren mit den Mokkatassen* (2005); and finally by indicating how Müller's use of the collage form reflects her own views on literature.[3]

Although she created the first collages as we know them shortly after her move from Romania to Berlin, Müller had both written poetry and cut details from magazine and newspaper pictures while she was living in Romania. Her German grade-school teacher has recalled that when she was fourteen to fifteen years old, Müller possessed a thick notebook in which she wrote her poetry (Knorz); her first published poem appeared when she was sixteen.[4] Although critical readers would agree with Müller that these early poems are, for the most part, "juvenile" [*pueril*] (Eddy 332), lines such as "Im Tische singt / der Holzwurm" [In the table the woodworm is singing],[5] "mandelbittres Lächeln / habe ich gekostet" [I have tasted almond-bitter smiles],[6] and "der Wind sucht ... / auf zertretenem Gras / unsere Sonnenuhr" [The wind seeks our sundial on trampled grass][7] reveal that Müller was already developing her own poetical language. She has declared that she stopped writing poetry upon entering the university; Müller's collage poems, then, signal a belated return to these early lyrical roots.

The development of Müller's artwork took a two-pronged route. A major impetus came from her desire to create her own art. She has commented on her frustration at being able to draw with her eyes but not with her hands.[8] In compensation for that, she turned to the personal pleasure of cutting pictures out of magazines and newspapers as room adornments. One of these early pictures was of Kafka's ear.[9] Viewed in isolation, Kafka's rather oddly shaped ear shows sensitivity, vulnerability, and transparency; this small body part captures Kafka's essence as a writer. As Müller puts it, "When you look at a detail, you see only a part of a whole, but I believe you see more deeply from this part than when you view the surface of the entire object" (Eddy 330).

In another example, Müller tells how a friend of hers cut Ceaușescu's eye from a photograph, mounted it on brown wrapping paper, and wrote beneath it, "The Eye of the Dictator." She remarks: "We laughed, laughed resoundingly, because the eye threatened us even more now. With this surveillance through the cut-out eye, [this friend] had stumbled on surveillance itself. It was palpable and no bigger than a fingernail.... It was a bad joke." As a result, "We tried to hold on to the sovereignty of laughter. The small, broken sounds that we managed were already sad ones. We had already recognized that which confronted us before we grew silent" (*Teufel* 27-28).

Kafka's ear, Ceaușescu's eye: both details captured the essence of their subjects in concentrated form, precisely *because* they were isolated details. These cutout details are, however, a form of dissection. Müller comments, "When one looks at ... people, one is ruthless. One dissects them. The detail is larger than the whole. One looks inside them. One doesn't see anything, but one suspects what is inside" (*Teufel* 25-26).

Müller further notes that the immobility of the photographic image is misleading: "We look upon the captured movement," she remarks. "For me frozen movement is often the same as agitation.... When one looks closely, and long enough, something rages beneath the rigidity" (*Teufel* 26, 27).

It was a small step for Müller to form larger photomontages of the elements that she cut from various pictures. Her novel *Reisende auf einem Bein* [*Traveling on One Leg*] relates how the heroine assembles a photomontage for her kitchen wall: "A big thumb nail next to a traveling bus. A watch next to a gate thrown open and the cobbled pavement in front of it led to emptiness.... An airplane in the sky next to a hand. A face ... next to a girl in a rocking chair.... A corpse in a suit. A water mill" (*Traveling on One Leg* 37). In this novel Müller also describes an important work technique: "She had to look and compare for a long time until two pictures fit together. Once they fit they fit automatically. The connections that appeared were opposites. They made one single, strange collage out of all the pictures. The collage was so strange that it could relate to everything. It was constantly moving. The collage was so strange that it reached the point where the smile of the girl in the rocking chair unveiled the same abyss as the corpse in its suit" (*Traveling on One Leg* 37–38).

The technique of the photomontage—the juxtaposition of contrasting images and contrasting sizes of these images—creates a "strange" or "foreign" entity, in which the various elements of the work impact one another to make an overpowering statement. In other texts Müller has described her art as the product of a "fremder Blick" [foreign gaze],[10] which leads to "erfundene Wahrnehmungen" [invented perceptions].[11]

Early on Müller added phrases or sentences to the visual artwork, much as her friend had done in the case of Ceaușescu's eye. In *Reisende auf einem Bein*, Müller describes a street sign that the heroine stole for her apartment while she was still living under the dictatorship: "There was a man with a digging shovel on it. On the sign Irene had written: Digging is always on the edge of the legal. It was a sentence from a book.... Irene had connected that sentence to her life too" (*Traveling on One Leg* 73).[12] "Found" objects and an appropriate commentary: these are the prototype for Müller's earliest collages.

Shortly after Müller moved to Germany, she began creating and sending self-made postcards in which she combined photos or photomontages with a brief collage text. These were done, she said, "just in fun" for friends (Eddy 338). Eleven of her early collages are included in her 1991 book of essays *Der Teufel sitzt im Spiegel*; five of them are especially typical of the earliest postcard collages in that they are dominated by the artwork and contain a single phrase. One, bearing the text "Frühstück mit geschäumter Milch" (Breakfast with foamed milk) (56), is illustrated by two hand-drawn cups placed upon a table. One of these cups is quite small and rests in a saucer; the other is oversized and has no saucer, but its handle resembles a drawn ear, and the body of the cup consists of the photo of that part of a face that includes a clear wide blue eye. It is typical of Müller to make close associations between people and objects in her work, often in such a way that they grow into one another in her collages. As she herself puts it in a collage she created for her friend Oskar Pastior: "Kommst in ein langbeiniges Glas Milch / Wäsche in Weiß graugrüne Zinkwanne / bei

Nachnahme entsprechen sich / fast alle Materialien" [You're coming into a long-stemmed glass of milk / linens into white gray-green zinc tub / nearly all materials / correspond upon delivery].[13] Particulated body parts juxtaposed into and against objects and landscapes remain common throughout Müller's artwork. She is particularly fond of cutting out half or quarter faces, feet, and parts of the human torso.

One of the most interesting of the collages in this early volume of essays shows two half (or nearly half) faces: both are of men in their sixties, but they suggest different character traits. The higher of the two faces is hidden in shadow and shows a heavy eyelid and the suggestion of a smile; the lower one is in light, and the face shows purpose and direction. The photomontage is topped with a picture of a large, official-looking building behind tall, leafless trees, while the collage text above it reads:

Fahrer und Mitfahrer frösteln,
nicht

[Driver and passenger are shivering,
not]

The text is typical of the early collages in that it is not made up solely of isolated cutout words or word parts; instead the phrase "Fahrer und Mitfahrer frösteln" is a single snippet from a single line of text. The commentary on the phrase is provided beneath it in the heavily weighted word *nicht*. Without the comma at the end of the preceding phrase, *nicht* would be simply a denial of the situation—or of the authority of the author of the original cutout phrase. With the comma, however, it suggests a secondary meaning of *nicht wahr* [isn't that so?]. The word *frösteln* lends further ambiguity to the text. Are the two men shivering (or not) from the cold, or are they shivering from fear? Finally, even the words *Fahrer* and *Mitfahrer* carry a certain ambiguity: who is in control here—is it the man doing the driving, or is he simply a chauffeur? In looking at the lower man's face in the photomontage, one sees that Müller has cut it in such a way as to preserve one eye and ear, half the man's mouth, and his entire nose, thereby turning the frontal half-view into a simultaneous near profile and creating further ambiguity in the image. One can find this technique of rendering half a frontal image as a simultaneous side view in many of the montages to be found in Müller's two most recent volumes, *Die blassen Herren mit den Mokkatassen* and her Romanian-language book *Este sau nu este Ion* (see fig. 9).

Müller has, in fact, preserved both the ambiguities and the playfulness of the earlier collages in her later collage collections, and she has retained the strict postcard format for all these works. In later collage collections, however, Müller introduces a second prong of her art, that of silhouette cutouts, or *Scherenschnitte*. Like the photos and photomontages, these also evolved out of Müller's personal correspondence, where, instead of cut-out photos, she drew outline figures to illustrate a written statement (see fig. 10). In her collages Müller transformed these outline figures into silhouette cutouts; approximately half of the illustrations for her earliest published collection of collages, *Der Wächter nimmt seinen Kamm. Vom Weggehen und Ausscheren* [The guard takes his comb: On leaving and going one's way], are composed of these cutouts, and the fact that Müller has designed them makes their selection deliberate rather than coincidental. They are dictated by her own fantasy, not by the details in photographs, and they show that despite Müller's protestations that she cannot draw, she has a talent for delineating actions and moods through the posturings of her figures.

These figures serve to underscore the primacy of the text. The text is no longer commentary to a picture; rather, the picture is illustrative, in some fashion, of an aspect of the text or "story." This is a striking evolution in these cards. As Müller herself has acknowledged, her earliest works began with the image, to which she then added text. These evolved to works in which the text comes first. They have, she has said, "probably changed . . . of necessity. More and more they became a literary craft. I put myself to the test as to whether I can do it, whether I am still able to. I could never write a poem, sit down and write by hand, with a pen. But by this method, when I have these printed words cut out upon the table, they fly together and become a story. They leave me outside and *still* inside, I can't explain why" (Eddy 338).

Der Wächter nimmt seinen Kamm: Vom Weggehen und Ausscheren is a box of ninety-four little "stories" on ninety-four cards of postcard size. The

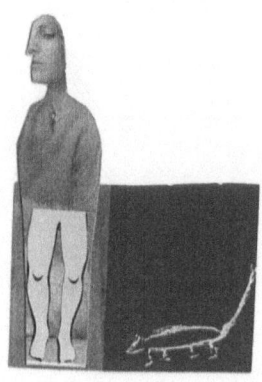

9. Frontal face view cut to suggest a slightly distorted profile and an undressed lower torso to suggest vulnerability. From *Die blassen Herren mit den Mokkatassen*. (Copyright Carl Hanser Verlag München 2005.)

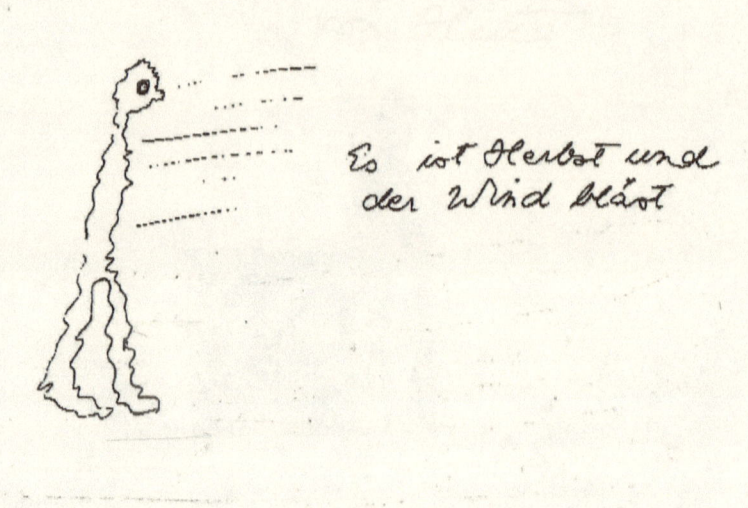

10. A typical sketch in a Herta Müller letter. (Copyright Herta Müller.)

subtitle of the work addresses not only "leaving" one's past, but also "veering off" or "going one's own way." There is a pun suggested in the last word of the title: *Ausscheren* is constructed from *scheren*, a verb meaning "to clip," and the collages are constructed by *clipping out* words and phrases, word parts, and images. Unobtrusive numbers on the back of these cards suggest an order, although the cards can, conceivably, be shuffled and read in any order. The overarching theme binding the cards together is the tension that exists between flight and entrapment: flight to the West to escape the fear and terror of the dictatorship and entrapment by images in the mind that do not allow one to be free of the past. The main title of the work is taken from card number 48, where Müller's text reads:

Dieser schwarze Kasten ist
keine Lampe und keine
Stille
es ist der Fahrstuhl
Fahrten mit Strom
im Spiegel Licht
wie eine Zahnbürste

und der Wächter
nimmt seinen Kamm
kann den Knopf
auf die Dauer
nicht halten

[This black box is
not a lamp and not a
silence
it is the elevator
Rides with electricity
light in the mirror
like a toothbrush
and the guard
takes his comb
cannot hold
the button
in the long run] (42)

The illustration for this text (see fig. 11) shows a cutout of an armless figure, encased within a door-like archway, bent over a table as if closely examining something upon its surface. There is little in the illustration to suggest a guard, a moving elevator, or an elevator button; the area with the table as seen through the archway is more suggestive of an office, museum, or library. The table, perhaps, suggests authority; the figure, perhaps, someone either trying to exert or to understand that authority. Contrary to the text, there is no intimation of flight—physical or mental—in the illustration, although the archway enclosure does suggest entrapment, just as does the elevator in the text. What is the nature of this entrapment? The similarities/differences between illustration and text create a tension that the reader is asked to resolve. Because it was chosen as the cover picture for the box in which Müller's work is lodged, the tension dissolves there, and the image becomes a self-portrait of the artist, entrapped by memories of her past, seeking words and picture fragments among the cutouts on her table. As Müller puts it in another of her cards:

11. Cover *Scherenschnitt* from *Der Wächter nimmt seinen Kamm*. (Copyright Herta Müller.)

Exil das ist nicht eng
außer wenn drinnen in der Stirn die Stimme so laut
wird wie auf dem Flur

[Exile is not narrow
except when within one's brow the voice is as loud
as in the hallway] (50)

Most of the silhouette cutouts in *Der Wächter nimmt seinen Kamm* show figures in varying postures: some are seated, some stand, some lie down; some slump over, some march stiffly; some, like dancers, have one leg raised high up in the air. Occasionally these cutout figures are mounted together with photo cutouts. On the title card, for example, a silhouette figure rests upon a cutout pillow. Whether silhouette cutouts, photos, or photomontages, nearly all the illustrations on the ninety-four cards of *Der Wächter nimmt seinen Kamm* are black and white; some are difficult to decipher, being blurred photographic images or fragments of faces or objects that cannot be discerned clearly. In some it is unclear whether part of a photomontage is a photograph fragment or a silhouette cutout. Although one can say that the blurrings, confused images, and image associations capture, in visual form, the state of mind of the exile, other images are quite clear and adhere closely to the text. In one poem about a man being driven to suicide by an interrogation into his writings, the text reads, in part, "In den täglichen Verhören will der Vernehmer wissen, ob die / Taube fliehen wollte, im Gedicht ob sie davon wußte daß der / Staat eine Holzkiste und das Land ein Wachsbild im Stiefel / ist oder . . ." [In the daily inquisitions the interrogator wants to know whether the / dove wanted to escape, whether she knew in the poem about the / State being a wooden box and the land a waxen image in the boot / or . . .] (36), while the photomontage shows the high brow and crest of hair of a man to the left and, to the right, two hands holding a manuscript and pencil. As Müller puts it, "There are collages where the picture mirrors the text, and there are pictures where the relationship is not obvious at all. I don't know why. Not everything lets itself be illustrated, perhaps most things don't let themselves be illustrated, and when one illustrates something, then it is just a tiny part of the whole, and not the entire thing. And I couldn't bear having the entire text repeated again as a picture" (Eddy 337). In spite of this, Müller defends her mix of image and text: "I frequently have the impression that language does not suffice, that it alone is unsubstantial. When you think about films, where there is image and sound and text, a medium that has the ability to work with all that at the same time" (Eddy 338).

There is a haunting quality to *Der Wächter nimmt seinen Kamm*, created both by the black and white visuals and the melancholy, poetic, and personalized nature of the texts. Nearly all the situations and memories captured there either echo or anticipate scenes in Müller's novels and short stories. Müller reflects: "Schon als Kind / war ich Mitte Dreißig" [Already as a child / I was in my midthirties] (65) and "Uns / gehört / die / Angst / der / Sanftheit" [To us / belongs / the / fear / of / gentleness] (25). She describes the Nazi past of many who lived in the Romanian-German villages: "Männer haben ihre Geheimnisse" [Men have their secrets], she writes (21), and "Ess ess sagt er Kopf ab noch ein Apfelstrudel also / Heillittla—von wegen Ermittler" [Eat eat he says heads off another apple strudel then / Heillittla—observer my foot] (93). In these villages, "Die Frauen fürchten und hüten das Lachen / die Männer sind Könige im Schnaps" [The women fear and guard their laughter / the men are kings in booze] (16), while "Die Muttersprache kichert Schwarz auf Kindesbeinen" [The mother tongue giggles black on children's legs] (92). In this latter collage, about a language where much is colored by the crimes of the fathers, "Alle Blumen heißen auf deutsch Bleiwurz und / Schwarze Susanne" [All the flowers are called in German leadwort and / black Susanne], the visual is one of the collection's rare color illustrations and shows the legs and feet of a chicken perched precariously on the edge of a board fence, framed against a blue sky. This photo cutout is shaped like, and suggestive of, a tie-dyed T-shirt. As is evident in these collages, "Die Ausnahme ist verboten" [Exception is forbidden] (35) in the environment of the German village.

Many of the collages describe the toll that the dictatorship takes on friendships. Müller writes: "Die Stühle sind kalt die Freunde ein wenig überlebt / und andere tot / wer hat wen ertragen / verhärtet geschwächt geblendet / benutzt vorgeschoben und verkauft / und dennoch behalten" [The chairs are cold the friends a little outlived / and others dead/ who sustained / hardened weakened blinded / used pushed and sold whom / and still retained him] (*Wächter* 39). She recalls a friend's treachery: "Ich darf sie nichts fragen, damit ich nicht weiß / sie täte es wieder" [I may ask her nothing, in order not to know / she would do it again] (*Wächter* 2), illustrating her text with one of her armless figures bent over in grief. She is haunted by memories of dead friends: "Ihre Särge sind jetzt im Hirn / reden leicht, und fressen mir die Stimme" [Their coffins are now in my brain / speak gently, and devour my voice] (*Wächter* 4). She describes the "dictator" or "president": "Jede Nacht legt er sich und beendet ein / Leben zeigt Zivilcourage Morgens um fünf / wird einer wegen zwei Zeilen verhaftet" [Every night he lies down and ends a / life shows civil courage at five in the morning / someone will be arrested because of two lines of text] (26), illustrating it with another of her *Scherenschnitt* cutouts, this time showing an armless figure bent over double, as if in pain. A number of collages are about guards and inquisitors. Müller writes, for example, to a graphic combining a *Scherenschnitt* figure standing tall with a photo of a cutout stone: "Ich schreib Spitzelberichte na gut. / die sind wie sich Näherkommen durch / die Knöchel ins Gesicht" [I write undercover reports fair enough. / they are like getting closer through / knuckles in one's face] (*Wächter* 28).

Other collages treat attempted border escapes, corpses at the border, bribes paid for passports, staged "suicides," reflections from the West, and comparisons of East and West. "Jetzt läuft mein Hund durch das Nachbardorf" [Now my dog runs through the neighboring village], she writes, to a *Scherenschnitt* of a figure leaning forward in a diving position, "Ich konnte ihn nicht mit mir nehmen. wie einen Löffel / in die Hand / Er hat es an sich besser als der Fremde hier / mit dem abgetragenen Glück in den Knochen / mit dem Humor der Wanderratten" [I couldn't take him with me. Like a spoon / in my hand / He actually has it better than the stranger here / with the worn-out happiness in his bones / with the humor of homeless rats] (*Wächter* 75).

Müller's second collection of collages, *Im Haarknoten wohnt eine Dame* [In the knot of hair there is a lady], was printed in book form rather than as a box of cards, both to save printing costs and to make it easier to market, and the pages are unnumbered.[14] It appeared seven years after *Der Wächter nimmt seinen Kamm* and shows several striking transformations in technique. Visually the work is considerably brighter. There are more colored illustrations, especially in pastel colors, and the *Scherenschnitte* are cut from colored and/or patterned paper as well as from black. There are several cutout "silhouettes" from magazine illustrations so that, for example, a rabbit appears in the head of a cutout human form (*Im Haarknoten* 80), while a sleeping human appears in the head of a dog or *Heimweh-*

12. Cutout from *Im Haarknoten wohnt eine Dame*. (Copyright Herta Müller.)

hund [homesickness dog] (*Im Haarknoten* 86; fig. 12). In general the visuals have more clarity and are simpler in form than those of the earlier volume, often serving as illustration for a given line or image in the accompanying verse. As in the earlier volume, one can find references to Müller's prose works: to the title of the novel *Heute wär ich mir lieber nicht begegnet* [I would rather not have met myself today] and the image used in that novel of a "Nase schmal wie eine Tabakblüte" [nose narrow as a tobacco blossom] (*Im Haarknoten* 63), and to the essay volume *Der König verneigt sich und tötet* [The king bows and kills] (*Im Haarknoten* 40).

Content-wise, *Im Haarknoten wohnt eine Dame* treats most of the same themes of the earlier collection: the Romanian-Germans' Nazi past, political persecution, sexual assaults, real and staged suicides, flight and emigration to the West, resettlement in Germany. And yet the tone of many of these poems is very different. Where deaths, staged suicides, and betrayal appear in the first volume to relate closely to specific traumatic events in Müller's life, they are now captured as little mini-tales about named (fictional) figures: Herr Wollstreicher (24), Marion (64), Ferstl (69), Emilia (74), and so on. Müller no longer writes about the "dictator" or "president," but she is clearly referring to the Romanian dictator when she identifies him as "king" in number 23 and quotes Ceaușescu directly:

"Mein König sagt nicht ohne Grund / ich liebe euch doch alle" [My king says not without reason / but I love you all]. Müller has said that the reason for choosing this term instead of "dictator" was because "the word 'king' sounds soft." As a child she thought of "king" as part of her grandfather's hand-carved chess set and the figure on a village weathervane; it was a figure that was both threatening and vulnerable. In this volume of collages the "king" is not just Ceaușescu, but the entire atmosphere of fear—and "appetite for life" that his reign created.[15]

In *Im Haarknoten wohnt eine Dame*, a naive, childlike perspective shapes many of the ninety-seven verses. Eighteen of them speak of "father" and/or "mother." Those that don't are still frequently dominated by phrases typical of a child living in the country. In one of several poems of suicide, a figure's hands are "locker wie ein Hampelmann" [loose like a jumping jack], and Müller adds to this a local superstition: "Dann heißt es Menschen / die ans Grab kommen seien / die Stühle des Toten / solange ihre Schatten auf der Erde liegen / muß er im Himmel nicht stehen" [It is said then that people / who come to the grave are / the chairs of the dead man / as long as their shadows lie on the earth / he does not have to stand in heaven] (30); in another she asks: "Wer hat im Sonntagshemd / die Katze bei den Birnbäumen begraben / und vorher totgeschlagen / sie schrie nicht laut ich hab geschaut / und nicht geweint" [Who buried the cat / by the pear trees in his Sunday shirt / and killed it previously / it did not cry out loudly I watched / and didn't cry] (31).

This second poem, like many in this volume, introduces rhyme into Müller's verses. This is another new development, for Müller initially had a strong dislike for "expressions or glib, rhymed sayings whose singsong immediately sticks in one's mind"; she traced such verses back to childhood, to rhymed weather predictions and childhood prayers, and to the rhymed poems composed in praise of dictator and fatherland. She found that in such rhymed verses, "nothing in them perplexes, they simply offer themselves for repetition." In spite of this, in this new volume of collages, Müller has turned to "the humorous effect of sentences and images" that one finds "in the free market economy" (*König* 33-34). The poem to the cover illustration is a good example: it shows a figure diving to its death, while the text tells of a man named "Ferdinand" who "springt vom Fensterrand / hält die Richtung schief / macht den Gehsteig tief" [leaps from the window ledge / keeps an inclined direction / deepens the walkway] (*Im Haarknoten* 66). By adopting the rhymes and singsong patterns of childhood and the techniques of the marketplace, Müller subverts the propagandistic aims of the Romanian socialist party. As she puts it, "It appeared that one could cope with the king through rhymes. One can present him. Rhyme forces him back into the heartbeats that he causes. Rhyme makes smooth swerves into the devastation that he has caused" (*König* 56-57).

In one of her speeches Müller has cited a comic rhyme used in Berlin to promote Paech-Brot [Paech bread] in its subway advertising: "Beim Ja-Wort schweigt die junge Braut / Weil sie noch rasch ein Paech-Brot kaut" [The young bride does not speak her vows / because she is quickly chewing another piece of Paech bread]. For Müller the word "Paech-Brot," or, as she read it, "Pechbrot" [bread of misfortune], captured the essence of her life under the Ceaușescu dictatorship: "At that time I really had no idea how one could capture the torment with which the secret service mishandled me in a single word. Not until the bread ad in the Berlin subway revealed 'bread of misfortune' as the right word for the wreckage of my nerves" (*König* 180). For Müller this word subverted the apparent harmlessness of the singsong advertisement, and the verse functioned instead like the punch line in the comic verses and pictures produced by the popular German satirist Wilhelm Busch (1832-1908). Müller produced for *Im Haarknoten wohnt eine Dame* a number of her own illustrated, comic-rhymed verses that introduce characters, tell a brief story, and end with a punch line. One of the most frequently cited of these states:

> Kurz darauf sagte Barbara
> mein Vater war Nazi
> mein Sohn ist ein Skin
> mein Mann Demokrazi
> mit Doppelkinn
> meine Tochter die wird Sängerin
>
> [A little later Barbara said
> my father was a Nazi

my son is a skinhead
my husband a democrat
with a double chin
my daughter is going to learn to sing] (*Im Haarknoten* 80)

Another, illustrated with a photomontage of oversized feet protruding to one side of a tall slim door, begins, in true Lizzie Borden fashion: "Hatten so ein schönes Haus / Mutter ging als erste raus / als man sie am Bahndamm fand / hieß es Leichnam unbekannt" [We had such a lovely house / mother was the first to leave / when they found her on the railway embankment / they called it corpse unknown] (*Im Haarknoten* 49).

Rather than trivializing the horrors of the dictatorship, the grotesque humor in these verse constructions represents a childlike defense mechanism that Müller admits to using in daily life. When, for example, she is disturbed by the store clerks in Berlin who constantly comment on her German and ask where she is from, she says,

> Immediately afterwards I imagine while walking on the street how it would be if all customers before and after me had to say where they come from. I go through place names, put their statements into rhymes: "Hello, I would like cough syrup and come from Lurup. Hello, I would like aspirin and come from Wien [Vienna]...." I make myself laugh and know that, first of all, I am laughing too late and, second, laughing at my own expense, because this battle of rhymes doesn't hurt anybody and will not help me the next time. I make music against the bell on the shop door, but not a thick skin. (*König* 179)

Rhyming is, as she puts it in another context, a case of humor used to battle a hopeless situation (*König* 33).

Singsong rhymes are not the only new points of departure in *Im Haarknoten wohnt eine Dame*, however. One verse is constructed as an elocution exercise for the letter "A" and reads, in part: "Anna war kalt am Tag danach / Lammhaar als Schal macht warm am Hals / Abraham trank Schnaps / da bat Anna / fang das Lamm Abraham / laß das Glas" [Anna was cold on the next day / lamb hair as a shawl makes the throat warm / Abraham drank schnapps / Anna asked then / catch the lamb Abraham

/ leave the glass] (*Im Haarknoten* 52). There is playfulness with word construction in her poems as well; one begins with the lines "Um sechs fuhr der Schachzug / um sieben der Frachtzug / um acht fuhr der Nachtzug / um neun hielt der Aufzug" [At six the chess play went / at seven the freight train / at eight the night train went / at nine the elevator halted] (*Im Haarknoten* 5) to a photomontage of two girls in identical dresses playing with a wagon that is off-kilter. Other poems play on parallel constructions: "*Hier* steht der Wind / und *dort* hängt die Glocke / *hier* liegt die Leiche / und *dort* friert die Socke" [Here is the wind / and there hangs the bell / here lies the corpse / and there the sock freezes] (*Im Haarknoten* 61), some play on altered repetitions: "Als die Zeit schlecht war wurde / man ärmer . . . / als die Zeit arm war / wurde man schlechter" [When the times were bad people / became poorer . . . / when the times were poor / people became worse] (*Im Haarknoten* 54).

Not all the poems in the collection are humorously written jingles. Some are strikingly beautiful in tone, with descriptive lines such as "Die Linden legen gelben Leichenzucker / in die Stadt" [The linden trees lay yellow corpse sugar / in the town] (*Im Haarknoten* 18); "Zwei Pappeln weit weg durchs Hinsehen nah / bei einander als gingen sie eingehängt" [Two far-off poplar trees that when one looked were close / to one another as if they were going arm in arm] (*Im Haarknoten* 87); and "Die Sonne läuft zu tief / gießt ihre letzte Milch / schief in mein Haar" [The sun is going too low / pours its last milk / lopsidedly into my hair] (*Im Haarknoten* 91). One, illustrated by a photomontage of a barren border landscape inside a coffee cup, reads:

> Die Pferde trinken am Fluß
> weil sie im Wasser den Himmel sehen
> wenn die Herren stürzen dann
> liegen morgen die Äpfel unten
> aber tief darunter wollt ich sagen
> sind wir
> von ihren Bäumen erschlagen
> und es werden wo wir liegen
> niemals Bäume stehen wollt ich sagen

sondern Pferde wollt ich noch sagen
die beim Trinken
den Himmel sehen.

[The horses drink at the river
because they see the sky in the water
when the great men fall then
the apples will lie down there tomorrow
but even lower I would say are we
slain by their trees
and there where we lie
trees will never stand I would say
but horses instead I would add
that while drinking
see the sky.] (*Im Haarknoten* 37)

In her various experiments with rhyme, imagery, word sounds, and word constructions, Müller's second collage volume demonstrates a new emphasis on poetic form and language, one directly related to the book's overriding theme of language and its elusive, often contradictory relationship with reality. Müller suggests this in the title of the work, *Im Haarknoten wohnt eine Dame*. This statement suggests the ludicrous state of affairs in a world where appearances are intended to override reality, and assertions truth. The poem in which this quotation appears is illustrated with pastel cutouts of a man's head leaning forward to touch a cloud from which a nail or peg protrudes.[16] The text shows the various stages of "truth" represented by what might be spoken as statements of fact:

Im Federhaus wohnt ein Hahn
im Laubhaus die Allee
ein Hase wohnt im Fellhaus
im Wasserhaus ein See
im Eckhaus—die Patrouille
stößt einen vom Balkon dort
über dem Holunder
dann war es wieder Selbstmord

im Papierhaus wohnt die Stellungnahme
im Haarknoten wohnt eine Dame

[In the house of feathers is a rooster
in the house of foliage the avenue
a rabbit lives in the house of fur
in the water house a lake
in the corner house—the plainclothes police
push someone from the balcony there
down across the elder bush
then it was suicide again
in the house of paper is the false statement
in the knot of hair there is a lady] (*Im Haarknoten* 76)

The parallel structure of *Im—haus* is broken with a dash and an action of violence. At the same time, the glib singsong rhythm of the poem is suddenly broken, with only a pretense of rhyme (*dort/Selbstmord*). The opening structures return in the last two lines with no resumption of disciplined rhythm. Through these techniques Müller demonstrates the futility of a repressive government's attempt to convince its citizenry of its official half-truths and lies.

Müller's third collection of collages, *Die blassen Herren mit den Mokkatassen* [The pale gentlemen with the mocha cups], appeared in book form in 2005 with 105 collages.[17] The cover of this book indicates a number of differences from the previous two volumes. Here the cover illustration is not one of Müller's visuals but is instead the text of the poem from which the title comes. This seems entirely appropriate since the texts in this volume are much more colorful than those that preceded it. Words, phrases, and word parts are now frequently cut from colored brown, green, gray, dark blue, and red paper, making the text look, in the words of one critic, like a colorful patchwork quilt (Segebrecht). Within the book the visuals, too, are not only more colorful, but also more unified. Several of the visuals include text (numbers 48, 60, 66, 94, and 104). The images constructed exclusively of black silhouette cutouts in the first two collections have now disappeared and are replaced by cutouts from magazine illustrations of tiny human figures (see fig. 12). In seventeen of these collage illustrations the figures are less than an inch tall, and they are set in isolated boxes or in landscapes that emphasize a condition of loneliness and enforced alienation. Müller also has a number of visuals of naked legs and feet in her photomontages, and she reintroduces half-frontal views of face images that are cut with full noses so that they appear to be slightly distorted profile images as well; this is a technique that offers a twofold visual perspective.

The title of the book is a descriptive phrase rather than an active statement; it appears late in the volume, in collage number 103. The visual shows the head and shoulders of a suited man; a square panel that covers the area where his torso would be; and, below, naked legs and feet. He is crowded to the left of the illustration into what appears to be a narrow doorway. The crowding, the gentlemanly dress of the top part of the man, and the utter vulnerability of the naked legs and feet serve as an appropriate visual to "die blassen Herren mit den Mokkatassen," who, in addition to edelweiss and feathers, wear explosive fuses in their hats, play a belligerent Bavarian drinking song that is directed against themselves ("Rätätä, rätätä, morgen hamma Schädelweh" [Tomorrow we'll have a hangover]), and threaten others with return transport "in die Heimat" [to the homeland]. The visual suggests the self-destruction inherent in these "pale gentlemen": if one looks beneath the suit jacket and necktie, one can see that they, like Hans Christian Andersen's emperor, are wearing no clothes.

Overall there is greater subtlety to Müller's visuals in this volume. And in general the visuals have become smaller and the accompanying texts longer, creating a greater unity between the variegated word cutouts and the accompanying images. As in the second volume, many of these poems are rhymed, and there continue to be some with the childlike singsong effect of the previous volume. Overall, however, the rhyme in this volume is less intrusive, especially since the length of lines appears to be determined by the width of the page as frequently as by meaning, rhyme, or rhythm. As a consequence, many of the old "end" rhymes now occur within a line, which deemphasizes it and subverts even further the singsong of Müller's earlier verses. One typical example, which Müller illustrates with a woman's half-face/profile with a monstrously shaped "something" on her head, reads:

> Wenn feine Leute meine Mutter ins Gesicht
> fragen wie kann man diese Haartracht aufgetürmt
> wie eine halb verpelzte Nähmaschine tragen
> muß ich mich schämen aber sie sagt
> die kämen doch im Grunde schier aus dem
> Nichts wie Sägemehl und Streunhunde
> und wir
>
> [When fine people get into my mother's face
> and ask how can someone wear this coiffure
> piled up like a half-furred sewing machine
> I am embarrassed but she says
> by all accounts they come virtually from the
> void like sawdust and stray dogs
> and us] (*Die blassen Herren* 7)

Here, in addition to what might be called typical end rhymes—*fragen/ tragen, schämen/kämen, schier/wir*—despite the vast disparity in length of rhymed line length, Müller includes another rhyme: *Grunde/Streunhunde*, which, given the placement of *Streunhunde* at the end of a visual line, might also be considered an end rhyme except for the location of *Grunde* right next to *schier*. Like the two-pronged perspective of the half-frontal profiles in her visuals, the use of two "final" end rhymes in the last three lines of the poem creates a twofold perspective.

Whereas in many of the collages in her second collection Müller had adopted rhyme and the thoughtless singsong rhythms of children's verses and product marketing as a defensive mechanism and survival technique, in this collection her uses of rhyme are generally more sophisticated and less pronounced because the rhythm is not so heavily regulated and because so many rhymes are internal. In addition, her use of near-rhymes and assonance rhymes within her texts makes it clear that most of these poems no longer satirize the rhymes of village weather and prayer verses but function instead on quite another level: the childlike quality of the second volume is replaced here with more sophisticated verse forms. Müller says that part of the motivation for using rhymes in these verses came about accidentally: "[I] accepted . . . the rhymes, for which I had done nothing, which had met up by accident on the table top. They were words that became acquainted with one another, because they had to share the place where they lay. I could not chase them away and acquired a taste for rhyming." She did this, she said, "trusting in the rhymes of Theodor Krämer and Inge Müller,"[18] who, like she, were artists who were damaged by brutal life experiences; their rhymes were *spröde* [aloof], and Müller "sensed cautious, vulnerable rhythms in them, as if one's breath would knock in one's temples at this kind of rhyming. I was obsessed with these poems" (*König* 55).

The themes of this new volume are the same as in the first two. Not all the poems relate directly to village life, state terror, flight, and the plights of emigrants, however. One, for example, relates how "Als der Film abriss schrie der Friedel du hast / den Mastroiani umgebracht rannte durch den / Saal kriegte dabei zwei Hände die er selbst / nicht kannte und erwürgte den Filmvorführer / mit einem groß karierten Schal" [As the film tore Friedel cried out you have / murdered Mastroiani ran through the / hall acquired two hands that he himself / did not recognize and strangled the projectionist / with a large checkered scarf] (*Die blassen Herren* 35). In this verse the placement of the rhymes *Saal/Schal* and *rannte/kannte* are a little less obvious than in the singsong rhymes of the earlier volume. On the other hand, Müller plays so much with internal rhymes and assonance rhymes in this third volume that it sometimes appears that there is more pure rhyme in a given poem than actually exists. This is evident in the following example, where pure rhymes are in italics, impure and assonance rhymes are underlined:

Einmal regnete es
Milch aufs Haus
in 3 Schichten
kamen alle Katzen trinken
die auf dem Arm ge*tragenen*
mageren die spitznasigen *klugen* die den
Himmel als Privatbesitz im Schädel *trugen*
die erschlagenen die begrabenen
Aber heimisch geworden mit den

Jahren—und mit granat*roten*
Pfoten über*fahren waren* die *bulgarischen*
die schönsten unter *ihnen*
in den Dach*rinnen*

[Once it rained
milk onto the house
in three shifts
all the cats came to drink
those carried on the arm
thin ones the pointed-nosed wise ones that bore
the sky as a private possession in their cranium
the slain the buried
But feeling at home through the
years—and overrun with pomegranate red
paws the Bulgarian ones were
the loveliest among them
in the gutters] (*Die blassen Herren* 70)

This use of obvious and hidden rhyme has by now become a technique that Müller uses more and more frequently. As she puts it, "Rhyme causes a stir and disciplines one at the same time. The whole line can change, coalitions can coalesce with other lines. One can comb the rhymes against the grain, hide them in the middle of sentences, spatially, and watch how they immediately swallow up again that which they reveal. And at the end of a sentence one can make them weighty, show them spatially, but in reading them not emphasize them, hiding them in one's voice" (*König* 57).

In all three published collections of German collages, Müller makes language a focus of her attention. "Wer hat den Vagabundenhund / erfunden dass ich Wörtern die / es nicht mehr gibt den Mund / abkauf" [Who has invented the vagabond dog / so that I buy from words / that exist no longer / my mouth], she asks (*Die blassen Herren* 46). Some of the words lost to the emigrant now appear in the poems of the third collection; in collage number 97, for example, she uses the word *Mundhimmel* [mouth sky], which is the German translation of the Romanian word for *Gaumen* [palate], and in collage number 64 she even introduces an entire line of

Romanian text into her poem: "mă cam doare bila" [my head hurts some]. Collage number 30 mentions *Antilopschuhe* [antelope shoes]; although this word has been corrupted into a brand name for shoes, Müller notes that in her childhood it was the Banat German dialect word for "high-heeled shoes" and that as such, it was pure "poetry."[19] She also reincorporates into her poetic vocabulary words like *Koffer* [suitcase], which were once censored by the Ceaușescu regime.[20]

In our study of the development of the collages, it becomes clear that they have evolved a great deal from the earliest ones published in 1991. Müller's techniques have changed: whereas she once took nearly all her words from the German newsmagazine *Der Spiegel*, she now uses many different magazines, a system that allow for greater variation in font and color. She has changed her storage techniques of word cutouts as well; where she once kept all of them spread across a tabletop, she has turned to storing many of them in drawers, and where she once sorted words by grammatical function, she has turned to sorting most of them alphabetically. Basically, however, the process of construction remains the same: she begins with a blank card and a tabletop covered with cutout words, and, like Irene with her photo cutouts in *Reisende auf einem Bein*, studies them until words find each other and come together into a foreign creation. Once they are created, they cannot be revised or changed.

Müller has often stated that it is impossible to put a person's life experiences into words; this is especially true of people forced to live for years in a state of constant fear: "That which one experiences never lets itself be captured at face value with words; it must be demolished and tailored to words."[21] She seeks "a direct word for long, complicated stories that contains so much that is unspoken, because it avoids all details. Because such a word shortens the course of the event to a single point, the ideas of countless possibilities are extended in one's mind." It is, she says, "the trick with language ... through which ... something beyond the word becomes real, when the trick is successful.... Contrived through the trick, therefore completely artificial."[22]

Müller's construction of collages is much more than a matter of selecting words for placement on a card. Although a single word or phrase often appears to set an entire collage in motion, sometimes Müller must create words from cutout letters to complete one of her new sentence constructions. In number 100 in *Die blassen Herren mit den Mokkatassen*, for example, she has a good many entire words and phrases, such as *habe ich*, *mit dem*, *die Lichter*, *der Grenzstation*, *torkelte*, *Buchhalters*, *Gewehr*, and *gleichaltrig*, but she has also pieced together words like *Nacht-a-ms-el*, *Schn-ab-el-lied*, *Ab-fahr-gl-eis*, and *Holzapfel-ger-ippe*. These words, phrases, and word parts, all meticulously placed and glued to a card, are then a visual representation of the artistic process and that "concurrence of fortuitous and calculated word deployment" of which Leitner spoke in his review.

They also represent Müller's personal take on artistry. She is adamant in her insistence that poets are not a special class of people. Her collages are visual demonstrations of her theory that writers and painters "do not have anything special, all their own. We can at the most put together something from what we see. And what we make—our so-called art—is better or worse, according to how well we put it together" (Aguilera) adding, "and when we are able to put things together in such a manner that something unexpected happens, then something like poetry arises."[23]

Notes

1. Leitner, *Das Gedicht* (14), in "'Wir sind Päpstin!'" All translations from German into English are my own unless a translator is named in my footnote reference.
2. One notable exception is Lyn Marven's study, which examines the collages as the visual representations of the forms of trauma.
3. A fourth volume of collages, titled *Este sau nu este Ion*, was published in Romanian in 2005, the same year in which *Die blassen Herren mit den Mokkatassen* appeared.
4. The poem was "Dämmerungseile," published in the student pages of the *Neue Banater Zeitung*, February 27, 1970. For a discussion of Müller's earliest publications, see Schneider, "Literatur und Literaturreflexion."
5. "Besprechung," in Schneider, "Literatur und Literaturreflexion" (337).
6. "Gegen Vorurteile," in Schneider, "Literatur und Literaturreflexion" (337).
7. "Am Schwengelbrunnen," in Schneider, *Wortmeldungen* (53).
8. Müller, "Mit dem Auge kann man keinen Stift halten."
9. Müller, "Kafkas Ohr."

10. This is the title of Müller's essay volume *Der fremde Blick oder das Leben ist ein Furz in der Laterne*.

11. Müller addresses this topic in *Der Teufel sitzt im Spiegel*, and Eke makes it the focus of his edited collection *Die erfundene Wahrnehmung*.

12. It is, of course, wrong to assume that the first-person narrator is identical with Herta Müller. She prefers to use Georges-Arthur Goldschmidt's term *autofiktional* [autofictional] for her novels (Müller, *In der Falle* 21).

13. Herta Müller, "für Oskar," trans. Philip Boehm. http://nobelprize.org/nobel_prizes/literature/laureates/2009/muller-lecture_en.html (February 3, 2010).

14. Although the pages are not numbered, I refer to specific collages by their order in the book.

15. See *Der König verneigt sich und tötet* (40-73) for Müller's elaboration on what the word "king" embodies for her. Here she states that the word *König* replaced for her the word *Herztier*, which she used as the title for her 1994 novel (54).

16. The illustration is reminiscent of the Gellu Naum poem that appears as an epigraph to Müller's novel *Herztier* and begins with the lines "Jeder hatte einen Freund in jedem Stückchen Wolke / so ist das halt mit Freunden wo die Welt voll Schrecken ist" [Everyone had a friend in every piece of cloud / that's the way it is with friends where the world is full of horror]. Similarly the illustration to collage number 86, which shows a woman's face above a dead fox, is reminiscent of Müller's 1992 novel *Der Fuchs war damals schon der Jäger*.

17. Again the pages are not numbered, but I refer to specific collages by their order in the book.

18. Müller, *Der König verneigt sich und tötet* (56). Müller wrote an appreciation (*Nachwort*) of Theodor Kramer (1897-1958) for a volume of his poems that she edited in 1999 titled *Die Wahrheit ist, man hat mir nichts getan: Gedichte* (Vienna: Paul Zsolnay, 1999) and published an essay on Inge Müller (1925-66) in her volume *In der Falle*.

19. Müller, "Der Himmelsschlüssel," *Die Nacht ist aus Tinte gemacht*.

20. In her first collection of collages, this word appeared only on the final card; in other places, *Koffer* had been replaced, as in the title poem, with coded words, such as *Kamm*. This most recent collection uses the word *Koffer* in eight collages. See Müller, *Heimat ist das was gesprochen wird*, for a discussion of how the word was censored by Romanian authorities as a metaphor denoting German minority emigration (27-28).

21. Müller, "Wenn wir schweigen, werden wir unangenehm" (15).
22. Müller, "Immer derselbe Schnee und immer derselbe Onkel."
23. Müller, "Mit dem Auge kann man keinen Stift halten."

Works Cited

Aguilera, Carlos A. "Mir war der rumänische Fasan immer näher als der deutsche Fasan. Ich will mit Utopien nichts mehr zu tun haben." Interview with Herta Müller. *Akzente*, October 5, 2008. Web. January 23, 2010. http://www.hanser-literaturverlage.de/ extras/specials/herta-mueller/herta-mueller-interview.html.

Eddy, Beverley Driver. "'Die Schule der Angst': Gespräch mit Herta Müller, den 14. April 1998." *German Quarterly* 72.4 (Autumn 1999): 329–39.

Eke, Norbert Otto. *Die erfundene Wahrnehmung: Annäherung an Herta Müller*. Paderborn: Igel, 1991.

Knorz, Christina. "Therese Vogel aus Eckersdorf unterrichtete Herta Müller." *Nordbayerischer Kurier Online*, October 9, 2009. Web. January 17, 2010. http://www.nordbayerischer-kurier.de/nachrichten/1284562/details_8.htm.

Leitner, Anton G. "'Wir sind Päpstin!' Viel dekorierte deutsche Autorin Herta Müller mit Nobelpreis ins Ziel eingelaufen." Wordpress, October 11, 2009. Web. January 16, 2010. http://antonleitner.wordpress.com/2009/10/11/wir-sind-papstin-viel-dekorierte-deutsche-autorin-herta-muller-mit-nobelpreis-ins-ziel-eingelaufen/.

Marven, Lyn. "'So fremd war das Gebilde': The Interaction between Visual and Verbal in Herta Müller's Prose and Collages." *New German Literature: Life-Writing and Dialogue with the Arts*. Ed. Julian Preece, Frank Finlay, and Ruth J. Owen. Oxford: Peter Lang, 2007. 123–41.

Müller, Herta. *Der fremde Blick oder das Leben ist ein Furz in der Laterne*. Göttingen: Wallstein, 2002.

———. *Der König verneigt sich und tötet*. Munich and Vienna: Hanser, 2003.

———. *Der Teufel sitzt im Spiegel. Wie Wahrnehmung sich erfindet*. Berlin: Rotbuch, 1991.

———. *Der Wächter nimmt seinen Kamm: Vom Weggehen und Ausscheren*. Reinbek: Rowohlt, 1993.

———. *Die blassen Herren mit den Mokkatassen*. Munich and Vienna: Hanser, 2005.

———. *Die Nacht ist aus Tinte gemacht. Herta Müller erzählt ihre Kindheit im Banat.* Dir. Thomas Böhm and Klaus Sander. Supposé, 2009. CD.

———. *Este sau nu este Ion.* Iași: Polirom, 2005.

———. *Heimat ist das was gesprochen wird.* Blieskastel: Gollenstein, 2001.

———. *Im Haarknoten wohnt eine Dame.* Reinbek: Rowohlt, 2000.

———. "Immer derselbe Schnee und immer derselbe Onkel, oder warum Worte beim Schreiben etwas anderes werden müssen, um genau zu sein." *Neue Zürcher Zeitung Online*, November 17, 2007. Web. January 23, 2010.

———. *In der Falle.* Göttingen: Wallstein, 1996.

———. "Kafkas Ohr." Speech upon receipt of the Franz-Kafka-Literaturpreis, Klosterneuburg, May 4, 1999. Author's notes.

———. "Mit dem Auge kann man keinen Stift halten." Discussion with Cornelia Niedermeier. *Der Standard* (Vienna), January 22, 2004. Web. January 10, 2010. http://www.lyrikwelt.de/hintergrund/muellerherta-gespräch-h.htm.

———. *Reisende auf einem Bein.* Reinbek: Rowohlt, 1995.

———. *Traveling on One Leg.* Trans. Valentina Glajar and André Lefevere. Evanston: Northwestern University Press, 1998.

———. "Wenn wir schweigen, werden wir unangenehm—wenn wir reden, werden wir lächerlich. Kann Literatur Zeugnis ablegen?" *Text und Kritik. Zeitschrift für Literatur.* Ed. Heinz Ludwig Arnold. 155 (July 2002): 6–17.

Schneider, Eduard. "Literatur und Literaturreflexion in der rumäniendeutschen Presse der Nachkriegszeit. Die *Neue Banater Zeitung* (Temeswar) und ihr Beitrag zur Förderung der literarischen Nachwuchsgeneration (1969–1975)." Veröffentlichungen des Instituts für deutsche Kultur und Geschichte Südosteuropas an der Ludwig-Maximilians-Universität München. Vol. 110. Munich: IKGS, 2007. 335–38.

———, ed. *Wortmeldungen. Eine Anthologie junger Lyrik aus dem Banat.* Timișoara: FACLA, 1972.

Segebrecht, Wulf. "Herta Müller: Die blassen Herren mit den Mokkatassen. Ich bin ein Wort, gebrauche mich!" *Frankfurter Allgemeine Zeitung*, September 29, 2005. Web. January 10, 2010.

10 In Transit
Transnational Trajectories and Mobility in Herta Müller's Recent Writings

Monika Moyrer

> Man verteilt die Gefühle ja oft auf seltsame Weise nach außen. Auf einige wenige Gegenstände, die sich ohne Grund dafür eignen, das Erinnern im Kopf zu verdeutlichen.[1]
>
> *(Müller, "In jeder Sprache" 16)*

Herta Müller's preferred collage technique correlates her affection for inconspicuous details and *Scherben* [broken pieces of china] as she invests specific objects with an array of biographical, political, linguistic, and literary meanings. These objects, which transcend genres and languages, relentlessly reappear dispersed (and broken) throughout her oeuvre (regardless of their disfiguration) and map out a visible path to Müller's process of remembering. In addition to empowering particular objects, this method highlights the new, more effortless mobility across borders, which resulted from the opening of the former Communist countries in

Eastern Europe. I contend that this flexibility has allowed Müller to create powerful material vessels that encapsulate the contradictions inherent in her memories. While essentially remaining dispersed, localized interventions, these objects further unsettle Müller's notions of "home" and "homeland(s)."

In this essay I focus on one particular cutout, the *Mokkatassen*, or mocha cups, as isolated, movable, and severed word objects that circulate in multiple Müller texts either as *Mokkatassen*, MOKKATASSEN, *M/okk/at/assen*, or *ceaş/ca/de/MOCA*. Specifically I examine these anachronistic, oriental objects and their function in Müller's German and Romanian texts and show how through her collage technique these inconspicuous word objects become what I call "memory bites"—material and tangible collector's items imbued with memory.

When Müller sides with Jorge Semprún by arguing that "die Wahrheit der geschriebenen Erinnerung muß erfunden werden" [the truth of the written memory must be invented] (*In der Falle* 21), she at the same time takes issue with notions of "truth" and "memory" that conceal their invented (or fabricated) origin. This also explains Müller's obsessive circling back to the same memory bites, through which the author simultaneously conceals and constantly reinvents her "truth." The fragments reflect postwar traumatic incidents while also exposing Müller's ambivalent or rather conflicted attitude toward Germany and Romania. I argue that the recurrent use of the same particular memory bites—in this case the tangible object of a mocha cup—results in spatial dispersions. These dispersions seemingly decontextualize the object from its "natural" surroundings while creating a trail of connections among texts. As material objects, these cups contain a bite of "truth" whose meaning must be assembled by the reader. Therefore I treat the different places where the mocha cups appear as Müller's textual collection.

Focusing on Müller's textual collection of mocha cups, I read her collage volumes in which the *Mokkatassen* appear—*Die blassen Herren mit den Mokkatassen* [The pale gentlemen with the mocha cups] (2005), as well as her Romanian collages in *Este sau nu este Ion* [Is it or is it not Ion] (2005)—as textual *Vitrine* [glass display case] in which the possibility of assuming agency over recollected memories is presented. In my analysis a proper visualization of Müller's entire collection of *Mokkatassen* would entail a basic partitioning of the glass display case into several separate shelves: the large, publicly visible German shelf would consist of the well-received *Die blassen Herren mit den Mokkatassen*—which also testifies to the collages' reception as visual "art"—and a second, smaller, almost invisible because not widely received yet audible Romanian shelf would consist of the volume *Este sau nu este Ion* and its accompanying audio recording. A third shelf would be reserved for the German prose texts in which the mocha cups appear—namely, in the speech "Die Anwendung der dünnen Straßen" [The exercise of the thin streets] (2004) and in Leopold Auberg's story in the novel *Atemschaukel* (2009). As a whole this particular imaginary glass display case then would bring together the scattered memory bites (i.e., *Mokkatassen*) and house Müller's textual mocha collection.

Missing Links

Scholars have often described Müller's critique of the Banat-Swabian village in which she grew up and the ethnocentrism of the region (particularly in the author's early texts) as one of the determining features of her writing (Kegelmann; Bozzi; Glajar). The traumatic collective incidents of the years 1945–49, which directly affected Müller's mother and indirectly the author herself, however, have not yet received adequate scholarly consideration.[2] Müller had already fictionalized her mother's deportation experiences in certain passages in *Niederungen* [*Nadirs*] (102) and *Der Mensch ist ein großer Fasan auf der Welt* [*The Passport*] (74), but she only recently started articulating them directly—for example, in the speech "Die Anwendung der dünnen Straßen" [The exercise of the thin streets]. "Drei Jahre nach der Heimkehr aus dem Lager kam ich zur Welt, die Deportation steckte noch in ihr und streute sich in meine Kindheit" [I was born three years after the return from the camp; the deportation was still inside her and dispersed into my childhood] (19). When Müller mentions her childhood, she speaks of a dispersed effect. Dispersal, then, becomes a key concept that connects the bites of her experiences and also influences her work aesthetically.

In her poetological essays Müller writes about the importance of the

Riß [split] (*Teufel* 75–77, 87), which Lyn Marven theorizes as the articulation of trauma that "becomes visible in the texts' content, and also in the aesthetic of fragmentation which structures their linguistic and narrative syntax" ("'In allem ist der Riß'" 397).³ Marven, however, locates the traumatic as rooted in Müller's physical experiences under the dictatorship, such as the interrogations and the threats of violence (49), without taking into account the larger collective traumatic context that the generation of Müller's mother and Oskar Pastior experienced. Indispensable in filling these voids and providing more accurate explanations—through an adequate articulation of remembrance caused by earlier traumatic incidents—is Müller's close collaboration with Pastior. He becomes the missing link between Pastior's mother's generation's bourgeois "innocence"—its uncritical stance toward the *Kulturnation* [the cultural nation with which Transylvanian-Saxons identified] and fascist Germany—and the inability of that generation to articulate its mourning after the deportation.⁴

When Müller identifies herself as the daughter of a father who had been an SS member (Müller, "Antrittsrede" 187) and a mother who had been deported ("Anwendung" 19), she engages in what Paola Bozzi describes as "konzentrisches Kreisen," a "concentric circling" around National Socialism (32). This is why Müller needs Pastior's remembrance: to come to terms with her parents' inability to develop a vocabulary that effectively copes with the conflicting spectrum of guilt, shame, and disturbing memories—in other words, with their "inability to mourn" (Mitscherlich and Mitscherlich 14). In addition to the official Stalinist and later Communist Romanian historiography that suppressed any memory discourse regarding deportations and reparation, German-Romanians were also reluctant to remember their ambivalent status as both perpetrators and victims. On the one hand, ethnic Germans exhibited a "considerable tendency to fascism" (Weber 3), and as Weber contends, "The expulsion and displacement of Germans from Eastern and Southeastern Europe has its origin not on May 8, 1945, but already on January 30, 1933" (6). On the other hand, ethnic Germans from Romania experienced the traumatic collective deportations to Soviet camps in January 1945.⁵ With the emigration of Romanian-Germans to Germany, this non-discourse of historical responsibility became displaced to Germany.⁶ In Germany

Müller strongly opposed groups such as the *Vertriebenenverbände* [expellee organizations] that held on to a one-sided view of victimization.

Müller's Romanian collages, which feature language as the site of memory work, have propelled a renewed shift of this memory discourse from Germany back to Romania. When Herta Müller eventually started collecting the stories and memories of formerly deported villagers, she attempted to counter her mother's "cryptic sentences" (Müller, *Herta Müller* 39). Pastior's historical and biographical details—such as the *Mokkatassen*—his descriptions, and his memories of the five years in the camp become an additional layer in Müller's collection, from where they start moving—as the succeeding examples demonstrate—among languages, genres, and historical periods.

Franz's *Mokkatassen* in "Die Anwendung der dünnen Straßen"

In 2004 in a speech at the opening of the Ingeborg-Bachmann Competition in Klagenfurt, Müller spoke publicly about "einem Mann in ihrem Alter, . . . der deportiert war wie sie. Ich nenne ihn Franz" [a man of her age, . . . who was deported as she (her mother) had been. I call him Franz] ("Anwendung" 19). Both the pseudonym and the fact that Müller refers to a joint visit with "Franz" to Ukraine directly links the author's mentioning of the inconspicuous *Mokkatasse* with Pastior's story. The purpose of their trip is the visit to the camps where Pastior and Müller's mother were imprisoned between January 1945 and November 1949 (Gündisch and Beer 221; Weber 1; Pastior, *sage* 359): the "DONBASS region" and, more specifically, "Dnjepropetrovsk, Gorlovka, Donezk, Enakieva, Krivoi-Rog" ("Anwendung" 20). Traveling with Pastior to the location gives Müller the opportunity to collect firsthand impressions of the landscape and obtain a visceral "feel" for the site. After Pastior's sudden death in 2006, Müller remains the main witness to Pastior's recollections. For the first time Müller completes a novel "secondhand," relying on Pastior's firsthand accounts rather than her own experiences.[7]

In Germany Müller's mostly well-received *Atemschaukel* benefits from what Ute Frevert calls the "memory boom," which started with publications such as Günter Grass's *Im Krebsgang* [*Crabwalk*] (2002). While a recuperation of traumatic memories—memories that attest to "German suffering" such as expulsions, bombings, or mass rapes (Taberner and Berger 1)—on the German side is necessary, Frevert argues for an adequate contextualization of these memories to avoid a "nationale Nabelschau" [national navel-gazing] that isolates the experiences of victims and perpetrators (12). Frevert calls instead for transnational memorials that support joint European memory sites (13).[8] Could Müller's *Mokkatassen* perhaps serve as examples of memory bites that encapsulate the ambiguity of victimhood? To put it even more bluntly: could they serve as condensed transnational memorials? They certainly function as intertextual symbols, crossing over from Pastior's into Müller's texts. Once in Müller's possession, they freely move among her texts—from the speech to the collage poetry to the novel—communicating with different audiences. In "Die Anwendung der dünnen Straßen" the listening audience and addressees are Austrian and German. Only later do the *Mokkatassen* move across languages: from the German into Romanian collages. This translingual move might open the door for difficult conversations around the topics of guilt, victimhood, and the repression of memory not only in Germany and Austria but also in Romania.

In the speech in Klagenfurt, Müller's mocha cups stand in for the remembered objects of the collection of Franz's mother. In a Transylvanian town in Romania in the 1930s and 1940s, Franz's father, an art teacher, collected paintbrushes, whereas his mother played guitar and collected mocha cups with golden rims. Here the mocha cup alludes to a passion for collecting and signifies a bourgeois urban upbringing in a family that is educated and interested in the arts.[9] Franz's middle-class background sheds light on his family's education, on its sensitivity to the arts and fashion, as well as on his mother's appreciation of *Kitsch*. Müller's stress on this aspect sharply contrasts with her own background. In most texts in which Müller meticulously gives a fictionalized account of her childhood (e.g., in *Niederungen*), she focuses on the lack of collecting and on the absence of such decorative objects. This "lack" specifies the differences between her rural, more secluded Banat-Swabian village—Paola Bozzi reminds us that Müller's work has developed "at the same time from and against a peasant culture" (33)—and Franz's middle-class Transylvanian-Saxon background. What Müller depicts in the village of *Niederun-*

gen is a culture characterized by a deficiency of education or higher aspirations.[10] Consequently she proceeds to distance herself from this culture.

Müller concludes her speech in Klagenfurt with the poem "Der Löffelbieger sagt" [The spoon-bender says], in which themes from *Atemschaukel* first occur: *Mokkatassen, Grammophonkistchen* [small gramophone box], and *Herzschaufel* [heart-shovel]. The same poem reappears later in *Die blassen Herren mit den Mokkatassen*, evidencing once again the effortlessness with which Müller's objects travel among genres.

Leopold's *Mokkatassen* in *Atemschaukel*

In *Atemschaukel* Müller introduces the same narrative constellation as in "Die Anwendung der dünnen Straßen" but expands on the symbolic significance of the *Mokkatassen*. In an earlier speech from 1994 Müller affirms that in totalitarian systems such as National Socialism and Stalinism, *Unschuld* [innocence] and *Grazie* [grace] have become *unwiederbringlich* [irrecoverable] (*Hunger und Seide* 10). The following scenes from *Atemschaukel* illustrate precisely this loss of innocence and grace through the fragmentation of the word *Mokkatasse* into the MOKKATASSE. The decomposition and the typographic accentuation of the word allude to Pastior's anagrammatic poetry as well. The chapters of *Atemschaukel* in which the mocha cups occur show once more Müller's ability to condense historical content, visual techniques, and material objects into one abbreviated poetical image that happens to be a "memory bite" loaded with ambivalence.

In the chapter "Exciting Times," the main protagonist, Leo, finds himself as a deportee in Ukraine. Begging for food in a village in exchange for coal, he has a flashback. Here the *Mokkatasse* comes up in connection with Dietrich, "aus dem Reich" [from the Reich] (57). This young soldier from Hitler's army is lodged in Leo's house and buys Leo's mother a birthday present: two *Mokkatassen*. The symbolic proximity between Transylvanian-Saxons and Hitler's army is present in other images as well—for example, when Leo remembers how eager neighbors, relatives, and teachers were to join the army (56). Like the *Mokkatassen*, the *Edelweiß*—which reappears later in *Die blassen Herren mit den Mokkatassen*—signifies the proximity to all things German (or Austro-Hungarian), especially the army. Leo observes that uniformed teachers wore the *Edelweiß* with other military emblems. In this climate, in which Jewish neighbors disappeared yet "mehr wollte man nicht wissen" (56) [no one wanted to know anything more (*The Hunger Angel* 47)], Leo tells Dietrich about his mother's collection and Dietrich ends up buying two pinkish mocha cups. Alternating between his memories of home and his actual presence in the Ukrainian village, Leo's flashbacks start when he thinks that he sees some petunias, which trigger the memory of his mother's glass display case:

> Ich sah Petunien in einem Hausgarten, eine ganze Vitrine voller blassrosa Tässchen mit Silberrand. Im Weitergehen schloss ich die Augen und sagte MOKKATASSE und zählte die Buchstaben im Kopf: zehn. Und dann zählte ich zehn Schritte, danach zwanzig für beide Tassen. Ich zählte bis einhundert für alle zehn Mokkatassen, die meine Mutter zu Hause in der Vitrine stehen hatte, und war drei Häuser weiter gekommen. Im Garten waren keine Petunien. Ich klopfte an die erste Tür. (*Atemschaukel* 58)
>
> [I saw petunias in someone's garden: an entire bed full of pale-pink little cups with silver rims. As I walked on I closed my eyes and said, DEMITASSES, then counted the letters in my head: ten. Next I counted ten steps, then twenty, for both cups. But where I stopped there was no house. So I counted to one hundred for all ten demitasses my mother had at home in her china cabinet and found myself three houses farther along. There were no petunias. I knocked on the door.] (*The Hunger Angel* 49)

Leo's "innocent" gesture of telling Dietrich about his mother's collection and accompanying him to the china shop, something about which he ends up feeling guilty and which he calls his *Schuld* [fault] (57) complicates his later memory.[11] Furthermore, Leo witnesses how Dietrich gazes at his mother with binoculars when she is sunbathing. Leo's assistance associates the mocha cups as well with Dietrich's desire. In the situation of *Sühne* [atonement] (Pastior, *durch* 153)—as the justification of the deportation as collective reparation suggests—the pinkish color turns into a cipher symbol for ambivalent emotions such as innocence, complicity, and possibly even desire. In Leo's current living conditions the imagined petunias and mocha cups have lost their significance. In fact in the camp the memories of pinkish, nostalgic, or sexually charged mocha cups are not only unnecessary—homesickness is out of place and hunger desexualizes (158)—but also dangerous because the slightest suspicion of homosexuality would be deadly (9).[12] As if to represent the breach with the past, the images of the collected objects fracture and disintegrate into single letters. A minor but potent symbol of the cultural nation and the aspirations of the middle class, the *Mokkatassen* have been emptied of their earlier semantic content. In other words, the atomization of the word *Mokkatassen* symbolizes for Leo how the continuity to the old system in itself has been broken. The cracks caused by larger historical dichotomies such as guilt/atonement, war/peace, and cause/effect openly display the dismemberment, amputation, and tattering of language for the individual caught between these oppositions.[13] In the end, a tonal montage of the sounds of the alphabet works like a magic spell. It offers Leo a typographically (meaning spatially) accentuated grid through which each letter gains an individual meaning for confronting his present situation: "Im Weitergehen schloss ich die Augen und sagte MOKKATASSE und zählte die Buchstaben im Kopf: zehn" [Moving along, I closed my eyes and said MOKKATASSE and counted the letters in my head: ten] (58).

Mokkatassen in *Die blassen Herren mit den Mokkatassen*

The initial idea of collage appears in connection with the postcard (*König* 56). The self-made postcard, a personalized greeting card addressed to a specific person, gives the collage a specific addressee. The recipient of the postcard is to make associations with the snippets and to acknowledge a personal connection. In this creative collage process of looking more carefully at words, Müller encounters certain *Gegenstände* [objects] ("In jeder Sprache" 16). As she explains it, the process happens "ohne Grund" [without reason]; in other words, feelings become dispersed "auf einige wenige Gegenstände, die sich ohne Grund dafür eignen, das Erinnern im Kopf zu verdeutlichen" [on a few objects which lend themselves without reason to clarify the remembrance inside one's head] (16). Again, the dispersal of *Mokkatassen* in different locations shows how pivotal the principles of collage have become for Müller's overall aesthetics.

At the most basic level Müller's collages were comprised of cutouts taken from outside sources. Fascinated by the excellent paper quality,

Müller goes through cast-off copies of magazines such as *Der Spiegel*, *Brigitte*, ADAC-*Motorwelt*, and *Karstadt-Katalog* (Müller, "Interview Anke te Heesen" 178); cuts words out; and strips them completely of their context. These cutouts are single paper objects that—as the example of the *M/okk/at/assen* demonstrates—are physically broken into even smaller units. On more than one occasion Müller explains: "Immer waren mir die Gegenstände wichtig" [Objects were always important to me] ("In jeder Sprache" 15). One reason is that objects—and one could add the mocha cups here as well—are *direkt* [direct] (*Teufel* 96). They reveal "was Menschen nicht zeigen könnnen" [what people cannot show] (96). In Müller's aesthetics objects are always related to specific people or characters: "Sie gehören immer zu dem, was und wie ein Mensch war, untrennbar dazu" [Even today they are intrinsically tied to what and how a person is] ("In jeder Sprache" 15). Moreover, objects gain more agency than people because the objects are *selbstsicher* [confident] (*Teufel* 96) and "tragen die Inhalte des Geschehens" [carry the substance of the action] (95). Hence, when asked to act in such a predetermined framework, people are unable to function and thus become "Karikaturen der Gegenstände" [caricatures of objects] (96). Did Leopold become a "caricature" of the objects he remembered? He created single-letter fragments while using the mocha cups as a grid, which underscored their agency. This observation corresponds with Müller's spatial description of objects as "der Plan, die überdeutliche Karte, das Schnittmuster, nach dem Personen handeln" [the plan, the obvious map, the pattern, according to which persons act] (96). Anja K. Johannsen's study on space in Müller's oeuvre affirms that the author's characters are always shown "in contact with something else, occasionally other people, often, however, with objects as the determining spatial components" (Johannsen 185). This relational aspect of objects and their agency underlines their prominent position in Müller's work.

Additionally objects stand out because they are made of material that is different from the human body. In collages they are—and this is crucial—different in that they are a found source. In this outside realm, where words/signs are encountering each other, they absorb traumatic impulses, create a poem, and then vanish into a postcard. In *Der König verneigt sich und tötet* Müller expands on the body as "der vergänglichste Stoff" [the most ephemeral material] (49), as opposed to wood or metal. Lyn Marven has shown how the "collapse of boundaries between the self and the world" (54)—and one could add the skin and the object—and the projection of fear onto "discrete, external objects" (57) are aesthetic strategies to confront the experience of trauma.

When the *Mokkatasse* is closely tied to Leopold Auberg's experience in the camp, it becomes a significant legible and audible memory bite—a material vessel—that evidences through the dismemberment and amputation of language "was und wie ein Mensch war" [what and how a person was] (Müller, "In jeder Sprache" 15). Moreover, the memory bite is at the same time a tangible, external object, not just an inner thought testifying to the greater "factualness of things" (Renneke 281). Consequently the mocha cups' mobility not only resembles the anagrammatic collage technique that generates an outer object, but it also visualizes the modern shift that the montage took at the beginning of the twentieth century, which Volker Klotz describes as the shift from "nature" to "technology" (Klotz quoted in Borchmeyer and Zmegac 287).

While Müller does not possess ornamental *Mokkatassen* in her own childhood, her later focus on writing and her technique of collage allow her to create *M/okk/at/assen* as tactile and physical objects. When Müller becomes a collector, she does not collect cups with golden rims (meaning precious objects) but instead turns to discarded magazines. Seeking inspiration from the sensual, exotic, or vernacular vocabulary (Müller, "Interview Anke te Heesen" 178), Müller randomly samples from disposed sources that rely on *Aktualität* [up-to-dateness] and *Neuigkeitswert* [novelty value] (Pürer 12; Heesen 10). Her collection thus contains multilayered pieces that are mixed with sensual and vernacular traces.

With such present-day words, Müller "writes" the following collage poem that inspired the title of her last collage collection, *Die blassen Herren mit den Mokkatassen*. In the poem "Wenn drei Straßen staubig auf dem Rücken schlafen" [When three streets dustily sleep on their backs], the word *M/okk/at/assen* is made of letters and phonemes with very accurate, fine cuts that are discretely assembled. The poem's text invokes the imagery in which men celebrate a traditional *Oktoberfest* (Müller, *Die blassen Herren mit den Mokkatassen* n.p.). The accoutrements of *Edelweiß* [edelweiss] and feathers on their hats set the scene of a petit bourgeois environment. In addition, the orchestra plays folk music [*rätätä*]. Yet the idyllic scenery deceives. It is about "Herren mit den Mokkatassen / am Hut hat jeder eine Zündschnur ein / Edelweiß und eine Vogelfeder" [gentlemen with mocha cups / on the hat everyone wears a fuse an / edelweiss and a feather]. The pale gentlemen are dangerous because they have not only an *Edelweiß* on their hat but also a *Zündschnur* [fuse].

The combination of *Mokkatassen* and *Edelweiß* foreshadows Leo Auberg's memories in *Atemschaukel*, in which the two objects stand for the close alliance in the 1940s between conservative and National Socialist ideas among Transylvanian-Saxons. The insertion of the mocha cups and the edelweiss in a recent collage might suggest the continuity of such conservative right-wing ideologies in present-day Germany. Müller implies that a regressive tendency, grounded in amnesia and in a lack of remembrance, is still present. What is more, this ideology operates along the lines of exclusion, especially targeting those who presumably do not belong to this *heimatlich* scenario: "Wer den Respekt verliert also vier Fehler macht pro Nacht wird in die Heimat überführt" [those losing respect, that is, those making four mistakes per night, will be transported back home]. In the last line, a female character is addressed who is threatened in this way: "Ja, ja, bei so einer wie dir spricht einiges dafür" [Yes, yes, for someone like you a considerable amount speaks for it]. The poem, then, relates a critical and ambivalent attitude. This is especially obvious in the beginning, in which a *gemein* [mean] moon taints the reunion of the pale gentlemen.

When the author searches for the slightly archaic *M/okk/at/assen*—not widely used in *Der Spiegel* or either of the sources from which Müller samples—she shows her trust in "das alte Wort" [the old word] (Renneke 263). Through the incorporation of this outmoded vocabulary Müller brings "back" into the present-day German language archaic, oriental, and historically traumatic connotations associated with Pastior's remembrance. In contrast to the prose texts in which the mocha cup is fully embedded in a narrative context (of Franz's or Leo's story), in her collages its semantic and syntactic context has been destroyed. In the collage poems the *Mokkatasse* has become a detail that acts *antienzyklopädisch* [anti-encyclopedic] (281), no longer participating in support of structures that seek to address a topic systematically and comprehensively. The fragment has been isolated from its original context and remixed with countless other words that Müller stores in her drawer. The effortlessly producible (and discardable) paper clipping permits the mocha cup an easy cross-textual and intertextual transition, helping the object move seemingly freely through texts and languages.

As mobile paper objects, the *Mokkatassen* contrast sharply with their material counterparts, the premodern mocha cups with golden rims. In addition, Müller's collaged *M/okk/at/asse* openly displays the cuts, rims, and edges, forcing the reader/viewer to see the pauses and the white gaps between the chosen fragments.[14] These gaps can produce an irritation for the reader. Only reading the collage aloud allows for a meaningful rhythm and aids in reconnecting the—visually broken—pieces through one's voice. Thus the memory bites—as paper objects that have absorbed the traumatic pieces—can be reassembled in a meaningful way through speech. And it is through personal conversations that Müller connected with Pastior's memory bites in the first place. However, the conversation between the reader and the text—which depends heavily on the reader's active construction of meaning rather than a passive reception—allows room for open-ended interpretation and underscores what Müller—relying on Semprún—has valued for the representation of memory: invention.[15]

Within *Die blassen Herren mit den Mokkatassen* the poem "Das Limit prahlt" [The limit vaunts] stands out because it is the only text in which the German and the Romanian languages meet within the space of one poem. This spatial encounter, finally, shows another one of Müller's transgressions: the overstepping of the language barrier (a first for Müller, who up until then had written and published exclusively in German).

The Romanian line at the end of the German poem offers evidence that Müller has started collecting Romanian word fragments as well in preparation for the handcrafting of collages in Romanian. The result is the Romanian collage volume *Este sau nu este Ion*. Here for the first time Müller intervenes directly—through the technique of collaging—in the Romanian language. The author admits that she cannot write in Romanian the same way she does in German but that she is able to collage with cutout words that "'există' ca material" [exist as material] (Müller, "Interviu Rodica Binder").

The Romanian collages add an important dimension to Müller's views on language and writing. In these collages Müller wrestles with particular experiences in Romania. In German speeches (especially about the impurity of *Heimat*), Müller stresses how fortunate she is to have been exposed to more than her native language because the knowledge of an additional language, in this case Romanian, helped her to move beyond a one-sided view. In an interview with Rodica Binder, Müller makes a different point as well. She describes her reason for writing in Romanian as a sort of revenge, as a wrestling with a (particular) language that is connected to particular past experiences of disempowerment and repression. The writer is now in the empowered position "să-mi iau puțin limba la întrebări să-i arăt că acuma fac eu cu tine ce vreau" [to question language, to show the language that now I am in charge to make of you what I want] (Müller, "Interviu Rodica Binder").

This empowerment comes from the possibilities that collage offers in finding a rhythm, developing a story, and coming to a punch line in the space of a postcard. Some affect-ridden Romanian words, spread out on the table in front of Müller, lose their power when they are moved in and out of poems. The playful and flexible possibilities allow Müller to resume agency over affect, emotions, and past experiences and to rewrite her stories. In addition, this open play with fragmented words becomes for many Romanian readers a vivid imagery of the present state of Romanian politics. The political element, hidden in the German collages, makes Müller's Romanian collages more engaging in current discussions and less artistic. Subsequently, shifting to collaging in Romanian becomes an experiment and a play through which she is able to demonstrate her agency and articulate her ambivalences in regard to politics and language.

*Ceaș/ca/de/*MOCA in *Este sau nu este Ion*

In *Este sau nu este Ion*, the *ceaș/ca/de/*MOCA appears in the poem "Ernest zicea" [Ernest spoke] in combination with three characters (Ernest, Oskar, and a third protagonist). Words like *gară* [train station], *valiză* [suitcase], and Ukraina [Ukraine] suggest a journey and could be linked to the joint trip with "Franz" to the former Ukrainian camp sites that Müller mentions in her speech in Klagenfurt. In the Romanian poem Müller uses Oskar's proper first name, which underscores the documentary aspect of the trip. Here Romania becomes a third site through which the main character and her companions pass in order to recuperate memories. Pastior and Ernest Wichner, who accompanied Müller and Pastior on their trip, are *Grenzgänger* [border crossers] themselves, translating from Romanian into German, and thus maintaining strong ties to the Romanian language.

Müller's collage brings the memory discourse "back" to Romania, where during the Communist regime the deportation of Romanian-Germans was not publicly addressed.[16] She acknowledges that it means something else to cut with scissors through Romanian magazines and admits it is "my small game with Romanian" ("An Evening with Herta Müller"), thus proving her agency. Furthermore, Müller's audio recording communicates her poems to a Romanian audience, showing that she is free to voice her "memory bites" directly. In addition, the sound of her voice articulates another possibility of connecting with the audience. The recording reduces the distance between the reader and the listener, easing the reader's difficult task of reading the poem aloud to "comprehend" the rhythm (and meaning). At the same time, Müller projects authenticity. The acoustic directness opposes the visual dispersals and accentuates her "memory bites."

Similar to the transformation of the *Mokkatassen* into MOKKATASSEN and *M/okk/at/assen*, the memory object easily transitions into *ceaș/ca/de/ MOCA*.[17] Another aspect of Müller's sensuality is revealed through her connection with the Romanian language. The Romanian language has the "sinnlicheren, auf mein Empfinden besser passenden Wörter" [more sensitive, better suited words for my perception] ("In jeder Sprache" 27). In her assessment the Romanian language has images that are "sinnlich, frech und überrumpelnd schön" [sensual, bold, and perplexingly beautiful] ("Wenn wir schweigen werden wir unangenehm" 11).

The inner poetic hybridity that Müller attributes to her German and Romanian language exposure, "wenn man beide Sichtweisen kennt, tun sie sich im Kopf zusammen" [when one knows both perspectives, they mix in one's head] ("In jeder Sprache" 25), however, does not extend to the paper material. The positive connotation of perfume connected to the German paper contrasts with the poor quality and the smell of petroleum of the paper in her Romanian days (Müller, "Interview Anke te Heesen" 175). Romanian everyday expressions and particularly the folk music of Maria Tănase ("An Evening with Herta Müller") touch her deeply, but she develops an aversion to the politically abused language of the newspapers ("Interview Anke te Heesen" 175). These asymmetries affect Müller's relationship with Romanian, reminding us of her complicated relationship with both languages and ultimately of the loss of grace through the political ideologies of the twentieth century: National Socialism, Stalinism, and communism.

In conclusion, Müller's glass display case shows significant ambiguities at play in her oeuvre. Filled with everyday objects and an abundant imagination, her cabinet holds an excess of words, which contrasts with the intellectual scarcity of her childhood. Paper objects that function as leitmotifs destabilize narratives by transitioning between languages, genres, and historical facts while circling back to voids left by personal and collective trauma. In this process, the *Mokkatassen* serve as mobile objects that illustrate the textual and linguistic border crossings within the context of Müller's close dialogic collaboration with Pastior. Since 1990 Müller has often returned physically, poetically, and materially to Romania. By collecting and reassembling words and meanings from Romanian magazines—for example, the *ceaș/ca/de/MOCA*—Müller establishes tangible memory places in Romanian as well that rest on similarly shaky (because cut), impure (because reassembled from diverse sources), and fragmented (because they display the cuts) textual grounds as her German counterparts. Finally, Müller's *ceaș/ca/de/MOCA* evidences the expanded possibilities that she has by "writing" collages in more than one language. Even if these localized interventions (in Romania and Ukraine) take place in collage poems that are not widely read, they still offer her a space for reinventions and articulations of "truth" and "memory."

Müller's memory work is not finished. Her collection of mocha cups with its multiple significations will not remain safely stored in a glass cabinet (or poetry collection) but will be submitted to continued critique. I hope that Müller's memory bites and their localized interventions through dispersed objects find their way into public discussions. As their effortless border crossings unsettle static notions of "home" and "homelands" and transcend "national navel-gazing," Müller's symbols have the potential to question one-sided notions of "truth" in favor of igniting a public dialogue about the ambiguity of victimhood and perpetration. Ironically Oskar Pastior's past as an informant of the Securitate—Müller's "authentic witness" (Assmann 90)—has just done that: brought to attention the fragile notion of "authenticity," "truth," and "memory."

The reader still retains an active role in constructing and assembling the ambiguity inherent in Müller's fragmented cups. Maybe this is a model for a poetic version of a truly "transnational memorial" (Frevert 13) that brings together Romanians, German-Romanians, Germans, and possibly Ukrainians in a dialogue about "what a totalitarian regime meant" (Şahighian quoted in Mediafax).

Notes

1. "One disperses feelings in peculiar ways. On a few objects, which lend themselves without reason to clarify the remembrance inside one's head." My translation.

2. Assmann's book on memory takes into account that trauma can be displaced on subsequent generations if no adequate forms of remembrance are developed (75). Traumatic incidences would need to be articulated in order to become integrated and embraced as part of one's identity (94).

3. Marven writes: "It is my contention that Müller's prose fiction and her collages respectively focus the content and form of trauma: her novels depict traumatic events and the processes of traumatization, while the collages codify the structures of fragmentation which are an effect of trauma" ("'In allem ist der Riß'" 398). In *Body and Narrative*, Marven develops her thesis on the articulation of trauma through the body: disassociation; collapse of boundaries between the self and the world; representation of the self as alienated, other, or double; and the experience of the fragmented body (54).

4. "The inability to mourn" refers, first of all of course, to Alexander and Margarete Mitscherlich's analysis, in which a large part of the population was blocking out its involvement with National Socialism and hence displacing it to the level of the unconscious, where it maintained its destructive force. Second, it also refers

to victims of traumatic incidents whose lack of mourning and verbal articulation are symptoms of trauma (Assmann 109).

5. Since the Treaties of Paris of 1919–20, Transylvania has been part of Romania, whereas Northern Transylvania became part of Hungary in 1940. However, Germany continued to be the cultural nation with which Transylvanian-Saxons identified (Gabanyi 10; Motzan 108). Consequently these Germans maintained strong connections with Germany and an often uncritical position toward fascist Germany. This one-sided and complete dependence on the German National Socialists had severe consequences for the entire German population in Romania. Although Romania was Germany's ally until August 23, 1944, when Marshal Ion Antonescu's regime was overturned, the occupation by Russian soldiers had grave outcomes for the Germans in Romania (Gabanyi 10). Under the rationale of collective reparation, with the purpose of rebuilding the Soviet Union, between seventy and eighty thousand men and women were deported in January 1945 to Soviet camps (Gündisch and Beer 211–20; Weber 3, 6). These deportations directly affected Oskar Pastior, as well as Herta Müller's mother, and indirectly Müller herself.

6. In Romania the Aktionsgruppe Banat started one of the few attempts to address the question of the legacy of the National Socialist past among the parents' generation (Wagner 162; see also Totok and Weber). On Müller's more specific argument about National Socialism, see Kegelmann.

7. In her search for reliable information, Müller turns to Oskar Pastior. His memory, Müller writes, neither separates nor represses the times spent in the labor camp; rather, he lived from the details and was complicated because of his lifelong *Beschädigung* [injury] (Müller, "Interview Ulrich Greiner"). Moreover, because he judged his experiences within the causality of Nazi Germany's aggression, Pastior became Müller's principal "moral witness" (Assmann 48) in a project that started as the personal recuperation of her mother's "cryptic sentences" and the memory voids that had remained unfilled. Most critics praised the novel *Atemschaukel* as a document that evoked a previously untold collective memory through exact descriptions, "bildersatten Sprache" [language rich in images] and "protokollarischen Poesie" [protocolled poetry] (Naumann 43). Iris Radisch sharply critiques *Atemschaukel* as inauthentic, declaring: "Gulag-Romane lassen sich nicht aus zweiter Hand schreiben" [Gulag novels cannot be written secondhand]. Radisch particularly takes issue with Müller's language, calling it "parfümiert und kulissenhaft" [perfumed and staged] (43).

8. One of Germany's controversial institutions, a foundation that is opposed to joint European memory sites and rather seeks to establish a Zentrum gegen Vertreibungen [Center against Expulsions] in Berlin awarded Müller the Franz Werfel Human Rights Award in 2009. In her acceptance speech Müller rejects her appropriation by stating she is not a supporter and urges the Romanian-German community to look deeper into the history of the persecution of Jews and their entanglement with National Socialism (Deutschlandradio Kultur).

9. This stands in contrast to the given social structure: until the end of World War II, 75 percent of the German population in Romania was working in agriculture (Gündisch and Beer 227).

10. Anja K. Johannsen describes Müller's perception of the entire village as "claustrophobic." This perception structures her relationship to the landscape in a complementary fashion (173). In the course of her study Johannsen shows the extent to which objects structure spatial relationships to Müller's characters (185). She argues that Müller's construction of space is flexible and variable, being the product of "specific perceptions and memories" that spatially complement Müller's "rebellion against powers trying to define her" (203-04).

11. "Es war meine Schuld, ich hatte ihm gesagt, dass sie Mokkatassen sammelt, und war mit ihm ins Porzellangeschäft gegangen" [It was my fault; I had told him that she collects mocha cups and had gone with him to the china shop] (*Atemschaukel* 57).

12. Leo's homosexuality is one important theme in *Atemschaukel*. It is not the focus of my analysis, but it casts Leo as an outsider in his homophobic German community, which condemns sexual encounters with a Romanian as *Rassenschande* [Nazi term for sexual relationships with a non-Aryan] (*Atemschaukel* 11).

13. I borrowed the pairs guilt/atonement, war/peace, and cause/effect from one of Pastior's texts with biographical background written between 1974 and 1980; these testify to the ambiguity of his situation in the camp (Pastior, *durch* 153). The ambiguity, as Combrink points out, also shows in Pastior's poems—for example, in "Lesungen mit Tinnitus" (1986), in which they "resist against any form of bipolar argumentation" (see Combrink n.p.).

14. Petra Renneke has analyzed the importance of the *Ränder* [edges] and has explored the modern dimension of Müller's collage poetry (260, 274).

15. Lavin offers an allegorical reading of Hannah Höch's collages, which allow the viewer to be an "active, creative proponent in constructing meaning rather

than a passive recipient" (24). Hannah Höch (1889–1978) was an artist associated with the Dada movement in Weimar Germany. She mainly created collages and photomontages.

16. One exception is the supplement that was published on February 18, 2003, in *Revista* (see "Deportări").

17. According to Müller's Romanian publisher Polirom, Mircea Dinescu's satirical magazine *Plai cu boi* served as Müller's main Romanian source (see Editura Polirom).

Works Cited

Assmann, Aleida. *Der lange Schatten der Vergangenheit. Erinnerungskultur und Geschichtspolitik.* Bonn: Bundeszentrale für politische Bildung, 2007.

Borchmeyer, Dieter, and Viktor Zmegac, eds. *Moderne Literatur in Grundbegriffen.* Tübingen: Niemeyer, 1994.

Bozzi, Paola. *Der fremde Blick. Zum Werk Herta Müllers.* Würzburg: Königshausen and Neumann, 2005.

Combrink, Thomas. "Pastior, Oskar. Poetische Texte." *Kindlers Literaturlexikon.* Web. March 30, 2010.

"Deportări—Tratarea germanilor și altor minorități in România comunistă." *Revista* 22, February 18, 2003. Web. May 5, 2011.

Deutschlandradio Kultur. "Menschenrechtspreis für Herta Müller." *Kulturnachrichten,* November 2, 2009. Web. December 11, 2010.

Editura Polirom. "Dosar de Presa." Web. March 20, 2010. http://www.polirom.ro/catalog/carte/este-sau-nu-este-ion-2006/presa_01.html.

"An Evening with Herta Müller." *Radio Romania International.* Web. August 17, 2007. http://www.rri.ro/arh-art.shtml?lang=1&sec=13&art=4641.

Frevert, Ute. "Geschichtsvergessenheit und Geschichtsversessenheit revisited. Der jüngste Erinnerungsboom in der Kritik." *Aus Politik und Zeitgeschichte.* B 40–41/2003. September 29, 2003. 6–13.

Gabanyi, Anneli Ute. "Geschichte der Deutschen in Rumänien." *Informationen zur politischen Bildung* (2000): 10–15.

Glajar, Valentina. *The German Legacy in East Central Europe as Recorded in Recent German-Language Literature.* Rochester NY: Camden House, 2004.

Gündisch, Konrad, and Mathias Beer. *Siebenbürgen und die Siebenbürger Sachsen.* Munich: Langen Müller, 2005.

Heesen, Anke te. *Der Zeitungsausschnitt. Ein Papierobjekt der Moderne*. Frankfurt: Fischer, 2006.

Johannsen, Anja K. *Kisten, Krypten, Labyrinthe. Raumfigurationen in der Gegenwartsliteratur: W. G. Sebald, Anne Duden, Herta Müller*. Bielefeld: Transcript, 2008.

Kegelmann, Rene. "'Der deutsche Frosch war der erste Diktator, den ich kannte. Vergangenheitsbewältigung, Nationalsozialismus und Totalitarismus im Werk Herta Müllers." *Deutsche Literatur in Rumänien und das "Dritte Reich." Vereinnahmung-Verstrickung-Ausgrenzung*. Munich: IKGS, 2003. 299–310.

Lavin, Maud. *Cut with the Kitchen Knife: The Weimar Photomontages of Hannah Höch*. New Haven: Yale University Press, 1993.

Marven, Lyn. *Body and Narrative in Contemporary Literatures in German: Herta Müller, Libuse Monikova, Kerstin Hensel*. Oxford: Oxford University Press, 2005.

———. "'In allem ist der Riß': Trauma, Fragmentation and the Body in Herta Müller's Prose and Collages." *Modern Language Review* 100.2 (2005): 396–411.

Mediafax. "Volumul 'Leagănul respirației' de Herta Müller, lansat la Bookfest." June 12, 2010. Web. December 13, 2010. http://www.mediafax.ro/cultura-media/volumul-leaganul-respiratiei-de-herta-m-ller-lansat-la-bookfest-6386111.

Mitscherlich, Alexander, and Margarete Mitscherlich. *Die Unfähigkeit zu trauern. Grundlagen kollektiven Verhaltens*. Leipzig: Reclam, 1990.

Motzan, Peter. "Die vielen Wege in den Abschied. Die deutsche(n) Literatur(en) in Rumänien (1919-1989)." *Wortreiche Landschaft. Deutsche Literatur aus Rumänien*. Ed. Renate Florstedt. Leipzig: Förderverein BlickPunktBuch, 1998. 108–16.

Müller, Herta. "Antrittsrede." *Jahrbuch*. Ed. Deutsche Akademie für Dichtung und Sprache. Frankfurt: Luchterhand, 1998. 187–89.

———. *Atemschaukel*. Munich: Hanser, 2009.

———. *Der König verneigt sich und tötet*. Munich: Hanser, 2003. 7–39.

———. *Der Mensch ist ein großer Fasan auf der Welt*. Berlin: Rotbuch, 1986.

———. *Der Teufel sitzt im Spiegel. Wie Wahrnehmung sich erfindet*. Berlin: Rotbuch, 1991.

———. "Die Anwendung der dünnen Straßen." *Die Besten 2004. Klagenfurter Texte*. Ed. Iris Radisch. Munich: Piper, 2004. 11–22.

———. *Die blassen Herren mit den Mokkatassen*. Munich: Hanser, 2005.

———. *Este sau nu este Ion*. Iași: Polirom, 2005.

———. *Herta Müller. Der kalte Schmuck des Lebens*. Ed. Reinhard Wittmann. Hefte zu Ausstellungen im Literaturhaus München 2 (2010).

———. *The Hunger Angel*. Trans. Philip Boehm. New York: Metropolitan Books, 2012.

———. *Hunger und Seide*. Reinbek: Rowohlt, 1997.

———. *In der Falle*. Göttingen: Wallstein, 1996.

———. "In jeder Sprache sitzen andere Augen." *Der König verneigt sich und tötet*. Munich: Hanser, 2003. 7-39.

———. "Interview Anke te Heesen mit Herta Müller." *Cut and Paste um 1900. Der Zeitungsausschnitt in den Wissenschaften*. Ed. Anke te Heesen. *Kaleidoskopien* 4 (2002): 171-80.

———. "Interview Ulrich Greiner mit Herta Müller: Ich hatte soviel Glück." *Die Zeit* 43 (2009). Web. March 19, 2012. http://www.zeit.de/2009/43/Interview-Herta-Mueller.

———. "Interviu Rodica Binder: Cu Herta Müller despre colaje." *România literară* 39 (2005). Web. March 20, 2010. http://www.romlit.ro/cu_herta_mller_despre_colaje.

———. *Niederungen*. Berlin: Rotbuch, 1984.

———. "Wenn wir schweigen werden wir unangenehm—wenn wir reden, werden wir lächerlich. Kann Literatur Zeugnis ablegen?" *Herta Müller*. Ed. Heinz Ludwig Arnold. *Text und Kritik* 7 (2002): 6-17.

Naumann, Michael. "Pro Herta Müller. Herta Müllers neuer Roman über den sowjetischen Gulag-Alltag ist ein atemberaubendes Meisterwerk." *Die Zeit*, August 20, 2009:43.

Pastior, Oskar. *durch—und zurück*. Ed. Michael Lentz. Frankfurt: Fischer, 2007.

———. "... sage du habest es rauschen gehört." *Werkausgabe* 1. Ed. Ernest Wichner. Munich: Hanser, 2006.

Predoiu, Graziella. *Sinn-Freiheit und Sinn-Anarchie. Zum Werk Oskar Pastiors*. Frankfurt: Peter Lang, 2004.

Pürer, Heinz, and Johannes Raabe. *Presse in Deutschland*. Constance: UVK, 2007.

Radisch, Iris. "Contra Herta Müller. Kitsch oder Weltliteratur? Gulag-Romane lassen sich nicht aus zweiter Hand schreiben. Herta Müllers Buch ist parfümiert und kulissenhaft." *Die Zeit*, August 20, 2009:35-43.

Rennecke, Petra. *Poesie und Wissen. Poetologie des Wissens der Moderne*. Heidelberg: Winter, 2009.

Taberner, Stuart, and Karina Berger. *Germans as Victims in the Literary Fiction of the Berlin Republic*. Rochester NY: Camden House, 2009.

Totok, Wilhelm. "Die Zwänge der Erinnerungen." *Wortreiche Landschaft. Deutsche Literatur aus Rumänien*. Ed. Renate Florstedt. Leipzig: Förderverein BlickPunktBuch, 1998. 120–49.

Wagner, Richard. "Die Aktionsgruppe Banat. Versuch einer Selbstdarstellung." *Wortreiche Landschaft. Deutsche Literatur aus Rumänien*. Ed. Renate Florstedt. Leipzig: Förderverein BlickPunktBuch, 1998. 162–63.

Weber, Georg, ed. *Die Deportation von Siebenbürger Sachsen in die Sowjetunion 1945-1949*. Cologne: Böhlau, 1995.

11 Osmoses
Müller's Things, Bodies, and Spaces
Anja Johannsen

After her Nobel Prize was announced, commentators never tired of emphasizing that Herta Müller lent her literary and political voice to the victims of Stalinism and the Ceauşescu dictatorship. Müller is without question a political author whose writing describes and indicts the mechanisms of surveillance and oppression and their effects on people. Harassment and surveillance by the authorities and secret police of the Romanian dictatorship frequently mark the day-to-day life of her protagonists. The living conditions of her characters have severely damaged them and considerably affected their perception of themselves and the world. What is interesting above all, in my opinion, is that beginning from the processes of changing perception to the consequences of political and social repression, Müller raises questions of perceptual structures in general that go far beyond the specific themes of the politically oppressed.

These perceptual structures are strikingly often debated by means of the description of spaces in Müller's texts. Such debate is especially remarkable against the background of the recent spatial turn in the field of cultural studies: literary studies have been increasingly preoccupied with the question of how theories of space can be applied to the analysis of literary texts, especially in terms of the relation between space and text. What does the description of a room or a landscape within a literary text tell us about the text itself or about the author's poetics? I argue that Müller's texts are particularly appropriate for tackling this question. In her literary texts space is dependent on the observer's frame of reference—that is, it is the product of sensuous perception and bodily practices. Space is always conceptualized relationally. In my analysis I will focus on the components of these spatial constructs—things and bodies—and their complex relation within the literary text as I argue that Müller's attention to questions of perception is instrumental in her creation of spaces.

The Russian formalist Viktor Shklovsky writes that our everyday perception tends toward automatization and does not conceive an object in its particularity but rather identifies and categorizes it—that is, reduces it to the characteristics necessary for instrumental rationality to deal with that particular object. Shklovsky refers to this automated seeing as the algebraic method of thinking (Shklovsky 13). The central function of the arts, in contrast, is to disturb and rupture this automated perception that dominates our everyday life. The literary text, in estranging the world we believe ourselves to know, sensitizes us. This sensitizing also has an eminently political and moral function for Shklovsky since it makes us once more receptive to that which automated perception has withheld and thus ultimately teaches us empathy. Following in the footsteps of the formalists, who focused primarily on the question of how a text is made, I discuss which processes and literary techniques Müller uses to break up and sensitize our automated perception—and how her literary and political voice maintains its distinctive and unmistakable sound.

Things

The presence of material objects is conspicuous and plays a decisive role in Müller's texts—whether in her fiction, her essays, or her collages. Her characters often find themselves confused by the things of everyday life. In her essay "Einmal anfassen—zweimal loslassen" [Catch hold once—let go twice; *König* 106-29], Müller explains the peculiar significance that things hold in her writing and thought and reflects on what constitutes her prose. She begins the text (a good twenty pages that were conceived for a lecture at the Tübingen Poetik-Dozentur in 2000) by recalling a train trip she took shortly after settling in West Germany at the end of the 1980s. Back then the German rail network was advertising its sleeper cabin in a poster featuring a relaxed young woman in a white nightgown with lace straps and the words "Inge Wenzel auf dem Weg nach Rimini" [Inge Wenzel on the way to Rimini; *König* 107].[1] This nightgown prompted three sorts of memory in Müller: first, the image of this item of clothing recalled her adolescent years, when her grandmother had sewn her a similar nightgown before she left her village for a boarding school in the city. Second, it reminded her of a terrifying journey in which she traveled in a sleeper car from Timișoara to Bucharest, when she feared for her life under the threat of the Securitate. In her purse she had a list of names of Romanian political prisoners for Amnesty International. On the platform the secret police had detained and threatened her. When they then let her on board, she assumed that they planned to have her thrown out of the train during the journey. Thus she suspected the woman with whom she shared the sleeper cabin of working for the Securitate. This woman was also wearing a similar white nightgown. The third memory is of a cheap polyester nightgown that Müller sold with the help of a friend at a flea market before emigrating to West Germany; he advertised it as a *Fickhemdchen* [fuck-nighty; *König* 120]. Thus the multiplicity of meaning held by this nightgown in the German advertisement bundled together several layers of memory and forced Müller to confront these various pasts. Inge Wenzel's sleeping attire triggered memories of persecution and death threats associated with the *Dorfabschiedshemd* [village farewell nightgown; *König* 119] and her Banat-Swabian childhood; with the nightgown of the woman in the sleeper car en route to Bucharest; and with the fuck-nighty and her dear friend, who two years later was found hanged in his apartment (*König* 121).

The polysemy of objects that Müller illustrates in this essay with the example of the nightgown is never explicit to the same extent in her fiction. Whereas the essay offers a full description of each individual narrative invoked by the piece of clothing, thus explicating the object's multidimensionality—that is, its multilayered meaning—her fictional works produce the illustrative connections only progressively in the course of the text. Scholars have pointed out that Müller's narrative texts consist of close-ups of details arranged into complex assemblages (Becker; Dawidowski; Eke). Since these close-ups typically introduce objects into the picture, the montage of these close-ups generates texts within these objects; the words or clusters of words naming objects take on a decisive role in the constitution of the text. The narrative material is unveiled to the reader precisely to the extent to which these words become charged with significance in the course of the text. *Herztier* [*The Land of Green Plums*], for example—the text that exercises this narrative mode most consistently—gives a leading role to concepts such as *Nagelschere* [nail scissors], *Nuss* [nut], *Blechschaf* [tin sheep], and *Holzmelone* [wooden melon], which return again and again in more or less variable contexts (Schmidt 61-63). This selection shows how Müller primarily works with concepts that sound rather banal outside of the narrative context, such as *Nuss* and *Nagelschere*, or with odd compound terms such as *Blechschaf* or *Holzmelone*. They seem strange the first few times the reader confronts them in the text: what should we make of a word like *Blechschaf*, where the two parts of the word seem quite alien to each other? Only the respective context created in the text imbues the words with significance, such that they establish connections among each other to form an increasingly multilayered organic text (Philipp Müller 119-20). Of course this describes a process that occurs to a certain extent within any text, even independently of any literary quality; the structure of meaning emerges only gradually. But Müller goes one decisive step further. Müller allows these semantization processes to come to light by building her texts upon words that at first glance seem to simply refer to insignificant household objects or do not make very much sense at all but that by the end of the text radiate polysemy.

    This is one of the reasons why it is considered more difficult to find one's way in Müller's fictional texts than in her essays. The term "hermetical" crops up in reviews again and again. Ralph Köhnen has quite rightly objected to this categorization. He argues that Müller's texts are idiosyncratically formed with the densest web of interconnections since many things are in conjunction with each other not because they are similar in themselves but because they were experienced together—that is, at the same time, within the same context (Köhnen 124). It is no accident that it is material objects that force together the disparate experiences and narratives. In "Einmal anfassen—zweimal loslassen" Müller writes in summary:

> Mir kommt es vor, als bestimmten die Gegenstände, wann, wie und wo einem vergangene Situationen und Menschen einfallen. . . . Es sind immer wieder die Gegenstände, die untereinander ihre eigene Komplizenschaft aufbauen, die Personen und Vorgänge um sie herum fügen sich ihnen. . . . Frappierend wie Überfälle schleppen die Gegenstände von jetzt meine Geschichten von damals herbei. In ihnen sitzt latent das Zeitübergreifende, funkelt mit seinen grellen Einzelheiten, bevor es sich wieder in die Gegenstände zurückzieht.
>
> [It seems to me as if the objects determine when, how, and where one is reminded of certain situations and people. . . . It's always the objects that find their accomplices among themselves, and people and processes around them yield to them. . . . The objects of today, striking like attacks, drag my stories of that time in front of me. Timelessness sits latently in these objects, glaring garishly with its details, before it withdraws again into the things.]
> (*König* 121–22)

Müller ascribes an independent life to the objects, a life that is usually hidden but comes to light under the vision of the reader who is receptive to these hidden dimensions of things. It is less a feat of human projection when we discover the hidden dimension of the object confronting us than a question of receptivity. Whether or not one perceives it depends on the reader's way of confronting it, but this independent life of the object is always there in Müller's texts.

In her essays Müller often describes the loss of receptivity in our interaction with things: "Niemand will Selbstverständlichkeit hergeben. Jeder ist auf Dinge angewiesen, die einem gefügig bleiben und ihre Natur nicht verlassen. Dinge, mit denen man hantieren kann, ohne sich darin zu spiegeln" [No one wishes to abandon what they take for granted. Everyone relies on things that remain compliant and stay true to their nature. Things one can handle without seeing one's own reflection in them] (*König* 147). In her fiction, by contrast, Müller utilizes this encounter between the sensitive and the susceptible, between the non-automated perception and the hidden dimensions of the object. Müller's characteristic narrative procedure is founded on the moment of bafflement produced by this confrontation: her vision first lifts the object out of the framework of meaning to which it seems to belong and allows it to enter into new contexts. Only by means of this interplay between the semantic discharge and recharge of the object can she create a flexible new textual framework. In *Herztier*, for example, the narrator sublets from a Hungarian Catholic woman who kisses the crucifix hanging on the wall before every meal. Müller describes this object as follows:

> Ihren Jesus hatte Frau Margit auf einer Augustwallfahrt in der Eile zwischen dem Bus und den Treppen der Wallfahrtskirche aus einem Sack voller Jesuskreuze gekauft. Der Jesus, den sie küßte, war der Abfall eines Blechschafes aus der Fabrik, das dörfliche Schachern eines Tag-und Nachtarbeiters zwischen den Schichten. Es war das einzig Gerechte an diesem Jesus an der Wand, daß er gestohlen war und den Staat betrog. Wie jeder Jesus aus dem Sack war auch dieser am Tage nach der Wallfahrt ein Saufgeld auf dem Tisch der Bodega. (*Herztier* 131–32)

> [Frau Margit had picked up her Jesus during an August pilgrimage, in the rush between the bus and the steps of the church where the pilgrims were headed, picking Him at random from a whole sack of Jesuses that were on sale. The Jesus she kissed was made of scrap off one of the tin sheep from the factory, the product of an off-shift cottage industry. The only righteous thing about the Jesus on her wall was that he was stolen property, a traitor to the State. Like every other Jesus in that sack, this one had been converted into drink at a bodega table the day after the pilgrimage.] (*The Land of Green Plums* 122)

The religious symbolism of the object is removed and the object is placed in a new framework of meaning. At first the new context refers to the economic circulation of goods on the black market. By reintroducing the tin sheep once more, however, Müller significantly expands that context. The *Blechschaf* calls up all of the frustration that pervades the daily life of those who have left their villages and farms to start a new life in the city as workers in the metal-processing industry, without knowing that they would face the same monotonous workday there as well. Thus in place of the conventionally established meaning of the crucifix the text embeds it into a multilayered, textually immanent context, undermining the order of things through such recodifications.

Things and Bodies

David Midgley argues that Müller gives the emotional events in a text such resonance primarily by attaching them to certain objects (35). As we have seen, things function as the bearers of memory, like the nightgown, as the state of the individual characters and their relations to each other manifest themselves in these things. In *Herztier* we find a passage where the narrator describes her regular meetings with three friends in a bar. The four have long been shadowed and threatened by the secret police and live in constant fear of arrest or assault:

> Weil wir Angst hatten, waren Edgar, Kurt, Georg und ich täglich zusammen. Wir saßen zusammen am Tisch, aber die Angst blieb so einzeln in jedem Kopf, wie wir sie mitbrachten, wenn wir uns trafen. Wir lachten viel, um sie voreinander zu verstecken. Doch Angst schert aus. Wenn man sein Gesicht beherrscht, schlüpft sie in die Stimme. Wenn es gelingt, Gesicht und Stimme wie ein abgestorbenes Stück im Griff zu halten, verläßt sie sogar die Finger. Sie legt sich außerhalb der Haut hin. Sie liegt frei herum, man sieht sie auf den Gegenständen, die in der Nähe sind. (*Herztier* 83)

> [Because we were afraid, Edgar, Kurt, Georg and I met every day. We sat together at a table, but our fear stayed locked within each of our heads, just as we'd brought it to our meetings. We laughed a lot, to hide it from each other. But fear always finds an out. If you control your face, it slips into your voice. If you manage to keep a grip on your face and your voice, as if they were dead wood, it will slip out through your fingers. It will pass through your skin and lie there. You can see it lying around on objects close by.] (*The Land of Green Plums* 74-75)

Müller's text reveals the psychological state of these characters not only on the surfaces of their bodies but also, in a kind of direct extension of their bodies, in the surrounding objects, thereby creating a fluid transition between bodies and things. Skin does not clearly delimitate the body from the outside; rather, both the body itself and the things at its extensions exist in a relational exchange. The permeability of the body exists in osmosis with the things surrounding it. Similarly in *Heute wär ich mir lieber nicht begegnet* [*The Appointment*], Müller recreates an oppressive context of fear and rage that overwhelms the narrator: "Während ich auf den Lift wartete, war mir, als sei ich nicht mehr in meiner Haut, sondern verteilt in den Briefkästen an der Wand" (*Heute* 139); [As I was waiting for the elevator I felt as though I'd left my body and been parceled out among the mailboxes fixed to the wall] (*The Appointment* 122).

In another passage in the same novel the narrator explains her tendency toward shying away from people and things:

> Bei den Menschen, die mir sofort nicht gefallen, wird das Fremdeln kleiner, wenn ich nicht darüber rede. . . . Bei Gegenständen fremdel ich aber, weil sie mir gefallen. Ich denk mir etwas hinein, was gegen mich ist. Wenn ich es nicht sage, verschwindet es, wie das Fremdeln vor Menschen. Ich glaube, es wächst mit der Zeit ins Haar. (*Heute* 190)

> [With people to whom I take an immediate dislike, the wariness soon wears off unless I talk about it. . . . But the reason I am shy of objects is because I like them. I transfer the thoughts that are against me onto them. Then these thoughts go away, unless I talk about them—just like my wariness of people. Maybe it all collects in your hair.] (*The Appointment* 169)

At that point only a thorough combing can remove the shyness: "Dieses Scheitelziehen von der Kopfmitte zur Stirn, man sieht das Fremdeln an den Taschenkämmen. Nur stummes Fremdeln läßt sich auskämmen, und der Kamm wird fettig" (*Heute* 190); [While they're parting their hair you can see their wariness of others collecting in their combs. But they can't comb it out completely if they go on talking about it. The fear of strangers sticks to the comb and makes it greasy] (*The Appointment* 169–70). An interplay is established between sensation (shyness), body (hair), and object (the comb)—that is, the bodily process, the accumulation of hair oil, becomes integrated into the processes of de- and re-semantization, which, as we have seen, are performed upon the things. The osmotic process between the insides of the body and the things shows that the body is not an area removed from or opposed to the ascription of meaning relative to situation and context but rather is very closely related to things. In Müller's descriptions the constitution of the body and that of things differ only in degree and not in principle. The human body and the object with which it comes into contact are conceived as two different "materials" distinguished only by their dissimilar physical properties. In the comparisons Müller drew as a child between herself, her own bodily material, and the material things surrounding her, the body always ended up beneath the object:

> Das Material, aus dem die Gegenstände bestehen, erfuhr beim Hinsehen jene Zuspitzung, mit der im Kopf der Irrlauf beginnt. Das Gewöhnliche der Dinge platzte, ihr Material wurde zum Personal. Zwischen zwei gleichen Dingen entstanden Hierarchien, und sie entstanden noch mehr zwischen mir und ihnen. Ich mußte mich den Vergleichen stellen, die ich aufgemacht hatte, und konnte nur den kürzeren ziehen. Verglichen mit Holz, Blech oder einem Federkleid ist Haut der vergänglichste Stoff.
>
> [The material that objects consist of began, upon closer inspection, that process of intensification with which the mind begins to go astray. Their commonness, ordinariness, cracked open; their material became personal. Hierarchies arose between two equal things, and even more so between me and them. I had to subject myself to the comparisons I had started, and I could only draw the shorter straw. Compared to wood, metal, or feathers, skin is the most ephemeral material.] (*König* 49)

Without any grounding in a stable framework of meaning, objects and bodies are equally "personal" and "material"; in this equation of bodies and objects it is inevitable that bodies cannot measure up to the objects due to their much greater fragility and vulnerability.

In *Herztier* Müller brings this comparison of things and bodies to a very fine point, clearly showing both the great resemblance between things and bodies and the striking difference concerning their vulnerability. The first-person narrator of *Herztier* confides in her friend Tereza as she tells her for the first time about Captain Pjele's interrogations:

Ich erzählte Tereza, was ein Verhör ist. Ohne Grund, als spreche ich laut mit mir selber, fing ich zu reden an. Tereza hielt sich mit zwei Fingern an ihrem Goldkettchen fest. Sie rührte sich nicht, um die dunkle Genauigkeit nicht zu verwischen.

1 Jacke, 1 Bluse, 1 Hose, 1 Strumpfhose, 1 Höschen, 1 Paar Schuhe, 1 Paar Ohrgehänge, 1 Armbanduhr. Ich war ganz nackt, sagte ich.

1 Adreßbuch, 1 gepreßte Lindenblüte, 1 gepreßtes Kleeblatt, 1 Kugelschreiber, 1 Taschentuch, 1 Wimperntusche, 1 Lippenstift, 1 Puder, 1 Kamm, 4 Schlüssel, 2 Briefmarken, 5 Straßenbahnkarten.

1 Handtasche.

Alles war aufgeschrieben in Rubriken auf einem Blatt. (*Herztier* 144)

[I explained to Teresa what an interrogation is. For no reason, as though I were talking to myself, I began to speak. Tereza clutched her gold chain with two fingers. She didn't move, so as not to blur the inky precision.

1 jacket, 1 blouse, 1 pr. trousers, 1 pr. nylons, 1 pr. panties, 1 pr. shoes, 1 pr. earrings, 1 wristwatch. I was stripped naked, I said.

1 address book, 1 pressed lindenflower, 1 pressed cloverleaf, 1 ballpoint pen, 1 handkerchief, 1 mascara, 1 lipstick, 1 powder, 1 comb, 4 keys, 2 stamps, 5 tram tickets.

1 handbag.

Everything was entered under different headings on a single sheet.] (*The Land of Green Plums* 134-35)

The leap from the first to the second paragraph in this passage is remarkable: the first merely describes the conversation, while the second begins where the report on what occurred during the interrogation seemed almost concluded. There is no transition describing the process as such—the coerced undressing. That the narrator had to completely undress in front of the captain is only conveyed by the list of the items of clothing; the belated "Ich war ganz nackt" [I was completely naked] only confirms what the list had already indicated. The reader learns of the existence of this list—a list the captain presumably made while she was undressing—after a calculated delay. "Alles war aufgeschrieben in Rubriken auf einem Blatt" [Everything was entered under different headings on a single sheet]. Classifying these objects—the items of clothing and the contents of her purse—

in this sober and businesslike mode, marked above all by the number preceding each entry, mirrors the psychological violence the narrator suffers in this scene.

> Mich selber schrieb der Hauptmann nicht auf. Er wird mich einsperren. Es wird auf keiner Liste stehen, daß ich 1 Stirn, 2 Augen, 2 Ohren, 1 Nase, 2 Lippen, 1 Hals hatte, als ich hierher kam. Ich weiß von Edgar, Kurt und Georg, sagte ich, daß unten im Keller Gefängniszellen sind. Ich wollte im Kopf die Liste meines Körpers machen gegen seine Liste. Ich kam nur bis zu meinem Hals. Der Hauptmann Pjele wird merken, daß mir Haare fehlen. Er wird fragen, wo die Haare sind. (*Herztier* 145)

> [Everything except me, whom Captain Pjele failed to write down. He will lock me up. There won't be any list saying that I had in my possession when I arrived here 1 forehead, 1 pr. eyes, 1 nose, 1 pr. lips, 1 neck. I know from Edgar, Kurt and Georg that there are prison cells in the basement of the building. I wanted to take a mental inventory of my body to counter Captain Pjele's list. I only got as far as my neck. Captain Pjele will realize that some of my hair is missing. He will ask where the missing hairs are.] (*The Land of Green Plums* 135)

This third list, the list of the narrator's body parts, is doubly coded in the text. First, it is imagined as an additional list in the secret police's files that had to be completed before her imprisonment. In this sense the list of body parts would be the continuation of the previous two lists of things, and it shows with the utmost concision the violence of categorization that records everything: the objects are also violated as Pjele categorizes, lists, and thus robs them of their individuality. And yet the absurdity of this procedure becomes much clearer when a body is subject to the same treatment as the objects. This complete parceling and listing of body parts negates every peculiarity of this body: everyone has "1 forehead, 2 eyes, 2 ears, 1 nose, 2 lips, 1 neck," just as various ballpoint pens, handkerchiefs, lipsticks, combs, keys, stamps, and tram tickets are found in countless purses. Every list of this sort suppresses any particular details of the objects and of the bodies that distinguish them from others of the same kind. The detailed language of the narrator, which reflects an abundance of shades and nuances of narration, stands in clear contrast to the purported precision of the lists. The grid work of the list denies the objects and the body any individuality and history. The list is the embodiment of what Shklovsky called "automated perception." According to him, thought as an "algebraic method of perception" only understands things "as numbers, or they are registered formulaically, without entering into consciousness.... Thus life goes missing and is transformed into nothing. The automation eats up the things, the clothing, the furniture, the woman, and the horrors of war" (Shklovsky 14–15).

However, the list of body parts raises one further question. The narrator makes this list of her body "to counter Captain Pjele's list," as she tells her friend. But she cannot succeed: "I only got as far as my neck. Captain Pjele will realize that some of my hair is missing" (*The Land of Green Plums* 135). She is referring to the few hairs she had plucked out and placed in her letters to her three friends, as arranged, so they would know whether or not the secret police were intercepting them. Her fear that the secret police would be able to notice individual hairs missing—an absurd fear, of course, seen realistically—is a sign of the terrible extent to which the power of the secret police had long since taken possession of her body. Her fear sits in each individual hair. Her body does not work as expected, as her autonomy would guarantee; its material is much too fragile for that. The body lacks the resistance that is so urgently needed since the violence has inscribed itself onto her body. Individual objects offer a refuge from humiliating interrogations such as the mother-of-pearl button in her blouse that the narrator in *Heute wär ich mir lieber nicht begegnet* wears to every interrogation, the turning of which in her hands gives her a certain equanimity at last. But reflecting on one's own body does not help at all. In fact panic grips the narrator in *Herztier* while she is making her counter-list, when she realizes the extent to which her body has become the scene of her battle with the political powers.

Homines Aperti

Most of Müller's texts place the body in an ongoing relation of exchange with the external space. The outside permeates the body just as the inside extends itself into outer objects; the osmotic exchange between inside and outside runs both ways. Yet the penetration of the outside into the human body is by no means always described as violence. In *Niederungen* [*Nadirs*], for example, the child's relation to the surrounding nature is presented as an osmotic relationship from the very beginning of the text. The child and its environment permeate each other continuously (Günther; Dawidowski)—a process that triggers equal amounts of desire and fear. Fear comes from the frequent admonishments of the grandfather, who as the upholder of tradition rejects any form of assimilation. Yet the child consciously seeks fusion with the natural environment. The following passage illustrates this point:

> Ich war eine schöne sumpfige Landschaft. Ich legte mich ins hohe Gras und ließ mich in die Erde rinnen. Ich wartete, daß die großen Weiden zu mir über den Fluß kommen, daß sie ihre Zweige in mich schlagen und ihre Blätter in mich streuen. Ich wartete, daß sie sagen: Du bist der schönste Sumpf der Welt, wir kommen alle zu dir. Wir bringen auch unsere großen schlanken Wasservögel mit, aber die werden flattern in dir und in dich hineinschreien. ... Ich wollte weit werden, damit die Wasservögel mit ihren großen Flügeln Platz in mir haben, Platz zum Fliegen. (*Niederungen* 78)

> [I was a beautiful swampy landscape. I lay down in the tall grass and made myself trickle into the earth. I waited for the big willows to come to me from across the river, to root their branches in me and spread their leaves in me. I hoped they would say: you are the most beautiful swamp in the world, we are all coming here. And we will bring our tall slender water birds with us, but they'll flutter around in you and will scream in you. ... I wanted to expand so that the water birds with their wide wings would have room enough in me, room to fly.] (*Nadirs* 62)

Critics have repeatedly pointed out that this dissolution of borders is the result of the child's imagination (Becker 36; Günther 45–46). However, as Müller's later fiction shows, descriptions of such osmotic processes are a recurring theme in all of her texts. *Herztier*, for example, speaks frequently of faces that reflect geographical regions, as in Lola's case:

> Lola kam aus dem Süden des Landes, und man sah ihr eine arm gebliebene Gegend an. Ich weiß nicht wo, vielleicht an den Knochen der Wangen, oder

um den Mund, oder mitten in den Augen. . . . In Lolas Heft las ich später: Was man aus der Gegend hinausträgt, trägt man hinein ins Gesicht. (*Herztier* 9-10)

[Lola came from the south of the country, and she reeked of poor province. I don't know where it showed the most, maybe in her cheekbones, or around her mouth, or smack in the middle of her eyes. . . . Later I read in Lola's notebook: Whatever you carry out of your province, you carry into your face.] (*The Land of Green Plums* 2, 4)

What can we conclude from this? What do the osmotic processes between the characters and the objects and areas surrounding them say about Müller's view of humanity? Müller's texts rely on an image of man that is related to Norbert Elias's. Elias had rejected the image of the *homo clausus* and criticized Freud, among others, for describing the person as a closed unity (Elias and Scotson 174-77) rather than viewing the person as a plurality that is open to its environment. Müller, entirely in line with Elias's vision, writes of people as components of complex and continually shifting nettings—nettings of things and other bodies. In dissolving those configurations typically seen as inflexible and steadfast, such as the borders between the body and its environment or between bodies and things, and replacing them with new flexible contexts of reference, Müller reveals static arrangements to be merely the cementing of dominant orders and thus undermines them. The structure of Müller's texts reflects the theme of her oeuvre: rebellion against every form of totalitarian claim to power and against definitional powers. Against ideological models of the world, which rely on the subsumption of details to the whole, Müller sketches only "gebrechliche Einrichtungen des Augenblicks" [fragile creations of the moment];[2] she prefers the detail to the whole because the idea of a whole as such bears a totalitarian core in her view. In an interview about her most recent novel, *Atemschaukel*, she explains why literature has to talk about details in order to mediate somebody's experiences: "Das muss man ja in Einzelheiten darstellen. Das Wort Trauma oder Deportation oder Beschädigung hat in der Literatur ja keinen Sinn. Das muss ja aufgelöst werden in Einzelheiten" [One has to depict that in details. The word trauma or deportation or damage makes no sense in a literary text. It has to be dissolved in details] (Müller and Schmidtkunz 12). Brigid Haines speaks in fact of Müller's insistence on detail as a "micro-politics of resistance" (Haines 125).

However, it is important to note how little Müller's texts can be reduced to the aspect of ideological critique. Ralph Köhnen shows how it is precisely the dissolution of boundaries that reveals a specific textual pleasure (Köhnen 136). Müller's images, he argues, are not just the despairing and aggressive visions of one suffering repression and facing death; her mix of linguistic images cannot be reduced to pure thanatography. Rather, the transgression of semantic agreements leads directly to the beginning of beauty—the violent prose of factual relations is complemented by another prose, confusing in its precision, that confronts and interrupts any kind of automated perception.

Things, Bodies, and Spaces

In Müller's prose, according to Friedmar Apel, everything is translated into spatial experience (*Deutscher Geist und deutsche Landschaft* 229). For spaces, in Müller's works, are nothing other than the contiguity of the material (things) and the personal (bodies). In line with Apel, I argue that in Müller's texts spatial perception involves the question of the transformation of the perceived through text. Thus the guiding question is to what extent Müller's texts are literary texts precisely at those points where they construct spaces. Her essay "Gegenstände, wo die Haut zu Ende ist" [Things, where the skin ends], for example, touches upon many of the points discussed above. Müller begins by describing a thought experiment from her childhood: "Ich sah der Reihe nach alle Gegenstände an, die man zusammen Zimmer nannte, oder Hof, oder Mittagstisch. Ich versuchte, mir alles, was ich sah, bei dem, was man Zimmer nannte oder Hof, wegzudenken. Da blieb mir nichts mehr. Die Orte selbst verschwanden. Zusammen mit mir" [I looked at all the objects, one by one, all of which together one called a room, or a yard, or a dining table. I tried to mentally subtract from what one called room or yard everything I saw. Then there was nothing left. The places themselves vanished. Together with myself] (*Teufel* 90). Even the first sentence in this passage is remarkable: she speaks of "Ich sah der Reihe nach alle Gegenstände an, die man zusammen Zimmer nannte, oder Hof, oder Mittagstisch" [(I looked at all the objects, one by one,) all of which together one called a room, or a yard, or a dining table]. Here the unnamed objects do not fill the space but rather comprise the space; Müller is operating with a concept of space that explicitly breaks with the traditional Euclidean notion of container space. The room and the yard are not seen as prior to the objects; rather they are the products of the aggregation of certain objects characteristic of a particular type of space, like a yard or a living room.

Michel Foucault proposes that in order to get a clearer conception of the various relations comprising our living spaces, we should begin with a description of those various emplacements (Foucault 38). He uses the concept of the ensemble of relations that form a space. Disentangling this ensemble and describing the individual components is for him the first decisive step toward the understanding of a space. What Müller describes in the quoted passage is very similar to what Foucault recommends for the purposes of analysis but with a sort of inversion: Müller describes the emplacements through negation, and the child imagines the ensemble of relations by imagining its erasure. She tries to picture her parents walking around in the empty room. Within this emptiness, she goes on to imagine, there would be "keine Arbeit für sie. Es gäbe nur sie selber für sich und einer für den anderen. Sie müßten sich selber, und einer den anderen, und ich mich, und jeder jeden langsam und immer zerstören.... Das taten sie auch. Und ich. Doch weil es die Gegenstände gab, fiel das nicht so auf, als wenn sie sich, und jeder jeden, ohne Gegenstände hätten zerstören müssen" [There wouldn't be any work for them. There would only be themselves for themselves and one for the other. They would have to destroy themselves, and each the other, and I myself, and everyone destroy everyone slowly and forever.... And they did. And I did. But because there were things, this wasn't so noticeable as it would be if they had to destroy themselves and everyone destroy everyone else without things] (*Teufel* 90–91). There seem to be two superimposed ensembles in the domestic space: the personal or emotional relations—that is, the evidently destructive relations among the family members—and the configuration of things, the function of which seems to be camouflaging the ineluctable destructive processes of normal family life and work life. The child observes both ensembles constituting her living space and their joint operation along with the absence of any alternatives, for, as the passage above shows, when the child tries to imagine the room or the yard without these sites of family members and objects, the places themselves disappear.

Following in Foucault's footsteps, the German sociologist Martina Löw has developed her own analytical models and a corresponding terminology for a precise investigation of the genesis of spaces. Whereas Foucault does not carry out the suggestion quoted above, Löw in *Raumsoziologie* (Sociology of space) works to develop a strictly relativistic conception of space to oppose the Euclidean model of container space still dominant both within sociology and in our everyday notions of space. Overcoming the structural division between space and material is central to Löw's argumentation; for Löw spaces consist of ordered material, and each space is a relational configuration of bodies, whereby spatial boundaries such as walls, doors, etc., as well as objects and people within these boundaries, all count for her as bodies, corresponding thus far to Foucauldian "sites." For Löw space is always a relational configuration of living creatures and social goods. And even though it is unusual, it is absolutely necessary to integrate people into the conception of space because it makes it more difficult to reflect on spaces since spaces, as Löw claims, are constituted by the involvement of the people present (Löw 154–55).

This insight is crucial for Müller's essay, although in reverse order; in the attempt to think away the objects that one calls "room" or "yard," not only do the places themselves vanish, but the narrator vanishes too: "zusammen mit mir." If the meshwork of objects and people comprising the space is dissolved, the individual components do not persist independently of the others; they simply disappear. The Müllerian child in this case is present in space—that is, as a placed person and at the same time as the perceiver of this space. These two indivisible functions of the child in the text fit the conception of space proposed by Löw, which denies any division between the constitution of space and the perception of space. For if the genesis of space is no longer to be seen as antecedent, the perception and the constitution of space become one.

Löw now distinguishes two processes of constituting space: alongside the placement of social goods and people that she calls *spacing*, the constitution of space also requires an activity of synthesis—that is, goods and people have to be combined to form spaces (Löw 159). *Spacing* and synthesis are not to be seen as two independent processes since the one cannot occur without the other; Löw only distinguishes them for the purposes of analysis.

The aspect of the constitution of space that interests Müller is synthesis. The decisive characteristic of synthesis is the variability and dynamism inherent in this model: a room is never the same if its constitution depends on who enters it, when, in what state, and which memories and associations he or she connects with the space.

Thus Müller's spatial descriptions make clear that her interest concerns people as components in a Foucauldian ensemble. All binary relations are made irrelevant in her literary texts or are seriously confounded. The usual parameters for describing spaces such as up/down, right/left, and closed/open lose their unequivocal meaning. Spaces are no longer Euclidean in Müller's texts; instead she conceives spaces as purely relational forms. What does this tell us about her understanding of text?

At the beginning, I argued that Müller's texts depict their own inner poetic structure by means of the description of spaces. What I have said above shows that those spaces are products of the observer's perception and memory. Every single room is simply a network of the components that reside within it and generate it respectively. The components of the room, on their part, are not entities with clear boundaries. On the contrary, they are all related through osmotic transitions. These nettings can be understood as images of the flexible polysemic network of the text itself.

Thinking about space strictly in non-Euclidean terms, as Müller does, means that there are no borders any more. Correspondingly in Müller's view the literary text is an open netting with loose ends that is always in progress. Unlike most modern and postmodern literature Müller's texts do not lament over the limitation of signification.

The following passage of "Gegenstände, wo die Haut zu Ende ist" illuminates this with particular clarity.

> In den weiten Landschaften schreit die Stille. Die Starre lauert. Landschaft ist Stilleben, mit dünnem grünem Boden. Der Einbruch wartet. Er fängt an

zwischen den Schläfen und hört unter den Sohlen der Schuhe nicht auf. Die innere Unruhe und die äußere Starre fallen übereinander her. Wir nennen es "Horizont," was sich eng ums Gesicht legt. Wir reden vom "Gesichtskreis." Wir sind eingekreist und werden lächerlich.

[The stillness screams through the wide landscapes. Rigidity lurks. Landscape is still life, with a thin green ground. The invasion is waiting. It begins between the temples and doesn't stop under the soles of the shoes. The inner disquiet and the outer rigidity fall on each other. We call it "horizon," that which lays itself so closely around one's face. We call it the circle of vision. We are encircled and become ridiculous.] (*Teufel* 100)

The first sentences of this passage return to the recurring theme that body and environment are intertwined in an osmotic relation. But what is most interesting is what follows: "Wir nennen es 'Horizont,' was sich eng ums Gesicht legt," she writes. In his *Geschichte des Horizonts* [History of the horizon] Albrecht Koschorke argues that the horizon motif differs from all other landscape motifs in literature and the visual arts because of its formal character since the basic structures of perception were negotiated using that motif and since the horizon is seen as a constituting referential axis for the empirical order as such (Koschorke 7). The horizon is not just one component in the field of perception but rather organizes the entire field.

If the horizon itself—that is, the line of demarcation between near and far—lays itself closely around the face, as in Müller's text, this makes null and void every possibility of orientation. Thus what Müller describes here is the consistent extension of the continued invalidation of all established parameters of perception. The oppositions of near and far, wide and narrow, have been entirely negated, inside and outside merge, and up and down can no longer be distinguished: "Wir bewegen uns durch den leeren Himmel, der hoch oben und so weit unten ist, daß er die Knöchel erreicht" [We move through the empty sky, which is so high above and so far down that it reaches the ankles] (*Teufel* 100). The complete loss of spatial coordinates manifests itself in the final rupture of the connection between perceiving and mastering space. If the horizon lays itself closely around the face, then this represents the radical inversion of the panoramic view in literature described as the high-water mark of "visual land acquisitions" that dominated literary descriptions of the landscape in the eighteenth and early nineteenth centuries as an expression of the viewer's omnipotence (Koschorke 155–58). Müller presents us with the complete inversion of this relation, whereby it is not the viewer who subjugates the landscape but vice versa: "Wir reden vom 'Gesichtskreis.' Wir sind eingekreist und werden lächerlich" [We call it "the circle of vision." We are encircled and become ridiculous]. We make ourselves ridiculous by clinging to a fiction of mastery of space, by speaking nonchalantly of the horizon and thus drawing on a traditional perceptual model, the validity of which has long since become doubtful. Müller uses the term "horizon" only in order to dismantle it; the concept entails a notion of a sovereign view over that selection of space revealed to the eye, a notion that is no longer valid here. Quite the contrary: the viewer is in the center of the horizon not because his or her view dominates the horizon but because the horizon encircles him or her. If we ask what or who subjugates the perceiver in Müller's view, the foregoing argument makes it clear that it can only be one's own perception of the external space that one cannot escape. For Müller, after all, in accordance with the synthetic model, space cannot conceivably be constituted independently of the perception of that particular space. Thus what she is describing is a self-relation.

Müller's image of the horizon closing in on the body is particularly revolutionary in light of the formal character of the horizon motif. In a division of near and far, as Koschorke explains, the horizon always divides the field of that which can be experienced and thus interpreted from its opposite, and the visible from the invisible. Thus the horizon motif is used to highlight the process of signification itself, if we conceive of the sign as a configuration of visibility and invisibility. Koschorke shows that the history of the horizon describes not just the continual renegotiation of the relation between space and sign, but also the internal structure of the sign. Thus argumentation at the level of cultural history and argumentation at the level of semiological theory come together when Koschorke examines the loss of validity that the reference to horizon experienced at the beginning of modernity. The explanation from cultural history has it that there is no longer any entirely foreign distance in a world absolutely permeated by restless travel. The irretrievable loss of the invisible object behind the horizon, which had always been the object of our longing, makes lacking omnipresent and, at the same time, our longing is deprived its location; it becomes completely erratic. The poetic motif of the journey that was so central to literature from the Middle Ages into the nineteenth century is thus rendered obsolete. This declaration of invalidity for motor activity in space, as Koschorke puts it, is followed by the motor activity of writing; literature, along with the other arts, becomes self-referential: that which at the level of representation is the devaluation of distance of perspectival depth presents itself semiotically as signification becoming absolute (Koschorke 321).

Koschorke follows the course of the horizon motif up to modernity, where he ends with the conjecture that the binary structure of the horizon will disappear entirely in favor of a new way of thinking no longer oriented toward the question of immanence and its transgression. The spaces Müller describes can be seen as such a new way of thinking, as her texts seek to offer a radical answer to the question of immanence and its transgression by replacing the distinction between identity and alterity with a system of continual transgressions. As we have seen, the concept of the human person on which Müller's works rely is no longer oriented around the demarcating line between self and other, as in psychoanalysis, for example, but rather describes the individual as part of a flexible ensemble. Moreover, these continual transgressions clearly go beyond the distinction between artistic and non-artistic experience: Müller does not distinguish between a literary and a non-literary access to the world. She once described this in an interview in her typical, laconic manner as follows:

> Ich glaube, es gibt nur eine Welt. Das was du glaubst, daß da eine zweite dahinter entsteht, das gehört für mich in die erste Welt hinein. Ich glaube, die Poesie ist in der Welt, nicht in der Sprache. Die Poesie der Sprache ist ein Nonsens, es gibt die Poesie der Welt.
>
> [I believe there is only one world. What you believe, that a second world arises behind it, is part of the first world to me. I think that poetry is in the world, not in language. The poetry of language is a piece of nonsense, but there is the poetry of the world.] (Quoted in Apel, "Wahrheit und Eigensinn" 41)

Notes

1. Quotes translated by Bettina Brandt unless otherwise noted.
2. In Müller's Kleist-Preis speech: "Es gibt für das, was das Leben ausmacht, keinen Durchblick. Nur gebrechliche Einrichtungen des Augenblicks" [There is no clear perspective on what defines life. Only fragile adjustments of the moment] ("Von der gebrechlichen Einrichtung der Welt" 7).

Works Cited

Apel, Friedmar. *Deutscher Geist und deutsche Landschaft. Eine Topographie*. Munich: Albrecht Knaus, 2000.

———. "Wahrheit und Eigensinn. Herta Müllers Poetik der einen Welt." *Herta Müller. Text und Kritik* 155 (2002): 39-48.

Becker, Claudia. "Serapiontisches Prinzip in politischer Manier. Wirklichkeits- und Sprachbilder in Herta Müllers *Niederungen*." *Die erfundene Wahrnehmung: Annäherung an Herta Müller*. Ed. Norbert Otto Eke. Paderborn: Igel, 1991. 32-41.

Dawidowski, Christian. "Bild-Auflösungen: Einheit als Verlust von Ganzheit. Zu Herta Müllers *Niederungen*." *Der Druck der Erfahrung treibt die Sprache in die Dichtung. Bildlichkeit in Texten Herta Müllers*. Ed. Ralph Köhnen. Frankfurt: Peter Lang, 1997. 13-26.

Eke, Norbert Otto. "'Überall, wo man den Tod gesehen hat.' Zeitlichkeit und Tod in der Prosa Herta Müllers. Anmerkungen zu einem Motivzusammenhang." *Die erfundene Wahrnehmung: Annäherung an Herta Müller*. Ed. Norbert Otto Eke. Paderborn: Igel, 1991. 74-94.

Elias, Norbert, and John L. Scotson. *The Established and the Outsiders: A Sociological Enquiry into Community Problems*. London: Sage Publications, 1994.

Foucault, Michel. "Andere Räume. Typoskript eines Vortrages am Cercle d'Études Architectural, Paris, 14. März 1967." *Aisthesis. Wahrnehmung heute oder Perspektiven einer neuen Ästhetik*. Ed. Karlheinz Barck et al. Leipzig: Reclam, 1993. 34-46.

Günther, Michael. "Froschperspektiven. Über Eigenart und Wirkung erzählter Erinnerung in Herta Müllers *Niederungen*." *Die erfundene Wahrnehmung: Annäherung an Herta Müller*. Ed. Norbert Otto Eke. Paderborn: Igel, 1991. 42-59.

Haines, Brigid. "'Leben wir im Detail': Herta Müller's Micro-Politics of Resistance." *Herta Müller*. Ed. Brigid Haines. Cardiff: University of Wales Press, 1998. 109-25.

Köhnen, Ralph. "Über Gänge. Kinästhetische Bilder in Texten Herta Müllers." *Der Druck der Erfahrung treibt die Sprache in die Dichtung. Bildlichkeit in Texten Herta Müllers*. Ed. Ralph Köhnen. Frankfurt: Peter Lang, 1997. 123-38.

Koschorke, Albrecht. *Die Geschichte des Horizonts. Grenze und Grenzüberschreitung in literarischen Landschaftsbildern*. Frankfurt: Suhrkamp, 1990.

Löw, Martina. *Raumsoziologie*. Frankfurt: Suhrkamp, 2001.

Midgley, David. "Remembered Things: The Representation of Memory and Separation in *Der Mensch ist ein großer Fasan auf der Welt*." *Herta Müller*. Ed. Brigid Haines. Cardiff: University of Wales Press, 1998. 25-35.

Müller, Herta. *The Appointment*. Trans. Michael Hulse and Philip Boehm. New York: Picador, 2002.

———. *Der König verneigt sich und tötet*. Munich and Vienna: Hanser, 2003.

———. *Der Teufel sitzt im Spiegel. Wie Wahrnehmung sich erfindet*. Berlin: Rotbuch, 1991.

———. *Herztier*. Reinbek: Rowohlt, 1996 [1994].

———. *Heute wär ich mir lieber nicht begegnet*. Reinbek: Rowohlt, 1997.

———. *The Land of Green Plums*. Trans. Michael Hofmann. London: Granta, 1999.

———. *Nadirs*. Trans. Sieglinde Lug. Lincoln: University of Nebraska Press, 1999.

———. *Niederungen*. Reinbek: Rowohlt, 1984.

———. "Von der gebrechlichen Einrichtung der Welt. Rede zur Verleihung des Kleist-Preises 1994." *Hunger und Seide*. Reinbek: Rowohlt, 1997. 7-15.

Müller, Herta, and Renate Schmidtkunz. *Ich glaube nicht an die Sprache: Herta Müller im Gespräch mit Renata Schmidtkunz*. Audiobook. Klagenfurt: Wieser Verlag, 2009.

Müller, Philipp. "*Herztier*. Ein Titel/Bild inmitten von Bildern." *Der Druck der Erfahrung treibt die Sprache in die Dichtung. Bildlichkeit in Texten Herta Müllers*. Ed. Ralph Köhnen. Frankfurt: Peter Lang, 1997. 109-21.

Schmidt, Ricarda. "Metapher, Metonymie und Moral. Herta Müllers *Herztier*." *Herta Müller*. Ed. Brigid Haines. Cardiff: University of Wales Press, 1998. 57-74.

Shklovsky, Viktor. "Kunst als Verfahren." *Russischer Formalismus. Texte zur allgemeinen Literaturhtheorie und zur Theorie der Prosa*. Ed. Jurij Strieder. Munich: Fink, 1969. 3-35.

12 Herta Müller's Art of Reverberation

Sound in the Collage Books *Die blassen Herren mit den Mokkatassen* and *Este sau nu este Ion*

Arina Rotaru

Herta Müller belongs to a generation of ethnic German writers born in Romania who were influenced by the rhetoric of the Aktionsgruppe Banat, a group that combined experimentation with realism. Among the influences on the Aktionsgruppe Banat, dismembered by the Romanian Securitate in 1975, critics count Franz Kafka, the surrealists, *konkrete Poesie*, the theater of the absurd, *le nouveau roman*, and New American lyric and pop art (Sterbling 75; Spiridon 75, 210, 214). Müller uses experimental literary techniques such as collage and montage, primarily as inherent components of her idiosyncratic verse. In this way, her work invokes multiple literary traditions from Cubism, futurism, and Dadaism to surrealism and concrete poetry. In both theoretical and practical form, collage is featured in her work, from her poetological writings in the early 1990s (Müller, *Teufel*) to more recent publications, such as the 2005 volumes in German (*Die blassen Herren mit den Mokkatassen*) and Romanian (*Este sau nu este*

Ion). Her particular theorization of collage and her style of actualization on paper render Müller unique among contemporary writers.

An analysis of the peculiar technique of collage and montage underlying Müller's verse and image puzzles in the volumes *Die blassen Herren mit den Mokkatassen* and *Este sau nu este Ion* will bring us beyond the intense critical focus on surrealist aspects in her work as art of the image (Brandt 74–83) and enable us to understand the role of montage and collage in her work as it comes across via sound and is articulated in performance. Since major commentators have focused in particular on her art of the image, Müller's preoccupation with sound has been less explored. In support of this new thread of inquiry it is important to note that with the collage volumes from 2005 on, the author delineates an aesthetic of sound that resides in the peculiar cinematic (Köhnen 23–24) and performative quality of her phrases as well as the grid-like disposition of her verses. The digitalization of some of Müller's collages and the author's own public performances of her collages contribute to an aesthetic of sound complementary to the aesthetics of the image in her work. In this essay I will focus on close readings of collage texts in German and Romanian and pay attention to the CD in Romanian and digital recordings in both German and Romanian as constitutive parts of her collages.

Norbert Otto Eke does not regard Müller's collages as "collages in the strict sense of the word" (Eke 67). He notes that despite their reliance on found elements, not on invented ones, the components of collages consist of "Wort-Material" [word material] rather than real quotes. Critics such as Jürgen Wertheimer have provocatively declared Müller's poems to be neither "surrealistic montages nor Dadaist collages," in that the author is disassembling words just to recreate them anew and does not attempt to criticize the material of language through the material of language, as her avant-garde predecessors have done (Wertheimer 81). Yet it is important to understand to what extent these labels might apply to her work and how they bear on the definition of her poems as sound/visual or concrete.

In an effort to catalogue early collage writings such as *Der Wächter nimmt seinen Kamm. Vom Weggehen und Ausscheren* [The guard takes his comb: On leaving and going one's way; 1993] or *Im Haarknoten wohnt eine Dame*

[A lady lives in the bun; 2000], Eke proposes the term *Gesamtcollagen*, by which he recognizes the special status of collages for the author, especially with respect to their more radical approach to syntax than her prose (69). Yet Eke minimizes the meaning of collages for Müller's overall artistic project and claims that "die 'grosse' Oper findet in den Collagen nicht statt, sie ist ihnen aber ablesbar" [in the collages one can get an insight into the "big" work but this "big" work does not happen here] (69). I argue that the simultaneous release in 2005 of collage texts in Romanian and German raises new questions with respect to the overall purpose of the author's recourse to collage and resituates the confluence of image and sound in her work. In contrast to earlier collage volumes, the latest collages also display a more intense dramatic and performative character through their integration of various voices along the "lyrical" I.

The Cubists' efforts to destroy hierarchic relations in art and the futurists' attempts at the destruction of syntax merged in Guillaume Apollinaire's so-called conversation poems. It is important that Apollinaire is also the one artist who undertook an early surrealist aesthetics of sound (Schiff 139). Since Müller does not do away with syntax in the sense preached by the futurists but instead allows free "guided" association, while including fragments of speech and/or inner monologues, her collage poems, especially the recent volumes, where the dialogic principle is more evident, come closest to Apollinaire's conversation poems. Apollinaire uses a form of verbal collage comprising fragments of overheard speech, random impressions, and onomatopoeic effects "pasted" together without connecting links (Poggi 196). Müller, by keeping the general structure of the conversation poems and conveying their principle of simultaneity through telegraphic messages, letters, dialogues, and snippets of talk, furthers the critique of Communist phantasms and ethnocentric fixations present in her prose and essays. Yet the tone of the collages is a seemingly innocent one, and conversation and monologues rather than descriptive, overt criticism play an important role.

The 2005 collage work displays a model of ethnography as collage, where Müller does not favor image but voices, speech effects, slang, invective, or cacophony. In order to understand this innovative use of ethnographic allusion, I propose to adopt James Clifford's (539–64) suggestion of a parallel analysis of ethnography and surrealism based on their historical vicinity and on their techniques of comparison of cultures; in the process, no homogeneous representation results but rather a compositum that points out the "raw" data or elements of suture. In Müller's case, sound, both as conversation and soliloquy, functions as the central linking element of this juxtaposition of voices and ethnographic allusions. The space chosen by the author for ethnographic investigation and conversation is the Romanian Communist past collated with fragments from the present. In these collage texts, rhymes, refrains, and interjected sounds and voices do not smooth out the dissonances between verbal content and image; they maintain, rather, the discrepancies inherent in the concept of collage and in the dialogue at a distance between the two languages, Romanian and German. The texts in the two volumes use typography as a design equivalent for speech, in the manner of the futurists (Perloff 106). Thus various densities of ink can be read as a sign for verbal emphasis; equally invested with meaning and agency or voice are the various word fonts, sizes, and colors. Capitalizations are used to suggest vocal intensity, and color is likely used for timbre. For Müller the images that seemingly illustrate the texts double the verses by their further references to collages or photomontages. Their lack of explicit semantic coherence with the text conveys a simultaneous sense of convergence and divergence between text and image. While spatially simultaneous, text and image are not necessarily conceptually fused. Rather text and image manifest their kinetic tension through this discrepancy. The poems do not have titles, as no element is especially privileged other than by virtue of typographic size, order, or color. The collage "Die blassen Herren mit den Mokkatassen" that gives the title of the volume in German shows how Müller blends references to the Communist past with surrealist allusions and simultaneously undermines the image through performance as play on voices:

Wenn drei Straßen staubig auf dem
Rücken schlafen ist der MOND
gemein und magisch wie ein
Teigtisch rundherum die blassen

Herren mit den Mokkatassen AM
Hut hat jeder eine Zündschnur ein
Edelweiß und eine Vogelfeder EINER sagt: wir reden
hier nicht nur fundiert über die Fuchsjagd am besten
funktioniert unser Orchester von acht Mann studenlang
pfeifen wir Lieder wie "Rätätä, rätätä, morgen hamma
Schädelweh" oder "Wenn wir uns gegenübersäßen
würden wir uns nicht vergessen." WER den Respekt
verliert ALSO vier Fehler macht pro Nacht wird
in die Heimat überführt
Ja, ja, bei so EINER wie *dir*
spricht einiges dafür

[When three streets dusty
sleep on their back is the MOON
mean and magic like a
pastry table all around the pale
gentlemen with the mocha cups tucked IN
their hat each has a matchcord
an edelweiss and a bird feather ONE says: we speak
here not only in a well-grounded manner about the fox chase but
our orchestra of eight works best for hours
we whistle songs such as "tatata, tomorrow we're gonna have a
headache" or "Should we sit across from each other"
we would not forget each other." WHOEVER loses face
THAT IS makes four mistakes per night will
be sent to one's homeland
Yes, yes, with ONE like *you*
there is reason to believe so]

    The poem starts with a dreamy incantation that aligns two disparate events based on a dislocated temporality and inverted logic: "Wenn drei Straßen staubig auf dem/Rücken schlafen ist der MOND / gemein und magisch wie ein / Teigtisch rund herum…" [When three streets dusty / sleep on their back / is the moon/mean and magic as a / pastry table all around…] The dreamy landscape is perturbed by the association of two antithetical adverbial modifiers, "magisch und gemein" [magic and mean], as attributes of the moon, whose importance is also highlighted through capitalization. These surrealist dreamlike poetic images and associations are framed by inner assonances (*Straßen, staubig*) and inner rhymes (*gemein ... wie ein*). It is important to regard the author's use of surrealist imagery here and elsewhere in the volume as a tribute to the early surrealists' closeness to verse and performance rather than to image. As Christopher Schiff points out, sound was important in particular for the early surrealists and Apollinaire, with André Breton and Marcel Duchamp being indebted to Jean-Pierre Brisset's theories of assonant language (Schiff 146). Apart from inner rhymes and assonances the writing style, in different sizes and shapes, recalls futurist and Dadaist plays with typography and their association with intonation and sound. A different level of dialogue between image and sound is realized through the intercession of the humans. The pale gentlemen with the mocha cups are dressed in alpine costumes and wear bird feathers tucked onto their hats. The descriptive tone of the first images turns into a dialogic one as soon as the "pale gentlemen" begin to speak and description becomes dialogue. Through its capitalization, the pronoun *einer* [one] draws attention to the later use of the plural *wir*, when "EINER sagt: Wir reden / hier nicht nur fundiert über die Fuchsjagd" [when ONE speaks in the name of many. ONE says: We do not only discuss here / in a rigorous manner the fox chase]. The semantic component *jagd* [chase] of the compound *Fuchsjagd* [fox chase] and the bureaucratic jargon used in relation to the chase, "wir reden hier nicht nur fundiert über die Fuchsjagd," enwrap the men in a dubious aura. Furthermore, the inexhaustible orchestra of eight ("funktioniert unser Orchester von acht Mann stundenlang") symbolizes an orchestrated mechanism of power conducting incessant nonsensical human chases disguised by the use of a synecdoche, *Fuchsjagd*. The real menace of these searches is attenuated by songs. The songs, one of them transcribed phonetically, "Rätätä, rätätä, morgen hamma Schädelweh," are part of children's repertoire and/or belong to popular German rhyme culture. The intercession of this performative fragment of children's language provides a disjunction from the serious tone adopted earlier by the "one." Nevertheless, the seeming innocence of these songs is corrupted by a warning tone: "WER den respect / verliert ALSO vier Fehler macht pro Nacht wird / in die Heimat überführt" [WHOEVER loses face / THAT IS makes four mistakes per night will / be sent to one's homeland]. The poem points here to the rules of an obscure game that has power over one's destiny. The ambiguity of *Heimat* [homeland] adds to the mystery regarding the exact function of the "gentlemen with the mocha cups" and their power over the individual. The menace of being sent to one's homeland is featured as a performative action, the possible negative outcome of a game. The words and rules of the game can turn into concrete realizations and enactments of the menace they announce. Compared to the figuration of *Heimat* in Müller's essay *Heimat ist das was gesprochen wird* (2001), where homeland represents what is (potentially) articulated in speech, the actualization of *Heimat* here would point to an ominous twist and a punishment. The impersonal dialogues in the first part of the poem end with a colloquial direct address: "Ja, ja, bei so EINER wie dir / spricht einiges dafür" [Yes, yes, with ONE like you/ there is reason to believe so]. The indicting voice is anonymous, yet it transpires as the voice of a hidden instance commanding over the individual—a *Heimat* that resounds as the menacing echo of one's conscience. The value of "ONE" [EINER] here is contrasted to "EINER," the instance that speaks in first place and issues the order about the fox chase. Dramatically this last indictment "Ja, ja, bei so EINER wie *dir*" [Yes, yes, with ONE like *you*] could also be interpreted as a monologue, the scary fusion of a commandment extraneous to the individual, and the voice of one's conscience. The poem concludes on an indefinite note—"there is a certain justification" (there is reason to believe so)—which carries with it an enduring menace: one like you should be sent to one's homeland. In a literal niche of the poem, a picture depicts a blurred passport photo, a body section covered in tape, and two dangling feet tied by lace. This phantasmagoric character is suspended above earth, and its unreality is emphasized by its composition: the upper part of the body, whose mouth is taped as well, is a photographic work, whereas the lower part is a cartoon image. The merging of two cinematic techniques results in the hybrid structure of cartoon work and photography. This generic unevenness of the image is reproduced at the level of rhyme; the poem tends to rhyme internally on the level of single words rather than through end rhymes. By aligning images with verse, Müller reclaims surrealism's origin in verse (Warning 324-36; Brandt 76) and challenges the movement's focus on the image as well as her commentators' analytical preference for her imagistic art. Müller's practice of surrealism relies rather on a collation of discrepant images with voices from a recognizably Romanian Communist past and songs from the German national folk repertoire or children's song culture.

Remarking on the connection between these collage cutouts and recitation, the critic Petra Renneke, who uses the terms "montage" and "collage" interchangeably but operates in particular with a definition of "montage" close to the one outlined above, refers to Müller's 2005 collage volume in German as follows: "Die Schnittstellen der Collage gleichen dem Tempo des Atemholens, den Denketappen in ihrer Sprödigkeit, dem An-und Absetzen neuer Zeilen. Sie sind wie die Lautmalerei einzelner Gedanken" [The cutouts of collage resemble the breath tempo and the thought stages in their brittleness; they also mark the beginning and ending of various verses. They are like the sonorous depiction of single thoughts] (Renneke 247). The image Renneke associates with sound here, in an attempt to find a deeper understanding of collage in Müller's work, is derived from the visual register. This comment inhabits, however, a quite exceptional status among other observations by the critic, which are strictly bound to the visual register. *Lautmalerei*, a word usually translated as "onomatopoeia," points both to the visual and the sonorous register. Nevertheless, through this ambiguous composite word, Renneke signals important tensions in the composition of collage and its vicinity to montage, whose development was most closely associated with inner speech. By the mid-1920s, as Ian Christie notes, the idea of montage had developed far beyond its beginnings as a theory of the specificity of film and had become linked to the formalist concept of "inner speech," a kind of subjective internal "accompaniment to the experience of film viewing which facilitated the connection between separate shots" (Christie 79). Montage as the *Lautmalerei* of inner thoughts provides, first, a sonic and visual venue, and second, a sense of physical movement or transfer between an interior and an exterior sphere of expression. However, the inner speech featured in Müller's collages is far from the universal language of hermeneutics or even from the Gadamerian notion of mediation between the language/sound of the heart and that of the intellect (Oliva 42); it suggests rather a need to read and hear beyond the confines of a singular language. With Müller, collage occurs in the form of cadenced breath transmitted across material "cutouts" that have cinematic and kinetic value.

"Nehmen wir an wir sitzen schweigend auf einer Bank" [Let's suppose we are sitting silently on a bench] is an improvisation on the meaning of speech. It turns into a seemingly absurd monologue on the material value of vowels: "Du kannst doch nicht ständig Vokale kaufen / Gut, dann kauf eben noch einen Vokal" [You cannot keep buying vowels / Okay, then buy another vowel]. This puzzling line alludes to a popular television game show, *Wheel of Fortune*. When in need, contestants can literally "buy vowels" to help them solve a crossword puzzle. The puzzle model turns this sequence into a paradigmatic instance for grasping the limits of the performative. Jonathan Culler (507), following on J. L. Austin's suggestions, understands the performative as a break between meaning and the intention of the speaker. The act of buying vowels then would emerge as a negotiation between the text and the public and restore meaning in the gaps left blank by the text. The ensuing line, articulated by an external voice, plays on the value of "A" as in *Anzüge* [suits]: "Wie viele Anzüge hast du im Schrank" [How many suits do you have in the wardrobe]. The next line is uneven, as it contains in a single square unit the idiomatic commandment: "solltest du dich ganz schnell aus dem Staub machen" [you should quickly disappear from here]. This is succeeded by onomatopoeia, "Pok, pok," which suggests a sound of rapid steps. The next line, emphasized through internal rhymes, shifts the menacing tone to a playful one: "Da hab ich mir gedacht, wir spielen es nochmal Hose und Rock / im kleinen Saal ist ohnehin SILVESTERBALL" [That's when I thought, let's play it again, pants and skirt / in the small performance hall there's already a NEW YEAR'S EVE BALL]. In the last fragment of the poem, letters take on different, bigger sizes, while a poetic "I" uses hyperbolic expressions to convey its monologue: "Ich denk IN jedem Fall mental/und körperlich noch AN dein Handgelenk" [I STILL think mentally and bodily OF your wrist]. An extraneous voice then interrupts these private reflections: "Und in der Zwischenzeit im SCHRANK natürlich wirklich/wohnt dreimal der Mond und sticht/Wer hat das denn gesagt Ach, was egal Ich nicht" [And in the meantime in the WARDROBE of course really / the moon lives three times and stabs / Who said that oh, it doesn't matter it was not me]. The "I" instance gives in to intruding voices, which point to a sacrificial ritual "the moon ... stabs." This inner chiasmus is also reflected in the image attached to the poem, which suggests lack of internal cohesiveness—an L-shaped figure that is placing itself between two halves of a building and alludes to the revolutionary futurist poeticized "L" as language of the stars, whose purpose was to govern the unconscious and establish a new audio reality. If collages such as "Die blassen Herren mit den Mokkatassen" convey, across soliloquies and snippets of songs, the uncanny interference of the Communist past in the present, in this poem, the past itself turns into an inner voice of uncertain origin, brought to light through the cutouts of montage. Austin's performative was not ready to associate an inward act with a speech act (Culler 507), but montage offers the possibility of the freedom of the performative as manifested through the crevices of inner speech as exteriorization in writing and through image. Mueller's collages/montages set free that value of the performative that manifests explicitly in literature as a force of social change.

Analyzed in the context of the Romanian avant-garde, Müller's use of montage/collage practices might count not only as a liberating strategy of the performative but also as an attempt at breaking away, in the spirit of the Romanian avant-gardes, from an ethnocentric canon (Cernat 34). One exemplification of the futility of ethnocentric ambitions is the poem "Das Limit prahlt" [The limit vaunts], which thematizes both semantically and figuratively a hypothesized clash or separation between languages (German and Romanian) in the spirit of ethnocentric pride. The limit, in this sense, performs its own rebellion against national, generic, and linguistic delimitation. The poem is accompanied by a cutout of a fantastic creature, half man, half animal; the two-dimensional profile has the outline of a dog, but the three-dimensional photographs that make up the dog's profile consist of totally different perspectives and include part of a white chef's shirt with protruding long sleeves that add human arms to the dog creature. The poem that follows describes not only a composite creature, "zweidrittel Hund in Anthrazit" [two-thirds dog in anthracite], but also a puzzle of languages that cannot be contained by one-dimensional spatiality or language:

> DAS Limit prahlt
> Als Vorteil im Zusammenhalt
> Zwei Drittel Hund in Anthrazit
> ZUM STREICHELN SCHÖN
> mir wird so kalt
> sein AUG rinnt aus
> du bist nicht da komm lass uns gehn
> die Laus TRINKT BLUT in LILA
> mă cam doare bil a. mă cam doare bil a.

> [THE Limit vaunts
> as an advantage of coherence
> two-thirds dog in anthracite
> GOOD FOR FONDLING
> I am getting so cold
> his EYE is trickling out
> you are not there come on let us go
> the louse is DRINKING BLOOD in PURPLE
> my gall/mind is hurting me]

The word *Zusammenhalt* [coherence or fusion], a key term for the unusual linguistic and imagistic fusion of this poem, has a colored background, three-quarters in red, and one-quarter in a lighter shade. The waning color of *halt* might indicate a lack of coherence or fusion. After an initial description in the third person, the poem switches to a moaning monologue and nightmarish scenery: "mir wird so kalt / sein Aug rinnt aus" [I am getting so cold / his eye is trickling out]. Vision extinguishes gradually and is replaced by sound in the form of a lone voice: "du bist nicht da komm lass uns gehn" [you are not there come on let us go]. The last two lines belong to an absurd repertoire, with the last line in colloquial Romanian: "mă cam doare bil a." This expression can be interpreted paronomastically, as it means both "I suffer slightly from headaches" and "my gall is hurting me." *Bil a* is written in a fractured manner and displays a physical gap between *bil* and *a*; the split identity of the poematic subject itself emerges in nuce here and is revealed as the result of a discomfort. If we consider Dick Higgins's vision of the sound poem as a new medium to be composed by means of mixtures between two languages of any origin, performed across puns (Higgins 52), then we have here, with this novel humorous hybrid combination of languages and semantics, not only a new genre but also a construct whose highlight, the phrase in Romanian, signals the impossibility to contain two languages in the single scriptural space of a poem without some seeming discomfort: "mă cam doare bil a." We could ask then whether Romanian is to be read/heard in this context as the unintelligible rest in a collage where German plays the main role or whether Romanian is rather the hermetic twist of the poem. The answer is offered neither by translation nor by visual correspondences but rather by sound as a euphonic non-translatable and non-visual element.

The volume *Este sau nu este Ion*, released in the same year as *Die blassen Herren mit den Mokkatassen*, is written entirely in Romanian, although it comprises a singular phonetic transcription in Russian, "Şto takoi," which seems to be used for the purpose of rhyme. If the volume in German contained its sounds in the phonographic space of writing (Schenk 43), the Romanian volume, with the author's performance on CD attached, probes the performance value of poems on tape. It should be noted, however, that the site www.lyrikline.org contains four collages in German in their recorded form. Through their articulation in Romanian, Müller's poems not only add a new valence to her graphics, shadows, and material bodies of verses but also complement her other collages in German with vocal impersonations.

The poem "Adio, patria mea" [Farewell, my homeland] features the crossed-out emblem of a saxophone—the possible symbol of a hymn to a country that no longer exists. The first line, indented as if for a paragraph heading, "Adio, patria mea cu î din i, cu â din a" [Farewell to my homeland written with î, written with â"], alludes to writing reforms that were introduced in Romania during Sovietization, beginning in 1953 and with the last of them in 1993, a few years after the fall of communism.[1] Except for a relatively brief period (1953-64), the country's name was spelled with an "î," as Romînia; all other words previously written with

Adio, patria mea cu î din i, cu â din a

Ăăă, rău, bă, dă-mi niște bani să mă ăsta
Bă, tu mă parcă văd că ăla dă
hai, bă, dînsul păr în gît îi cîine mă
cît îl mîngîi mînca sîrmă
Bă, mă vîr o săptămînă
pînă îmi dă zahăr mă
O să fie găinărie
că și ăstia bătuți măr
mîine o să-și ia țigări

13. "Adio, patria mea." From *Este sau nu este Ion* (Editura Polirom).
(Copyright Herta Müller.)

an "â" continued to be written with an "î" until the most recent reform. The reform of 1993 was said to return Romanian words spelled with an "î" to an earlier spelling before Stalinization with an "â." Numerous Romanian linguists have deplored this reform since it apparently introduced chaos in writing.² In the first line, the auctorial voice is bidding farewell to two homophonous countries, one before and one after the spelling reform. Unusual for a volume where verse lines are cut out and written against backgrounds in different colors and nuances, the first line of the collage is written against a uniformly orange background, and only one cut separates "Farewell my homeland" from the next sequence colored in gray. This phonic and written farewell can be interpreted as an irony directed at the impossibility of a spelling reform to return Romania to pre-Communist times. After the first symbolic farewell, a strikingly different tone is set in place. Dialogues conducted in slang reproduce interactions between men who seem to belong to the Romanian underworld. The world of the properly written "â" is replaced by numerous words featuring "ă," one of the vowels of the Romanian alphabet that does not exist in other languages: "Ăăă, rău, bă, dă-mi nişte bani să mă ăsta / Bă, tu mă parcă văd că ăla dă / hai, bă, dînsul păr în gît îi cîine mă / cît îl mîngîi mînca sîrmă" [In approximate translation: Ăăă, it's bad, man, give me some money or I blow it off / come on, man, the one with dog hair in his throat is a dog / when I pat him he eats wire]. Other lines allude to the extreme austerity of Communist times and stage it in colloquial terms: "Pînă îmi dă zahăr mă / o să fie găinărie" [Until I get sugar listen to me buddy / there will be a mess]. Nowhere in the poem does the author adopt the exigencies of the reform: she spells all words with an "î," as was customary in the country she left in 1987. Multiple voices, whose colorful speech is almost "tangible" through intonation, are heard within the frame of the poem and complement the lyrical I. The numerous argotic repetitions and invocations have almost a formulaic nuance, as they all hypostasize the "ă." The assonant rhymes in "ă" also perpetuate this unusual vowel, which is mirrored by multiple argotic *bă* [hey man] and informal *mă* [hey you]. The country's pretentious hymns and formal rigors have been replaced by a new liberty of expression encrypted, ironically, in the prolonged "unmelodious" "ă." In her recitation on CD, the author accents the letters in a way that is directly mirrored on the graphic level: higher and lower pitches dictate higher and lower letter/unit levels. In "hai, bă, dînsul păr în gît îi cîine mă" we can follow precisely the cadence of the voice that raises the pitch when articulating *păr* and lowers it when pronouncing the following words, with *mă* on the lowest scale.

The arrangement of word units on the page corresponds to the inflections of the voice. For instance, "rău, bă, dă-mi nişte bani," which shares the same unit and colored background, is read almost in a single breath. Phonetics dictates graphics and is filling in the blanks of the image in a collage whose pictorial correspondent, the crossed-out saxophone, points to forbidden or erased sounding. If the first image of the poem, the crossed-out saxophone, signals a canceled performance, the dialogic performance that follows seems to enact this erasure and embody it in a recognizable past of attrition. The notion of homeland invoked in the title evades official hymnic intonation and is articulated instead through a vocal and argotic farewell. In an earlier essay Müller defined *Heimat*, in the sense of Jorge Semprún, as "what is spoken/articulated in speech" (Müller, *Heimat ist das was gesprochen wird* 26) and thus emphasized the volatile performative nuance and the potentiality inherent in the concept. In the present collage, "homeland" is removed from the sphere of potentiality and articulated, by contrast, as a past of voices encrypted on the tympanum. The writer as reciter contributes to the humorous reconstruction of facts from the underworld through the staccato accentuation of words as in "o să *fie*, găinări*e*" [there will be a mess] or the phonetic elision of the "i" in the final word of the collage, *ţigări* [cigarettes].

The title poem of the volume, "Este sau nu este Ion," carries a subtitle, "Roman naţional pe scurt interval" [National novel on short wavelengths]. This poem is the only one in the volume that has an identifiable title, separated from the rest through a spatial gap. The piece "rewrites" the famous 1920 Romanian novel *Ion* by major interwar writer Liviu Rebreanu in two very schematized parts and a conclusion. Rebreanu's novel, favored by the Communist regime for illustrating the attachment to one's homeland, documents the life of peasants before World War I against the background of a family drama. The national ethnographic style of the novel is, however, the exact opposite of what the Romanian avant-gardes, in particular the Dadaists and the surrealists, attempted to perform through their dissolution of ethnographic boundaries during the same timeframe (Wichner n.p.). Müller's "rewrite" performs its own dissolve of the novel and its embodiment of love for the homeland by using color, graphics, and word fonts to suggest a dissolve of printed space. In this spatial dissolve, two genres are conflated, a novel and a poem, as well as two media, a printed novel and a broadcast novel. In Müller's vision the first part of the novel reads: "un strat de muşte pe gard confuz în sus, / o coadă simplă de lopată zdrăngăne bum, bum- / plecăm fără batistă oarecum" [a flight of flies confused up on a fence, / a simple shovel handle is thrumming bum, bum- / we leave without a handkerchief somehow]. End rhymes disguise a lack of semantic unity, whereas the line "we leave without a handkerchief" at the end of a series of descriptions of rural life points to the failure of a performance to impress the audience. In my reading, this may be an allusion to the very strategy of collage and montage to steer away one's audience from a cathartic effect or identification of the audience with the work. In light of Müller's 2009 Nobel Prize speech, "Plecăm fără batistă" can be interpreted as leaving behind the possibility of any shelter or existential anchorage (Müller, *Every Word Knows Something of a Vicious Circle* 5). The lack of coherence or unity in the genre of montage/collage is reproduced at the level of consonants and harsh sounds: *zdrăngăne* is a highly cacophonic word through its dental alveolars "d," "t," and "z," and so is the plump noise "bum, bum." Cacophony could also be the result of the discordant transference of genres, from the written to the short wavelengths of the ether. The second section of the collage removes the action into another spatial and temporal dimension dominated by grim borders: "iar vameşii din Giurgiu (şase) nici măcar nu se/uită la mine, atîta vreme cît trece un cîine" [and the custom-house officers in Giurgiu (six) don't even look at me, as long as a dog is passing]. The conclusion reads abruptly: "Nimic bre, / că intri la pîrnaie" [Nothing, dude, or else you end up in jail]. The poem thus ends hermetically on a stifling and menacing note. If the first part is narrated from the perspective of a "we," in the second part an "I" comes to the fore, while in the conclusion an impersonal voice takes the floor. The mock existential dilemma of the title ("Este sau nu este Ion"; Is there an Ion or not; it might also be read, anagrammatically, as "Is there a 'noi' [an *us*], or not") concludes on a colloquial note overwritten "Concluzie" [Conclusion], which offers the laconic option to end the dialogue abruptly for fear of jail: "Nimic, bre" [Nothing, dude]. It is hard to determine where the present ends and where the pre-Communist past begins in this ironic transcription of a national emblematic novel rewritten as if for a broadcast-simplified transmission. The narrative is dispersed in voices that simulate the cuts of montage and correspond to fragments of exteriorized speech. On the CD recording, the voice of the author uses clear caesuras as markers for the change of color on the page. The second part of the verse lines has a deeper and heavier intonation, as in "confuz în sus" or "zdrăngăne bum, bum" and thematizes the bathos created by this ironic sonic "rewrite" of a national novel. The image, integrated in a niche of the poem, is marginal, but it reinforces the sense of a barrier or limit not to be transgressed: against a grim background, the scribbled silhouette of a dog is heading in the opposite direction of a fence.

Müller's CD recitation of her poems in Romanian can be interpreted along the lines provided by Charles Bernstein's reflections on the acoustic inscription of an author's voice (Bernstein 144–45). According to Bernstein, who analyzes the early recordings of modernist poetry, the gramophonic inscription offers a "thicker" description of the voice, especially by highlighting what he calls "vocal gestures": "the cluster of *rhythm* and *tempo* (including *word duration*), the cluster of *pitch* and *intonation* (including *amplitude*), *timbre*, and *accent*" (Bernstein 144). In Bernstein's vision, rhythm and pitch/intonation are not something inherent in the alphabetic script of the poem but are extended, modified, improvised, invented, or enacted in performance.

The recorded CD in Romanian displays a case of mediatization as opposed to live performance (Auslander 51), with the author's voice accompanying in ether, via the audio recording, the cuts of collage. In addition, the digitalized collages from the Internet site www.lyrikline.org (eight in number, four in Romanian and four in German) turn one form of media, the CD, into a digitalized voice resounding from a screen. In the 2010 exhibition on Müller's work, Der kalte Schmuck des Lebens [The cold ornament of life], organized by the Literaturhaus Berlin, collages are magnified as posters, adding one more dimension to the possibility of experiencing them in a double fashion, visually and on an audio guide.

The recitation on CD mediates between an ethnographic space of image and verse and its dormant sonorities and regionalisms. This mixture of ethnography and sonority as gesturing voice comes forth in the collage "Băăăăăă," present in digital form on the lyrikline.org portal. The poem starts with the argotic "Băăăăăă" [Hey dude] and continues in telegraphic form, with rhyming single-word or elliptical verse structures: "secetă / Mitică / pierdut vacă, / căutat geaba mă / nu găsit / trezit şopîrlă, / mică / indoielnică / tare frică / omorît" [drought / Mitică / lost cow / looking hopelessly / not found / awoken lizard / suspicious / terrified / killed]. In the image, still nature is represented as a slice of melon with holes instead of seeds, an allusion to the missing parts of verbal ellipsis. Words occur in rapid succession and are articulated on tape as a cavalcade of telegraphic details. One could say that collage, the alliteration of text and image, becomes here alliteration of text, image, and enacted sound, as the cuts of collage are also reproduced at the level of phrase and recitation as dramatic sectioning of the flux of speech. Through the repetitive pun on the vowel "ă" and its functioning as a micro particle generative of an echo, the poem displays features of nonsense and sound poetry. Furthermore, the colloquial and argotic *mă* or *bă* act as found sound material. The effect of vision and sound in the digital recording creates a performance in the absence of the author, a performance that is, nevertheless, animated by the gestures of colloquial speech, the body of letters, and the cadence of voice.

According to Quintilian's theory of performance as *actio*, the delight derived from the recitation and listening of poetry surpasses the pleasure of the written text (Quintilian 2–4). Furthermore, as Quintilian emphasizes, the speaking body is not something placed outside but rather inside the text. In this grounding theory of rhetoric, it is not as important to watch the body of the speaker in space as it is to pay attention to its movements in writing, where they manifest as performance. In "Da, înăuntru şi-n afară" [Yes, within and without], also present on lyrikline.org, the detail of a hand is superimposed next to a tambourine. The hand is not beating the drum but barely touching it. The performative dimension of recitation has its physical embodiment not in the text itself, as Quintilian would have it, but in the image. Since the first word of the poem is "yes," the poem appears to start as the continuation of a dialogue. However, the lines do not seem to belong to a particular "actor" but rather to a sententious instance. The impersonal voice here, a type of "voiceover," is the correspondent of a hand reaching out of frame in the accompanying image:

Da, înăuntru și afară:
parcă pentru prima oară,
viața e în ordine
e pornită
este unsă paradită
e umflată de pe stradă
confundată
e făcută bicicletă
pardon, nu se împrumută

[Yes, within and without:
maybe for the first time,
life is in order.
it is set out
it is anointed ruined
it is sequestered from the street,
mixed up
it is made into a bike
sorry, not for rent]

The colors in the poem mirror the constitution of the objects in the image: the cutout hand is in orange tones and set in relief over a fragment from a fresco painted in rusty brown, white, and black. The poem plays on the sizes and versions of "be": the conjugated verb "be" appears in four instances in the beginning of verses, and thus true rhyming seems to be achieved through anaphors "e pornită/este unsă paradită/e umflată de pe stradă." By contrast to an analysis that reads the collages as bodies in fragments and as an expression of a disjunction between mind and body (Marven 103–14), I see here, in this poem and elsewhere, rather a continuity of mind as recitation and gesturing poematic body. On screen and on the sheet, on tape and on stage, the body of the poem transgresses the limits of scripturality and manifests as performance. The decision of the author to write and record a volume of collages in Romanian can be regarded as an effort to give sonic expression to the generic cuts of montage and collage, in addition to reevaluating conventions that have collages read as text-image binaries. The recorded collages also display the author's return to Romanian as sound.

Müller highlights the original sound rhetoric inherent in collage and montage by allowing for her collages' technological processing on tape and by reciting them in front of international audiences. Through these live and recorded performances, and through the simultaneous release of the two volumes, two languages are inaugurated that do not translate each other, nor look at each other, nor contain each other but rather reverberate and gesture to one another.

Notes

1. See http://www.acad.ro/alteInfo/pag_norme_orto.htm.
2. See www.pruteanu.ro/103deceidini.htm.

Works Cited

Auslander, Philip. *Liveness: Performance in a Mediatized Culture*. London: Routledge, 1999.

Bernstein, Charles. "*Hearing Voices*." *The Sound of Poetry/The Poetry of Sound*. Ed. Marjorie Perloff and Craig Dworkin. Chicago and London: University of Chicago Press, 2009. 142-49.

Brandt, Bettina. "Schnitt durchs Auge. Surrealistische Bilder bei Yoko Tawada, Emine Sevgi Ozdamar und Herta Müller." *Text und Kritik* 9 (2006): 74-83. Sonderband. Ed. Heinz Ludwig Arnold. Munich: Richard Boorberg Verlag.

Cernat, Paul. *Avangarda română și complexul periferiei*. Bucharest: Polirom, 2007.

Christie, Ian. "Soviet Cinema Making Sense of Sound." *Wide Angle* 15.1 (1993): 35. *Sound and Music in Film and Visual Media: An Overview*. Ed. Graham Harper. New York and London: Continuum, 2009.

Clifford, James. "On Ethnographic Surrealism." *Comparative Studies in Society and History* 23.4 (1981): 539-64.

Culler, Jonathan. "The Fortunes of the Performative." *Poetics Today* 21.3 (Fall 2000): 503–19.

Eke, Norbert Otto. "Herta Müllers Weg zum Gedicht." *Text und Kritik* 155 (July 2002): 64–80.

Higgins, Dick. *The Poetics and Theory of Intermedia*. Carbondale and Edwardsville: Southern Illinois University Press, 1984.

Köhnen, Ralph. "Terror und Spiel. Der autofiktionale Impuls in frühen Texten Herta Müllers." *Text und Kritik* 155 (July 2002): 18–29.

Marven, Lyn. *Body and Narrative in Contemporary Literatures in German: Herta Müller, Libuse Monikova, and Kerstin Hensel*. Oxford: Clarendon Press, 2005. 103–14.

Müller, Herta. *Der Teufel sitzt im Spiegel. Wie Wahrnehmung sich erfindet*. Berlin: Rotbuch. 1991.

———. *Der Wächter nimmt seinen Kamm. Vom Weggehen und Ausscheren*. Reinbek: Rowohlt, 1993.

———. *Die blassen Herren mit den Mokkatassen*. Munich: Carl Hanser, 2005.

———. *Este sau nu este Ion*. Iași: Polirom, 2005. Print and CD.

———. *Every Word Knows Something of a Vicious Circle*. Trans. Philip Boehm. Nobel Foundation, 2009.

———. *Heimat ist das was gesprochen wird*. Blieskastel: Gollenstein, 2001.

———. *Im Haarknoten wohnt eine Dame*. Reinbek: Rowohlt. 2000.

Oliva, Mirela. *Das innere Verbum in Gadamers Hermeneutik*. Tübingen: Mohr Siebeck, 2009.

Perloff, Nancy. "Sound Poetry and the Musical Avant-Garde: A Musicologist's Perspective." *The Sound of Poetry/The Poetry of Sound*. Ed. Marjorie Perloff and Craig Dworkin. Chicago and London: University of Chicago Press, 2009. 97–118.

Poggi, Christine. *In Defiance of Painting: Cubism, Futurism and the Invention of Collage*. New Haven and London: Yale University Press, 1992.

Pruteanu, George. "De ce scriu cu î din î." Web. http://www.acad.ro/alteInfo/pag_norme_orto.htm.

Quintilian, Marcus Fabius. *Ausbildung des Redners*. 12 vols. Trans. Helmut Rahn. Darmstadt, 1975. Vol. 11:3, 2–4.

Renneke, Petra. *Poesie und Wissen. Poetologie des Wissens der Moderne*. Heidelberg: Universitätsverlag Winter, 2008.

Schenk, Klaus. *Medienpoesie: Moderne Lyrik zwischen Stimme und Schrift*. Stuttgart: Metzler, 2000.

Schiff, Christopher. "Banging on the Window Pane: Sound in Early Surrealism." *The Wireless Imagination*. London: MIT Press, 1992. 139-91.

Spiridon, Olivia. *Untersuchungen zur rumäniendeutschen Erzählliteratur der Nachkriegszeit*. Oldenburg: Igel, 2002.

Sterbling, Anton. *"Am Anfang war das Gespräch": Reflexionen und Beiträge zur 'Aktionsgruppe Banat' und andere literatur- und kunstbezogene Arbeiten*. Hamburg: Krämer, 2008.

Warning, Rainer. "Der Traum der Surrealisten." *Fragment und Totalität*. Ed. Lucien Dällenbach and Christiaan L. Hart Nibbrig. Frankfurt: Suhrkamp, 1984. 324-36.

Wertheimer, Jürgen. "Im Papierhaus wohnt die Stellungnahme. Zu Herta Müllers Bild-Text-Collagen." *Text und Kritik* 155 (July 2002): 80-85.

Wichner, Ernest. "In einer anderen Zunge reden wir. Zwischen Avantgarde und Anpassung—Die Literatur Rumäniens." *Stuttgarter Zeitung*, March 24, 1998. Print.

13 Accumulating Histories
Temporality in Herta Müller's "Einmal anfassen—zweimal loslassen"

Katrina Nousek

On May 11–13, 2000, eight authors came together at the University of Tübingen to speak on the topic "Zukunft! Zukunft?" [Future! Future?]. The lectures addressed the possibility of and limitations to thinking a notion of time that includes the idea of a future. Many sought to articulate a future-oriented indebtedness to past and present moments that could adequately represent subjective experience. Among these efforts was Herta Müller's contribution, later published under the title "Einmal anfassen—zweimal loslassen" [Catch hold once—let go twice].[1] Though the essay underscores the inextricability of past and present, it also implies an important potential for change dependent on individuals' ability to locate their subjective experience historically and socially. The narrating subject of Müller's essay reflects on her association of her past experiences in Communist Romania with her contemporary experiences in Germany. She is unable to shed these associations despite the time that has passed, her spatial relocation, and the end of the Communist dictatorship in Romania. Representing the narrator's subjective experience therefore requires articulating a post-socialist future that recognizes the influences of past experience under a Communist dictatorship. In what follows I wish to shed light on the complex literary strategies Müller develops to demonstrate the inadequacy of representing subjective experience within a temporal structure divided into past, present, and future. Her interrogation of temporal conceptions may be read as the potential for articulating a post-socialist future that does not collapse into a mere repetition of the past despite recognizing a fundamental connection with experiences in a Communist dictatorship. By actively appropriating her history, the narrating subject opens the potential for future change that requires a confrontation with history, a future in which history must be acknowledged but not necessarily relived.

Müller's essay opens with an allusion to the narrating subject's project of demonstrating the inadequacy of existing temporal categories for representing subjective experience: "Die Splitter aus der Vergangenheit könnten mir selber nicht so unerhört grell und neu durch die Gegenwart gehen, wenn ich sie seinerzeit, als sie gelebter Augenblick waren, durchschaut hätte" [The shards from the past could not get to me so shockingly garish and new through the present if I had seen through them at the time when they were experienced moments] (29). This sounds at first like a confirmation that hindsight is always perfect, but as the text unfolds, it becomes clear that the relationship between past and present time is not simply one of knowledge gained too late. Rather the present moment in the text is one of recycled pasts or new events that reveal themselves as returning variations of old ones. The early experiences of the autobiographical narrator in German communities in the Romanian Banat and later during the dictatorship of Ceaușescu provide a vocabulary through which she interprets the rest of her life. Her past imprints not only her memories but also her experiences to come. The relationship between past and present that constitutes her experience requires a complex mode of narration for its representation. Convoluted syntax and word plays in expressions such as "Ich treff meine Vegangenwart in der Gegenheit seit meiner Zukunft" [I meet my past-present in the present-past since my future] reveal the narrator's dissatisfaction with the existing categories of temporality that distinguish three main stages and often suggest a linear progression from past through present toward future (Müller 29).[2] Though the narrator foregrounds this difficulty explicitly, I hope to show how the text builds an implicit network of temporal associations based on a common vocabulary of images *not* foregrounded for the reader's attention. The text thus presents a stylistic solution that works in tandem with the author's theoretical articulation of temporal relations to bring the present moment and its temporal implications to light.

Andreas Huyssen's discussion of conceptions of temporality at the turn of the twenty-first century provides a useful point of orientation for thinking about Müller's essay and the aims of the Tübingen conference in general. In *Twilight Memories*, Huyssen argues that the growing concerns with memory, monuments, and commemoration in the German context can be read as a crisis of conceptions of temporality. Whereas the turn of the twentieth century marked the rise of a modernist discourse that celebrated innovation, a utopian moment of radical difference, and a type of memory that forgets the objectifying course of history in the capitalist present, the turn of the twenty-first century marks an interest in memory as the possibility of finding temporal grounding amid an increasingly innovative and heterogeneous culture. Huyssen suggests, "Perhaps what we are currently witnessing as the exhaustion of utopian energies vis-à-vis the future is only the result of a shift within the temporal organization of the utopian imagination from its futuristic pole toward the pole of remembrance, not in the sense of a radical turn, but in the sense of a shift of emphasis" (87–88). His analysis further elaborates the complexity with which specific artistic works, postmodern theories, and commemoration attempts in contemporary culture engage with history.

Huyssen's reframing of the conceptual challenge toward which diverse examples of post-1960s German culture are directed can help bring important aspects of Müller's essay to light. Though Huyssen formulates the structure of temporality in various aspects of contemporary culture in terms of a shift in the utopian moment—"utopia," a word that appears relatively infrequently in the Tübingen conference contributions and not at all in Müller's essay—and his discussion of destabilized categories of national identity in the contexts of immigration and German unification does not delve into the specificities of the German-speaking populations in the Banat, his formulation of a general cultural attempt "to think memory and amnesia together rather than simply to oppose them" is highly relevant to Müller's text (7). Whereas previous scholarship, especially that developed through trauma theory, foregrounds the effects of fragmentation in and through Müller's literary style, I wish to bring into relief the deep-set connectedness at work in her narration, whereby multiple points of a text are joined through association. Instead of reading her narrative as the articulation of subjective experience interrupted by trauma, I propose a reading that emphasizes her exploration of a particular structure of temporality in which future possibilities must necessarily and consciously be understood in historically inscribed terms. In "Einmal anfassen" this exploration occurs on the level of explicit theorization of temporal relations, a thematization of these relations through examples from the narrator's life, and an implicit demonstration of temporal relations for the reader. Theoretically and thematically the first-person subject attempts to narrate what are described as physical objects in a manner that can access multiple associations existing seemingly simultaneously within them. Images and objects accrue associations that, at the point one describes them, take the form of a history of the object in terms of the various contexts that have come to define it—in other words, what is called in German an *Entstehungsgeschichte*, or history of origins. Recognizing and recalling this history allows for a means of location or positioning that, although it may be invoked in part through the use of temporal categories such as past, present, and future, also recognizes the instability and inadequacy of these categories.[3] According to this reading, the circulation of images and the use of repetition characteristic of Müller's style can be seen less as a traumatic stutter and more as the gradual formation of another history that works in tandem with the histories explicitly described. The reader is encouraged to find a kind of grounding by engaging with these explicit and implicit histories as well.

In what follows I focus on three moments in Müller's text that can be read as confrontations with the *Entstehungsgeschichte* of physical objects as represented in the text. All of these moments are in some way related to the image of a nightgown, around which most of the reflections in the text are organized. The main confrontation involves the history of this nightgown as it develops through the narrator's association of four nightgowns she sees at different periods in her life. The first nightgown, a gift from her grandmother, becomes a point of relation to which she connects a nightgown she sees on another woman on a train, a nightgown an employer gives her, and a nightgown she sees on a woman called Inge Wenzel in an advertisement for the Deutsche Bahn or DB. As the narrator describes how she associates these four nightgowns, she repeats the capitalized phrase "INGE WENZEL ON THE WAY TO RIMINI" several times. The association among nightgowns and the repeated phrase (later revealed to be a citation from the DB advertisement) both foreground and demonstrate the process of constructing a history. The two other confrontations with *Entstehungsgeschichten* are moments within the nightgown history that become crucial to my reading. One involves slogans that the narrator's friend develops to sell two of the nightgowns at a flea market, and the other involves the history the narrator imagines for the woman wearing the nightgown as pictured in the advertisement. Keeping in mind Huyssen's arguments about the possible grounding that a future-oriented preoccupation with history may offer, I argue that Müller's text can be read as a search for this grounding and a testament to the emancipatory possibilities that make it worth finding.

The mutual inextricability of various temporal dimensions in Müller's text is explicitly thematized in the image of a nightgown that the narrator purports to encounter four times since her childhood in both Romania and Germany. The narrator reflects, "Wie bei den Nachthemden gehen von Anfang an Vergangenheit, Gegenwart und Zukunft durcheinander" [Like the nightgowns, past, present, and future mix together from the beginning on] (27). These four recurrences of the nightgown become pivotal for narration. The first was sewn for the narrator, we are told, by her grandmother as her "Nachthemd für mit auf den Weg vom Dorfzuhause in die Welt" [Nightgown for taking on the way from village-home into the world] when Müller began secondary school as a young girl in Romania (Müller 32). The second is worn by a railway passenger with a hairstyle resembling in surrealistic fashion "einer pelzüberzogenen Teekanne" [a fur-coated teapot] (34).[4] This passenger slept in the narrator's train compartment on a trip from Timișoara to Bucharest during which the narrator was smuggling documents for Amnesty International. The third nightgown, made of Hungarian nylon, was a gift from the owner of a fur factory in Romania whose children the narrator had tutored in German; the fourth is modeled by someone called Inge Wenzel in what is revealed to be an advertisement on the walls of the train on the way to Marburg.

For the reader the experience of the nightgown unfolds on two levels. The first level is explicit: the "Hin und Her vom Anfassen und Loslassen" [back and forth of catching hold and letting go], essential to Müller's articulated theory of temporal relations as laid out in the first paragraph of the text, is mirrored by the content of the narrative as the essay moves restlessly from the first-person narrator's current experiences in Germany to her past in Romania through her associations with the objects and surroundings she encounters. The reader is first introduced to the nightgown motif in the train advertisement—the most recent form of the nightgown in the narrator's life—and learns of the original nightgown and its subsequent forms from the narrator's memories as the image of a nightgown spurs them. As the narrative continues, the stories behind the nightgowns become increasingly gruesome. When the narrator smuggles a manuscript between Timișoara and Bucharest, she gets a feeling of mortal fear [*Todesangst*] that becomes connected with the nightgown she sees on the train. This fear is then associated with an actual death when she recalls a friend in Romania who had sold the other two gowns at a flea market. The narrator remembers that shortly before the end of Ceaușescu's reign this friend was found hanged in his house and the death was officially reported as suicide. The longer the narration continues, the deeper the reader penetrates into the narrator's increasingly gruesome associations. On one level the narration can be seen as Müller's working through of a traumatic past. It serves as a space for articulating events one could not otherwise confront. Much scholarship has productively probed Müller's work in relation to trauma theory, and I will return to this point below. On another level, however, the repetition of a textual element within the narrative becomes for the reader a process of accumulation whereby the textual element accrues associations as the narrator presents it in various contexts. The first-person narrator may articulate traumatic experiences, but something different happens on the level of the reader. By exploring this latter experience, my reading goes against the grain of the dominant approach to Müller's work through trauma theory to focus on the development of a history through the repetition of textual fragments within the essay.

Scholars such as Brigid Haines, Beverley Driver Eddy, and Lyn Marven have gained insight into Müller's work by using trauma theory to show how the literary strategies and subjectivity present in her texts are the result of Müller's expression of her repressed past.[5] These analyses address the impact of Müller's biography on her literature and compellingly examine the implications of trauma for the author's style of narration. Paying specific attention to Müller's collages, Lyn Marven notes, "Müller's corporeal images of trauma center on three key forms: dissociation, the experience of the self as other and the splitting of the self into two (or more) elements or identities; the dissolution of the boundaries between the body and the world; and the fragmentation of the body" (399). I wish to retain this apt description of the text but also to shift the emphasis from a representation of trauma to an interrogation of stable categories. "Einmal anfassen" opens a space that contests categories of subjectivity and temporality alike even in reference to experience that is in part traumatic. The essay emphasizes not the psychological consequences of this experience but rather the social contexts that mediate it.

Müller's autobiographical narrator develops a mode of social and historical location via a network of associations through which the textual subject and the reader may navigate an *Entstehungsgeschichte* that also allows for a future. The narrator's vocabulary, derived from her past, is composed of a finite set of images that circumscribe her language. By calling on the reader's existing associations as well as associations gleaned by the reader from the text, Müller is able to represent the way in which the trauma of the narrative subject's past has permanently infiltrated her perceptive capacities. The result for the reader is not so much a traumatic narrative but rather the development of an associative network that connects a repeated textual fragment across the various contexts in which it appears within the essay—in short, a history. Although the psychological working through of traumatic experience might also be understood as the articulation of a subjective history, the history developed in Müller's essay calls attention to the social constraints beyond the narrating subject that are at work in the representation of her subjective experience.

The textual transformations of the nightgown are primarily responsible for the trajectory of the narrative, but in order to understand more fully what is at stake in its transitions from one form to another, I will first focus on the narrator's description of her early experience in Marburg after she left Romania. This episode, itself associated with the nightgown, occurs as a diversion immediately after the first appearance of the Inge Wenzel advertisement on the train. In Marburg the narrator lives near the river Lahn. One day she sees several ducks feeding and preening there. As she describes the sight, she recognizes that her interpretation of it is derived from her experience of the excesses of Ceauşescu's dictatorship in Romania:

> Sie tranken nicht, sie aßen Wasser—ihre Schnäbel waren goldenes Besteck, ihre Schwimmhäute goldene Wasserhähne, die das kalte und das warme Wasser mischten. Sowas denkst du dir jetzt nicht, nahm ich mir vor, als ich es beobachtet und mit dem goldenen Besteck und den goldenen Wasserhähnen des Diktators verknüpft hatte.
>
> [They did not drink, they ate the water—their beaks were golden cutlery, their webbed feet golden faucets that mixed the cold and the warm water. You don't think that sort of thing to yourself now, I resolved when I had watched it and connected it with the golden cutlery and golden faucets of the dictator.] (Müller 30)

Two aspects of this passage are particularly significant for my reading: the imagery of material worth used to describe the ducks and the second-person pronoun you [*du*] with which the narrator addresses herself. The translation of the ducks' bills from yellow [*gelben*] in the preceding description to gold [*golden*] here marks a reinterpretation of the scene from optical perception to terms of material worth. The narrator explicitly links her thoughts to Ceauşescu, but there is also an implicit connection here to the fur-teapot haircut of the passenger on the train to Bucharest. In both instances animate objects acquire the figurative qualities of highly valued luxury goods. The political and socioeconomic connotations of this imagery suggest many interesting readings, but here I will focus on the recognition of the connection that the shared imagery creates between the yellow-turned-golden beaks and the hair-turned-fur coiffure. This connection is not as explicitly described as the connections among the nightgowns are, yet it also functions to bring otherwise unassociated elements of the narrative together. The subtle affiliation generated through the imagery of material worth forms a net of associations below the descriptive surface of the text that, whether remarked by the narrator or not, guides the reader's associations as well.

The narrator recognizes in her reaction to the ducks her inability to communicate her thoughts about them to others in a way that will change the hold her associations allow the ducks to have on her:

> Meine Verachtung für den Parvenu-Diktator war alt, mein Kopf kannte sie. Und sie ging mir damals aus dem Kopf in den Mund, es war wie Anfassen und Loslassen *im Wort*.... An der Lahn aber war dieser Verachtung etwas beigemischt, das man *im Sprechen* nicht loslassen konnte.
>
> [My contempt for the parvenu dictator was old, my head knew it. And back then it went out of my head into my mouth; it was like catching and letting go *in a word*.... On the river Lahn, though, this contempt was mixed with something that one could not release *by speaking*.] (Müller 30, my emphasis)

Unlike Müller's rational and expressible reactions to Ceauşescu while she was still in Romania, the way her experiences have defined her perception since leaving Romania takes the form of a corporeal reaction that cannot be cast off by speaking. The associations spurring her memories do not obey the superficial logic of the present conversation but rather stem from a response to multiple associations:

> Gerade weniger als nichts öffnet die Komplizenschaft gegen die Selbstverständlichkeit an der Lahn.... Vom Gold der Enten beim Essen und Wassermischen aber kannst du niemandem erzählen, davon, daß du so logisch, glasklar normal verrückt bist.... Du hütest dich, dir die Lahn anmerken zu lassen, schweigst und läßt andere glauben, daß du kein Auge hast für die Gegenwart in diesem Land.
>
> [It takes less than nothing to open up naturalness (*Selbstverständlichkeit*) to complicity on the Lahn.... But you can tell no one about the gold of the

ducks as they eat and mix the water, about how you are so logically, crystal clearly normal crazy.... You are wary to let on about the Lahn; you remain silent and let others believe that you do not notice the present in this country.] (Müller 31)

The last reference to the present is a moment of not only time, but also a specific place in the narrator's experience. Her "selbstgebaute[r] Ekel" [self-constructed disgust] is the result of previous experiences inextricably encoded in the surface of the objects in the present that conjure the past (Müller 31). The ducks on the river in Germany should have nothing to do with Ceaușescu's self-enrichment under his dictatorship or the luxurious meals he devours despite his country's impoverishment, yet the narrator cannot distance the association with the dictator from her train of thought, and this association becomes an integral component of her present experience in space and time that finds no outlet in dialogic exchange.

As this passage develops, the difficulty in communicating these experiences is revealed to be as much a problem with the social contours of language as it is with the experiences themselves. Until this moment the text had been narrated entirely in the first-person I [*ich*]. The invocation of the second-person you [*du*] coincides with the first example of the narrator's deep frustration at her inability to prevent herself from associating past and present experience. The narrator's reflections probe both temporal and subjective categories, but neither seems able to give the narrator a stable vantage point for evaluating her reflections. In these passages a transition occurs from the first-person narrator I to the informal second-person you [*du*]. Though Müller employs the formal second-person pronoun you [*Sie*] in other passages that will later be shown to refer to the reader, I would suggest that the narrator addresses herself when she uses the informal you. The content of these passages and their interrogative or self-injunctive tone support this. Ashamed of her silence or the vapid conversation that replaces an actual description of her perceptions, she reevaluates the historical contingency of her impressions. The formulation of her self-injunction demonstrates how temporally convoluted her perceptions are. She recalls how she tried to suppress her associations when the ducks reminded her of Ceaușescu: "Sowas denkst du dir jetzt nicht, nahm ich mir vor, als ich es beobachtet und mit dem goldenen Besteck und den goldenen Wasserhähnen des Diktators verknüpft hatte" [You don't think that sort of thing to yourself now, I resolved when I had watched it and connected it with the golden cutlery and golden faucets of the dictator] (Müller 30). This single sentence combines present "think," past "resolved," and past perfect "had watched" and "had connected" verb tenses, as well as a deictic reference to "now" that blurs the relationship between the self-reflective moment of writing the essay and the remembered moment of viewing the ducks in Germany, which itself encodes a still earlier moment in Romania. The narrator's effort to describe and assess her experience requires collapsing three different temporal layers, a process that eventually recombines the temporal layers on the level of the words themselves, resulting in compositions such as "unerlaubt entsteht Vergangenwart und Gegenheit" [without permission past-present (*Vergangenwart*) and present-past (*Gegenheit*) emerge] (30). Unable to locate her perspective in the subjective and temporal categories at hand, the narrator attempts to articulate a different means of subjective and temporal location in the course of the text.

This means of subjective and temporal location, it will turn out, involves developing a history for objects that influences the future. The value of such an *Entstehungsgeschichte* becomes clear in the scene in a flea market briefly referenced above. In this scene the narrator and her friend sell two of the four forms of the nightgown. To help attract customers, the friend develops advertising slogans. In the case of the original nightgown made by the narrator's grandmother, the friend develops a slogan that invokes its previous context: "Da er [der Freund] seine Entstehungsgeschichte kannte, warb er mit dem Text: 'Sie werden darin so schön und ruhig schlafen wie eine Winterlandschaft'" [Because he (the friend) knew its history, he advertised with the text: "You will sleep as beautifully and peacefully as a winter landscape"] (Müller 35). The reference to a winter landscape alludes to winter in the small Romanian village of Nitzkydorf, where the narrator was as her grandmother carefully sewed and embroidered a nightgown in anticipation of her granddaughter's departure for the secondary school in the city. In contrast, the nylon nightgown from the Hungarian fur factory owner—described as a "vulgäre Imitation" [vulgar imitation] when compared to the first—is advertised as "Schön und zart wie Eisblumen und Meeresschaum" [beautiful and delicate like frost flowers and sea foam] (35). This labeling has nothing to do with the previous history of the nightgown and simply attempts to make the object more appealing through a comparison with delicate natural phenomena. In so doing, it also obscures the narrator's previous description of the poor quality of the nightgown and her allusion to the futility of imagining the dissolution of capitalism while attempting to imitate its products: "Wie sich der mittellose Osten die Verlotterung des Kapitalismus vorstellt, war das Plastikhemd des Pelzmeisters" [The fur-master's plastic shirt was like the destitute east imagines the ruination of capitalism] (35). The potential buyers at the flea market, however, are not privy to these reflections and make their decision based on the nightgown they see and its accompanying slogan. The importance of the *Entstehungsgeschichte* woven into the advertising slogan of the original nightgown is subsequently affirmed by the buyer it attracts.

Whereas the first nightgown appeals to a young, freckled woman, the vulgar imitation is bought by an old woman whose gold teeth conjure for the reader the negative associations of the golden bills of the ducks guzzling water. The old woman has bad values and bad taste. On one level she is associated with the greed of the Ceaușescu regime, and on another she lacks the aesthetic sensibility to distinguish the nightgown as a mediocre copy. The figure of the younger woman, however, opens the possibility for a new generation with redefined values. In gravitating toward the original gown and the slogan used to advertise it, this younger woman consciously or unconsciously attributes worth to an object that has been translated into language sensitive to its history and origins. The shift in values over the generational difference of the two women marks the potential of change over time. In this case the younger woman's preference for an *Entstehungsgeschichte* that alludes to the nightgown's history instead of similes that invoke nature to divert attention from the synthetic material and factory production of the nylon nightgown demonstrates a shift to a mode of perception that includes rather than ignores history.

This is the very language that Müller may hope the reader will achieve through the repetition of the phrase "Kennen Sie Inge Wenzel auf dem

Weg nach Rimini?" [Do you know Inge Wenzel on the way to Rimini?] in the course of her essay. Repeatedly the narrator half-asks, half-pleads, "Kennen Sie Inge Wenzel?" [Do you know Inge Wenzel?] (Müller 31), and later, "Kennen Sie INGE WENZEL AUF DEM WEG NACH RIMINI?" [Do you know INGE WENZEL ON THE WAY TO RIMINI?] (38). The narrator does not know Inge Wenzel's origins and admits, "Oft möchte ich wissen, wo Inge Wenzel geboren und aufgewachsen ist" [Often I'd like to know where Inge Wenzel was born and raised] (39-40). If she knew Wenzel's history, perhaps she would be able to transform the object to which she refers—an image of a woman modeling the nightgown in an advertisement—into text in the way her friend who had successfully marketed the nightgowns did, but instead the narrator can at first only hope for the reader to bring something derived from a different experiential vocabulary to bear on the text. The first address to the reader formulates the question with Wenzel's proper name, capitalized according to convention, as though searching for resonances the reader may have with the figure as a person outside the text. The next time the question appears, though, it asks for knowledge acquired through reading the text. This time the phrase is entirely capitalized in order to search for resonances with the advertisement as a linguistic object in the text. Whereas the first presentation of the question "Do you know Inge Wenzel?" seems to inquire about information the reader might have from outside the text, the recapitulation engages the reader's understanding of the phrase as derived from the structure of the essay. The narrator does not inquire, "Do you understand?" but rather deploys a phrase recurring throughout the work to develop understanding through the process of reading. By tracking a textual object that can only be constructed, apprehended, and explained within the horizon of Müller's text, the reader constructs an *Entstehungsgeschichte* for a textual object. The previously unfamiliar phrase "INGE WENZEL ON THE WAY TO RIMINI" accrues associations during the course of essayistic narration. These associations allow the reader to relate to the object as translated into language with an understanding of its history in the process of reading. The associative process in which readers engage through the course of the text allows them to grasp the subjective experience that Müller attempts to represent. Defiant of linear temporal progression that would ultimately dissociate the past from the present or future, the narrating subject's experience can only be represented through an associative network developed by the reader in the process of reading Müller's prose.

Near the conclusion of the text a third history emerges. Admitting that she often wonders where Inge Wenzel was born and grew up, the narrator says, "Dann probiere ich ihre Gegenstände aus in Reimen" [Then I try her objects out in rhymes] (Müller 40). A series of rhymes that pair aspects of the Deutsche Bahn advertisement with cities and towns in Germany follows: "Am Hals zu ihrem Gold paßt Detmold / zu ihren Nachthemden paßt Emden / zu ihren Fahrten paßt Hinterzarten / zu ihrem Schlafen paßt Bremerhaven / zu ihrem Bett paßt Helmstedt / zu allen Dingen paßt Sindelfingen / zu ihren Kleidern der Saison paßt Iserlohn" [On her neck with her gold goes Detmold / with her nightgowns goes Emden / with her trips goes Hinterzarten / with her sleep goes Bremerhaven / with her bed goes Helmstedt / with all things goes Sindelfingen / with her seasonal clothes goes Iserlohn] (40). In the absence of information about the figure in the advertisement, the narrator writes a history according to the phonetic correspondence of the objects associated with the figure as she is pictured and the names of places through which the train (or other Deutsche Bahn trains with the same advertisement) likely has passed. Place and object are joined with the verb "passen zu" [to go with/match], which both describes and instantiates a relationship of belonging in tandem with the rhyme. By locating parts of the figure in various places, the narrator destabilizes notions of both a unified subject and a single point of origin. This figure belongs where the sounds of the words of which she is composed place her.

The language of belonging resonates with an earlier passage in the text that describes a social tendency to divide past and present according to spatial divisions dependent on notions of affiliation:

> Die Trennung der beiden [Gegenwart und Vergangenheit], die Auffassung von Zeit gehorcht hierzulande räumlichen Kriterien. Eigentlich sind es Zugehörigkeitskriterien. Wenn ich über zehn Jahre Zurückliegendes aus Rumänien schreibe, heißt es, ich schreibe (noch immer) über die Vergangenheit. Wenn ein hiesiger Autor über die Nachkriegszeit, das Wirtschaftswunder

oder die 68-er Jahre schreibt, liest man es als Gegenwart. Das hiesig Vergangene, wie weit es auch zurückliegen mag, bleibt Gegenwart, weil es sich hier zugetragen hat, weil es durch Zugehörigkeit bindet.

[The separation of the two (present and past), the conception of time here obeys spatial criteria. Actually they are criteria of belonging. If I write about something from Romania ten years back, people say I write (even still) about the past. If a local author writes about the postwar period, the economic miracle, or the events of '68, they read it as the present. The local past, as far back as it may be, remains present because it happened here, because it binds through affiliation.] (Müller 37)

Described in the context of authors writing about historical events, this passage brings to light the relationship between conceptions of temporality and a notion of location deeply dependent on a set of socially defined criteria of belonging or membership [*Zugehörigkeitskriterien*] that mark affiliation with a particular group. In the context of Germany, a "local" author writing about historical events or time periods acknowledged as influential to the development of Germany will be characterized as writing about the present. The narrator's reflections on Romania, however, despite their engagement with more recent moments, are characterized as reflections on the past. As an author living in Germany writing about Romania, Müller cannot be separated from contemporary authors writing about Germany in terms of spatial remove. The exclusion of her works from those of the group of local authors is thus maintained through temporal instead of spatial categories. The narrating subject's experience reveals temporal and spatial categories to be socially defined means of distinguishing what belongs in the local present and what is excluded into the remote past. When the narrator writes Inge Wenzel's history, however, she develops her own criteria for determining where the figure in the advertisement belongs. Instead of insisting on stable categories of identity, this history foregrounds the multiple origins of the various parts of the figure. Space and time become secondary to a non-semantic logic of rhyme and a repeated sentence structure that locate the figure via phonetic correspondence. The narrator appropriates not only Inge Wenzel's history, but also the very means whereby this history is written.

The appropriation of the means to establish location plays out thematically in the concluding paragraphs of the text. The narrator notes her tendency to look for the Inge Wenzel advertisement when choosing a train compartment in which to sit and describes the advertisement's importance for helping her establish her position: "In Begleitung von Inge Wenzel machte ich Standortbestimmungen" [With the company of Inge Wenzel I established my location] (Müller 40). Her immediate surroundings change as passengers come and go, and her location in Germany changes as the train moves from town to town. The advertisement in the train compartment, however, travels with her without changing. She keenly observes the passengers around her, but the commonalities she identifies in their habits while eating croissants undermine the possibility of a stable point of view. As she ponders the way the passengers dust crumbs off their clothing, she wonders whether she has actually identified a meaningful relationship external to her or if she has simply demonstrated her own insecurity in the need to find a meaningful relationship: "Hatte die Mühe, etwas über die beiden übers Krümelwischen abzuleiten einen Sinn. Oder zeigte die ganze Beobachtung lediglich, wie unsicher ich selber war" [Did the effort of deducing something about the two from brushing away crumbs make sense. Or did the whole observation only demonstrate how insecure I was myself] (40). In the constant flux of her surroundings the advertisement seems to offer the only ground whereby she may locate herself. Whereas previously she had located parts of the advertisement in specific places according to rhyme, in the train she uses the advertisement to locate herself. Anchored linguistically, the poster becomes the means for the narrator to establish her own position both socially and historically.

The establishment of location enabled by the advertisement in the moving train serves also as an establishment of subjectivity when the narrator steals the advertisement to hang in her bedroom. The security derived from locating herself socially and historically by way of the poster allows her to act in the present moment to directly influence her future. Acknowledging the uncertainty resulting from her assessment of the passengers around her, the narrator recognizes without hesitation that she wants to have the advertisement and be able to look at it while she is at home. When the narrator steals the poster she appropriates the *Entstehungsgeschichte* that has become her means of location and resists the social currents that threaten to take this means of location away from her: "Die Deutsche Bahn hat sie [INGE WENZEL AUF DEM WEG NACH RIMINI] bald darauf durch andere Bilder ersetzt. Sie wäre mir gestohlen worden, wenn ich sie nicht rechtzeitig gestohlen hätte" [The Deutsche Bahn soon replaced her (INGE WENZEL AUF DEM WEG NACH RIMINI) with other pictures. She would have been stolen from me if I had not stolen her in time] (Müller 40). The grounding for her subjective experience that she is able to find by way of the advertisement enables her to assume a role of agency and consciously secure her means of location. She knows what she is stealing and what it means to steal it. By hanging the advertisement in her bedroom, the narrator resists the process of constant relocation to which it is subject by both the moving position of the train and the marketing strategies that will replace it with the development of new advertising campaigns over time. Having used the advertisement to establish a subjective location in the moving train, she further stabilizes her ability to do so in the future by actively securing the object that is the means for this establishment.

Another reference to stealing also underscores the importance of the narrator's acts of appropriation as acts of resistance dependent upon an assertion of subjective experience. The narrator describes how in Romania she felt that her own hopelessness [*Aussichtslosigkeit*] motivated her petty thievery of clothespins and noodles (Müller 39). Looking back from the reflective moment of writing, however, she sees how her shoplifting was also an act of resistance against the dictatorship that she felt had stolen her life:

> Als hätte mich die Tugendhaften des Regimes nicht schon genug in Angst gejagt, mußte ich mir das Herz zusätzlich und maßlos riskant selbst flattern lassen. Ich war mit den Nerven so fertig, daß ich stehlen mußte. Dem Staat wenigstens Wäscheklammern oder Nudeln stehlen, weil er mir das Leben stahl.

> [As if the virtuous people of the regime had not driven me to fear enough, I had to additionally and excessively hazardously make my own heart flutter. I was at the end of my nerves that I had to steal. To steal at least clothespins or noodles from the state because it was stealing my life.] (Müller 39)

Though she had not recognized her resistance as such at the time, the narrator reinterprets her motivations when she reflects on her experience. She recognizes how stealing had been in part a way for her to locate her affective reaction to her social and historical conditions. She appropriates the general fear she experiences as part of life under the dictatorship by grounding it in a reason to feel fear that is a result of her actions. Far from inspiring regret or remorse for not having recognized her capability of resistance at the time, these retrospective observations are part of the process that allows her to initiate change in the present moment. When she steals the advertisement, she does so with the future in mind and remarks on the timeliness of her actions. Having recognized her need to establish her subjective experience, she is aware that appropriating her means of location in the train is also part of a larger resistance to subjective dislocation that she has experienced before. A far cry from the futile repetition of history, the moment when the narrator steals the advertisement, by maintaining an explicit connection to the past moments of stealing as well as all the other associations contained in the advertisement's *Entstehungsgeschichte* as traced through the text, allows her to affirm her subjective position and resist the social forces threatening to dislocate it. The result is a future-oriented, historically informed perspective that not only opens the possibility for change in the future, but also actively enables it.

Despite the essay's inclusion in a conference addressing the possibility of conceptualizing a future—and my strong emphasis on the importance of the notion of future it articulates—Müller's "Einmal anfassen" contains strikingly few references to the word "future." After explicitly theorizing the relationship of past, present, and future when introducing her reflections, the narrator invokes "future" only once before the concluding paragraph. In this reference the future takes the form of an analogy in which the present is to the past as the future will be to the present: "Vergangenheit, das ist die Zuspitzung der Gegenwart durch die Einsicht, daß sich das Leben weniger durch den Kopf und die Hände als durch die Füße und Gegenstände ändern läßt. Und daß sich das auch in der Zukunft nicht ändert. Zukunft, das wird wiederum die Zuspitzung einer gewesenen Gegenwart" [Past, which is the culmination of the present through the insight that life may be changed less through heads and hands than through feet and objects. And that this will not change in the future. Future, which becomes in turn the culmination of a passed present] (Müller 39). This passage formulates the future as the interdependence and inextricability of past and present that suggest the potential for change. The influence of history on the present does not mean that the future will be merely the reliving of history but rather that recognizing the way in which the present includes history can have consequences for the future. The accumulation in objects of associations from past contexts allows for a subjective positioning via the material conditions of life, despite social changes that may obscure, threaten, or propose to erase the history that these objects may be read to contain. Once recognized, this history may be appropriated and refashioned according to contemporary subjective experience.

In Müller's essay the recognition and appropriation of an *Entstehungsgeschichte* occurs in the associations for both reader and narrating subject that the phrase "INGE WENZEL ON THE WAY TO RIMINI" accrues through its repetition within the narration. The implicit accumulation of associations demonstrates performatively the development of an *Entstehungsgeschichte* that is accomplished thematically with the invention of Inge Wenzel's history through rhyme, the use of the advertisement as a means to establish a position socially and historically, and the appropriation of this means of location in the service of the future. The existing temporal categories of past, present, and future are rendered inadequate by the very subjective experience they cannot represent through the literary strategies that work in tandem to bring the narrator's subjective experience to light. The stakes of representing subjective experience in this particular case are no less than articulating a post-socialist present moment that both allows for a future and does not deny its relation to a Communist past. Adequate representation of this subjective experience is not to be found in the invention of new temporal categories that may change as quickly as the advertising campaigns in the Deutsche Bahn but rather in the *Entstehungsgeschichte* inscribed in the terms and objects that compose the present.

Notes

1. Müller's lecture, as well as the other presentations, can be found in Wertheimer. Translations from the German are my own.

2. My use of hyphenation to combine the nouns past and present unfortunately does not quite capture Müller's word play, which creates two new words by recombining the syllables of the German words for past [*Vergangenheit*] and present [*Gegenwart*].

3. Though I focus on categories of temporality in this essay, the gist of the argument is applicable to other categories relevant to Müller's works and related scholarship. Categories of national and ethnic identity, inner and outer spaces, and individual subjectivity tend to reduce the complexity of her work into paradigms that collapse rather than foreground the tension between dynamic associative processes and a coherent point of view that finds a delicate balance in them.

4. Bettina Brandt (74-83), Thomas Roberg (27-42), Ralph Köhnen (123-38), Nicole Bary (115-21), and Norbert Otto Eke (7-21) have made great contributions to analyses of the affinities of Müller's work to surrealism. Interesting to note in this context is also Huyssen's consideration of intertextual references in contemporary works. Instead of reading the engagement in these works with aesthetic traditions as an empty citation that foregrounds the impossibility of doing otherwise, Huyssen shows how the references can also be read as the invocation of aesthetic history. As such, Müller's borrowing of avant-garde strategies may suggest a means of location via other aesthetic projects as well.

5. See Eddy (56-72), Haines (260-81), and Marven.

Works Cited

Bary, Nicole. "Grenze—Entgrenzungen in Herta Müllers Prosaband: *Der Mensch ist ein großer Fasan auf der Welt*." *Germanica* 7 (1990): 115-21.

Brandt, Bettina. "Schnitt durchs Auge: Surrealistische Bilder bei Yoko Tawada, Emine Sevgi Özdamar und Herta Müller." *Literature und Migration*. Ed. Heinz L. Arnold. Munich: Edition Text und Kritik, 2006. 74-83.

Eddy, Beverley Driver. "Testimony and Trauma in Herta Müller's *Herztier*." *German Life and Letters* 53.1 (January 2000): 56-72.

Eke, Norbert Otto. "Augen/Blicke oder: Die Wahrnehmung der Welt in den Bildern. Annährung an Herta Müller (Einleitung)." *Die Erfundene Wahrnehmung*. Ed. Norbert Otto Eke. Paderborn: Igel, 1991. 7-21.

Haines, Brigid. "'The Unforgettable Forgotten': The Traces of Trauma in Herta Müller's *Reisende auf einem Bein*." *German Life and Letters* 55.3 (July 2002): 260-81.

Huyssen, Andreas. *Twilight Memories: Marking Time in a Culture of Remembrance.* New York: Routledge, 1995.

Köhnen, Ralph. "Über Gänge. Kinästhetische Bilder in Texten Herta Müllers." *Der Druck der Erfahrung treibt die Sprache in die Dichtung: Bildlichkeit in Texten Herta Müllers.* Ed. Ralph Köhnen. Frankfurt: Peter Lang, 1997. 123-38.

Marven, Lyn. "'In Allem ist der Riß': Trauma, Fragmentation, and the Body in Herta Müller's Prose and Collages." *Modern Language Review* 100.2 (2005): 396-411.

Müller, Herta. "Einmal anfassen—zweimal loslassen." *Zukunft! Zukunft? Tübinger Poetik Vorlesungen.* Ed. Jürgen Wertheimer. Tübingen: Konkursbuch, 2000. 29-40.

Roberg, Thomas. "Bildlichkeit und verschwiegener Sinn in Herta Müllers Erzählung *Der Mensch ist ein großer Fasan auf der Welt.*" *Der Druck der Erfahrung treibt die Sprache in die Dichtung: Bildlichkeit in Texten Herta Müllers.* Ed. Ralph Köhnen. Frankfurt: Peter Lang, 1997. 27-42.

Wertheimer, Jürgen, ed. *Zukunft! Zukunft? Tübinger Poetik Vorlesungen.* Tübingen: Konkursbuch, 2000.

Selected Bibliography

Herta Müller's Major Works in German

Atemschaukel. Munich: Hanser, 2009.
Barfüßiger Februar. Berlin: Rotbuch, 1987.
Cristina und ihre Attrappe, oder, Was (nicht) in den Akten der Securitate steht. Göttingen: Wallstein, 2009.
Der fremde Blick oder Das Leben ist ein Furz in der Laterne. Göttingen: Wallstein, 1999.
Der Fuchs war damals schon der Jäger. Reinbek: Rowohlt, 1992.
Der König verneigt sich und tötet. Munich and Vienna: Hanser, 2003.
Der Mensch ist ein großer Fasan auf der Welt. Berlin: Rotbuch, 1986.
Der Teufel sitzt im Spiegel. Wie Wahrnehmung sich erfindet. Berlin: Rotbuch, 1991.
Der Wächter nimmt seinen Kamm: Vom Weggehen und Ausscheren. Reinbek: Rowohlt, 1993.
Die blassen Herren mit den Mokkatassen. Munich and Vienna: Hanser, 2005.
Die Nacht ist aus Tinte gemacht. Herta Müller erzählt ihre Kindheit im Banat. Dir. Thomas Böhm and Klaus Sander. Supposé, 2009. CD.
Drückender Tango. Bucharest: Kriterion, 1984.
Heimat ist das, was gesprochen wird. Blieskastel: Gollenstein, 2001.
Herztier. Reinbek: Rowohlt, 1994.
Heute wäre ich mir lieber nicht begegnet. Reinbek: Rowohlt, 1997.
Hunger und Seide. Reinbek: Rowohlt, 1995.

Im Haarknoten wohnt eine Dame. Reinbek: Rowohlt, 2000.
In der Falle. Bonner Poetik-Vorlesungen. Göttingen: Wallstein, 1996.
Niederungen. Berlin: Rotbuch, 1984.
Reisende auf einem Bein. Berlin: Rotbuch, 1989.

Herta Müller's English Translations

The Appointment. Trans. Michael Hulse and Philip Boehm. New York: Metropolitan Books, 2001. (Translation of *Heute wäre ich mir lieber nicht begegnet.*)

The Hunger Angel. Trans. Philip Boehm. New York: Metropolitan Books, 2012. (Translation of *Atemschaukel.*)

The Land of Green Plums. Trans. Michael Hofmann. New York: Metropolitan Books, 1996. (Translation of *Herztier.*)

Nadirs. Trans. Sieglinde Lug. Lincoln: University of Nebraska Press, 1999. (Translation of *Niederungen.*)

The Passport. Trans. Martin Chalmers. London: Serpent's Tail, 1989. (Translation of *Der Mensch ist ein großer Fasan auf der Welt.*)

Traveling on One Leg. Trans. Valentina Glajar and André Lefevere. Evanston: Northwestern University Press, 1998. (Translation of *Reisende auf einem Bein.*)

Selected Secondary Literature

Bauer, Karin. "Tabus der Wahrnehmung: Reflexion und Geschichte in Herta Müllers Prosa." *German Studies Review* 19.2 (1996): 257–78.

Bozzi, Paola. *Der fremde Blick. Zum Werk Herta Müllers.* Würzburg: Königshausen and Neumann, 2005.

Brandt, Bettina. "Schnitt durchs Auge: Surrealistische Bilder bei Yoko Tawada, Emine Sevgi Özdamar und Herta Müller." *Literature und Migration.* Ed. Heinz Arnold. Munich: Text und Kritik, 2006. 74–83.

Dascalu, Bogdan. *Held und Welt in Herta Müllers Erzählungen.* Hamburg: Kovacs, 2004.

Eddy, Beverley Driver. "'Die Schule der Angst': Gespräch mit Herta Müller, den 14. April 1998." *German Quarterly* 72.4 (Autumn 1999): 329–39.

———. "Testimony and Trauma in Herta Müller's *Herztier.*" *German Life and Letters* 53 (2000): 56–72.

Eke, Norbert Otto. *Die erfundene Wahrnehmung: Annäherung an Herta Müller.* Paderborn: Igel, 1991.

———. "Herta Müllers Weg zum Gedicht." *Text und Kritik* 155 (July 2002): 64-80.

Gauss, Karl-Markus. "Das Lager ist eine praktische Welt. Ein europäisches Ereignis: Herta Müllers Roman *Atemschaukel* über die Deportation der Rumäniendeutschen in die Sowjetunion nach 1945." *Süddeutsche Zeitung*, August 20, 2009.

Glajar, Valentina. "Banat-Swabian, Romanian and German: Conflicting Identities in Herta Müller's *Herztier*." *Monatshefte* 89.4 (1997): 521-40.

———. *The German Legacy in East Central Europe*. Rochester: Camden House, 2004.

Günther, Michael. "Froschperspektiven. Über Eigenart und Wirkung erzählter Erinnerung in Herta Müllers *Niederungen*." *Die erfundene Wahrnehmung: Annäherung an Herta Müller*. Ed. Norbert Otto Eke. Paderborn: Igel, 1991. 42-59.

Haines, Brigid, ed. *Herta Müller*. Cardiff: University of Wales Press, 1998.

———. "'Leben wir im Detail': Herta Müller's Micro-Politics of Resistance." *Herta Müller*. Ed. Brigid Haines. Cardiff: University of Wales Press, 1998. 109-25.

———. "'The Unforgettable Forgotten': The Traces of Trauma in Herta Müller's *Reisende auf einem Bein*." *German Life and Letters* 55 (2002): 266-81.

Haines, Brigid, and Margaret Littler. "Gespräch mit Herta Müller." *Herta Müller*. Ed. Brigid Haines. Cardiff: University of Wales Press, 1998. 14-25.

Hartwig, Ina. "Der Held heißt Hungerengel. Herta Müllers neuer, wagemutiger Roman *Atemschaukel* begibt sich in die Innenwelt eines sowjetischen Arbeitslagers." *Frankfurter Rundschau*, August 21, 2009:22-23.

Haupt-Cucuiu, Herta. *Eine Poesie der Sinne: Herta Müllers Diskurs des Alleinseins und seiner Wurzeln*. Paderborn: Igel, 1996.

Henneberg, Nicole. "'Die Zumutung des Lagers sollte in der Sprache spürbar werden': Herta Müller about Her Novel and Her Work with Oskar Pastior." *Frankfurter Rundschau*, August 21, 2009:23.

Johannsen, Anja K. *Kisten, Krypten, Labyrinthe. Raumfigurationen in der Gegenwartsliteratur: W. G. Sebald, Anne Duden, Herta Müller*. Bielefeld: Transcript, 2008.

Kegelmann, Rene. "'Der deutsche Frosch war der erste Diktator, den ich kannte.' Vergangenheitsbewältigung, Nationalsozialismus und Totalitarismus im Werk Herta Müllers." *Deutsche Literatur in Rumänien und das "Dritte Reich." Vereinnahmung-Verstrickung-Ausgrenzung*. Munich: IKGS, 2003. 299-310.

Köhler, Andrea. "Das Buch vom Hunger. Herta Müllers ungeheurer Roman *Atemschaukel*." *Neue Zürcher Zeitung*, August 25, 2009. Web. August 27, 2009.

Köhnen, Ralph. *Der Druck der Erfahrung treibt die Sprache in die Dichtung. Bildlichkeit in Texten Herta Müllers*. Frankfurt: Peter Lang, 1997.

———. "Terror und Spiel. Der autofiktionale Impuls in frühen Texten Herta Müllers." *Text und Kritik* 155 (July 2002): 18-29.

———. "Über Gänge. Kinästhetische Bilder in Texten Herta Müllers." *Der Druck der Erfahrung treibt die Sprache in die Dichtung. Bildlichkeit in Texten Herta Müllers.* Ed. Ralph Köhnen. Frankfurt: Peter Lang, 1997. 123-38.

Marven, Lyn. *Body and Narrative in Contemporary Literatures in German: Herta Müller, Libuše Moníková, and Kerstin Hensel.* Oxford: Clarendon, 2005.

———. "'In allem ist der Riß': Trauma, Fragmentation, and the Body in Herta Müller's Prose and Collages." *Modern Language Review* 100.2 (2005): 396-411.

———. "'So fremd war das Gebilde': The Interaction between Visual and Verbal in Herta Müller's Prose and Collages." *New German Literature: Life-Writing and Dialogue with the Arts.* Ed. Julian Preece, Frank Finlay, and Ruth J. Owen. Oxford: Peter Lang, 2007. 123-41.

Mayr, Walter. "Gift im Gepäck. Die Enthüllungen über Spitzeleien des Dichters Oskar Pastior haben Streit ausgelöst unter rumäniendeutschen Schriftstellern. Im Zentrum der Debatte um Schuld, Verrat und den aufrechten Gang in totalitärer Zeit steht die Nobelpreisträgerin Herta Müller." *Der Spiegel*, January 17, 2011:128-31.

Melzer, Gerhard. "Verkrallt in Aussichtslosigkeit. Eine rumänische Kindheit. Zu Herta Müller und ihrem Roman *Herztier*." *Durch Abenteuer muß man wagen viel: Festschrift für Anton Schwob zum 60 Geburtstag.* Ed. Wernfried Hofmeister and Bernd Steinbauer. Innsbruck: Institut für Germanistik, 1997. 291-98.

Michaelis, Rolf. "In der Angst zu Haus. Ein Überlebensbuch: Herta Müllers Roman *Herztier*." *Die Zeit*, October 7, 1994. Web. February 18, 2011.

Midgley, David. "Remembered Things: The Representation of Memory and Separation in *Der Mensch ist ein großer Fasan auf der Welt*." *Herta Müller*. Ed. Brigid Haines. Cardiff: University of Wales Press, 1998. 24-35.

Müller, Philipp. "*Herztier*. Ein Titel/Bild inmitten von Bildern." *Der Druck der Erfahrung treibt die Sprache in die Dichtung. Bildlichkeit in Texten Herta Müllers.* Ed. Ralph Köhnen. Frankfurt: Peter Lang, 1997. 109-21.

OSA/RFE (Open Society Archives/Radio Free Europe) Archives. Romanian Fond, 300/60/5/Box 6, File Dissidents: Paul Goma.

———. Romanian Fond, 300/60/3/Box 18, File Open Letters: The Group of Seven.

Patrut, Iulia-Karin. *Schwarze Schwester—Teufelsjunge, Ethnizität und Geschlecht bei Paul Celan und Herta Müller.* Cologne: Böhlau, 2006.

Predoiu, Graziella. *Faszination und Provokation bei Herta Müller: Eine thematische und motivische Auseinandersetzung*. Frankfurt: Peter Lang, 2000.

———. *Rumäniendeutsche Literatur und die Diktatur.* "Die Vergangenheit entlässt dich niemals." Hamburg: Kovacs, 2004.

Radisch, Iris. "Contra Herta Müller. Kitsch oder Weltliteratur? Gulag-Romane lassen sich nicht aus zweiter Hand schreiben. Herta Müllers Buch ist parfümiert und kulissenhaft." *Die Zeit*, August 20, 2009:35–43.

Schmidt, Ricarda. "Metapher, Metonymie und Moral: Herta Müllers *Herztier*." *Herta Müller*. Ed. Brigid Haines. Cardiff: University of Wales Press, 1998. 96–107.

White, John J. "'Die Einzelheiten und das Ganze': Herta Müller and Totalitarianism." *Herta Müller*. Ed. Brigid Haines. Cardiff: University of Wales Press, 1998. 75–95.

Contributors

Paola Bozzi is a professor of German studies at the University of Milan. She received her PhD in modern German literature at the Humboldt University in Berlin in 1996. Her dissertation has been published as *Ästhetik des Leidens: Zum Werk Thomas Bernhards* (1997). Her research interests and publications include German literary and cultural studies of the eighteenth and twentieth centuries, modernity and postmodernity, philosophy and literature, gender studies, media aesthetics, and culture. She has written a monograph (*Der fremde Blick: Zum Werk Herta Müllers*, 2005) as well as articles on Herta Müller's work. Her recent books include *Vilém Flusser. Dal soggetto al progetto: Libertà e cultura dei media* (2007) and *"Durch fabelhaftes Denken": Evolution, Gedankenexperiment, Science und Fiction. Vilém Flusser, Louis Bec und der Vampyroteuthis infernalis* (2008).

Bettina Brandt grew up in Germany, the Netherlands, and French-speaking Belgium. She received MA degrees in French and German from the University of Utrecht and a PhD in comparative literature from Harvard University. Brandt taught at MIT, Columbia University, and Montclair State before joining the faculty of the Department of Germanic and Slavic Languages and Literatures at Pennsylvania State University. Her research interests include literatures and theories of the avant-garde(s); the literatures of migration; literary multilingualism and translation studies; gender studies; and global early modern relations. She has published articles or book chapters on the above topics and is currently completing a book-length study about the intersection of migration and avant-garde in the works of Herta Müller, Emine Özdamar, and Yoko Tawada. Her latest book publication (with Désirée Schyns) is a Dutch translation of a collection of writings by Yoko Tawada: *De Berghollander: Teksten van een Japanse in Duitsland* (Voetnoot, 2010).

Beverley Driver Eddy is a professor emerita of German at Dickinson College. Many of her publications are in the area of German-Scandinavian literary relations; she has also edited a volume of essays on the Austrian poet Evelyn Schlag and published biographies of the Danish feminist writer Karin Michaëlis and Felix Salten, the author of *Bambi*. She has published interviews with, and articles on, Herta Müller.

Valentina Glajar is a professor of German at Texas State University–San Marcos. She is the author of *The German Legacy in East Central Europe* (Camden House, 2004); (with Domnica Radulescu) *"Gypsies" in European Literature and Culture* (Palgrave Macmillan, 2008); and *Vampirettes, Wretches, and Amazons: Western Representations of East European Women* (East European Monographs, 2004). Glajar has also cotranslated (with André Lefevere) Herta Müller's *Traveling on One Leg* (Northwestern University Press, 1998, 2010). Her latest book (with Jeanine Teodorescu) is *Local History: Transnational Memory in the Romanian Holocaust* (Palgrave Macmillan, 2011). Currently she is working on a monograph on German-Romanian writers and the secret police.

Brigid Haines is a reader in German at Swansea University, Wales. She specializes in German women's writing and the "eastern turn" in contemporary German culture. Her books include *Herta Müller* (University of Wales Press, 1998); (with Margaret Littler) *Contemporary Women's Writing in German: Changing the Subject* (Oxford University Press, 2004); (with Lyn Marven) *Libuše Moníková in Memoriam* (Rodopi, 2005); and (with Lyn Marven) *Herta Müller* (Oxford University Press, 2013). She is a founding member of Women in German Studies (WIGS).

Anja Johannsen studied German literature and philosophy in Berlin; Providence, Rhode Island; and Freiburg. She is the author of *Kisten,*

Krypten, Labyrinthe: Raumfigurationen in der Gegenwartsliteratur: W. G. Sebald, Anne Duden, Herta Müller (Transcript, 2008) and has published broadly on contemporary German literature and the literary industry. Since 2010 she has been the director of the Literarisches Zentrum Göttingen, a cultural institute in Lower Saxony, Germany.

Monika Moyrer received her PhD from the University of Minnesota. She has published on Herta Müller, the FrauenMediaTurm Köln, and Robert K. Eissler's Psychoanalytic Goethe study. Currently she teaches German in the Department of World Languages and Cultures at the University of Scranton.

Katrina Nousek is a PhD candidate in the Department of German Studies at Cornell University. Her interests include contemporary German-language literature, historiography, and epistemology. In 2009 she was the second-place recipient of the Cornell University Goethe Essay Prize for a comparative work on Bertolt Brecht and Lázló Moholy-Nagy's theories of perception. Her recent activities include presentations at the University of Pennsylvania and the German Studies Association about structures of temporality in Herta Müller's prose.

Cristina Petrescu is a lecturer in comparative politics and recent history in the Department of Political Science, University of Bucharest. She has also worked as an expert for the Presidential Commission for the Analysis of the Communist Dictatorship in Romania and coauthored its *Final Report* (Bucharest, 2007). Her studies on communism and the process of coming to terms with the Communist past in East Central Europe have been published in Germany, Great Britain, Spain, Hungary, Poland, and Romania. Her forthcoming book is *From Robin Hood to Don Quixote: Resistance and Dissent in Communist Romania*.

Arina Rotaru is a PhD candidate in the German Studies Department at Cornell University. She has studied and done research at the Universities of Bucharest, Heidelberg, and Innsbruck and at the Pontifical University Urbaniana. Her teaching and research interests include questions of canon formation and literary periodization; transmission of literary patterns, motifs, and tropes; lyric poetry; sound and performance studies; "minority" literatures; the avant-gardes as transnational phenomena; and Afro-Caribbean and German confluences. She has presented papers on Jacques Derrida, Herta Müller, W. G. Sebald, and Botho Strauss at American and international conferences and has published translations of German expressionists in a Romanian anthology. Her work has been sponsored, among others, by the DAAD, the Scalabrini Foundation, and the Mario Einaudi Foundation. At present Rotaru is working on a dissertation provisionally titled "Poetics of Resonance: Sonic Legacies of the Past in post-1989 Literature."

Olivia Spiridon teaches German literature at the University of Tübingen and is a researcher at the Institute of Danube Swabian History and Regional Geography in Tübingen, Germany, specialized in the German literature of Southeastern Europe. She is the author of *Untersuchungen zur rumäniendeutschen Erzählliteratur der Nachkriegszeit* (Igel, 2002, 2009, and 2010). Her latest book is *Gedächtnis der Literatur. Erinnerungskulturen in den Ländern Südosteuropas* (coedited with Edda Binder-Iijima, Romanita Constantinescu, and Edgar Radtke) (2010). Recently she has published a bilingual (German and Romanian) anthology, *German Writers from Romania after 1945* (Curtea Veche, 2012).

Allan Stoekl is a professor of French and comparative literature at Pennsylvania State University. He has translated a number of works by Georges Bataille, Maurice Blanchot, and Paul Fournel. His most recent book is *Bataille's Peak: Energy, Religion, Postsustainability* (University of Minnesota Press). His current project is a study of avant-garde theories of the city from the perspective of questions of sustainability and gleaning.

Ernest Wichner is a German-language writer, translator, and editor from the Banat, Romania. He was a founding member of the literary circle Aktionsgruppe Banat (1972–75) in Romania and is a member of PEN, Germany. Since 2003 he has served as director of the Literaturhaus Berlin. His latest volumes of poetry are *Neuschnee und Ovomaltine* (2010) and *In ganz wie aufgesperrt* (2010). He has translated numerous texts by Norman Manea, Mircea Cartarescu, Nora Iuga, Christopher Middleton, M. Blecher, and many others. His edited works include *Ein Pronomen ist verhaftet* worden. *Die frühen Jahre in Rumänien. Texte der Aktionsgruppe Banat* (1992); *In der Sprache der Mörder. Eine Literatur aus Czernowitz, Bukowina* (1993); *Das Land am Nebentisch. Texte und Zeichen aus Siebenbürgen, dem Banat und den Orten versuchter Ankunft* (1993); and several volumes of Oskar Pastior's complete works.

Index

Page numbers in italics refer to illustrations.

Adam Müller-Guttenbrunn Circle, 38, 68, 79n35
"Adio, patria mea" (Müller), 241-45
Agamben, Giorgio, 18-19
Aguilera, Carlos A., 180
Aktionsgruppe Banat: credo of, 76n24, 79n36; Helmut Frauendorfer's reports on, 80n39; Herta Müller's interactions with, 37-38; influence of, on Herta Müller, 58, 65-70; influences on, 78n31, 230; Securitate and, 42-44; and surveillance of Herta Müller, 81n42; views of, on literature, 43
Allein die Hoffnung hielt uns am Leben (Stieber-Ackermann), 132-33
"Als der Abriss des Mondes" (Müller), *35*
Apel, Friedmar, 221
Apollinaire, Guillaume, 232
Appadurai, Arjun, 123
Arendt, Hanna, 87, 88-89, 104
ascending interest rates, 29
Ash, Timothy Garton, 83n50
Assmann, Aleida, 200, 200n2, 200n4
Atemschaukel (Müller): criticism of, 201n7; debates generated by, 144-47; and deportation of ethnic Germans, 130-33; detail in, 141-42; genesis of, 133-36; guilt in, 143-44; homesickness in, 137-38; hunger in, 137-39; influence of, 49-50; memory boom and, 188-89; *Mokkatassen* in, 190-92; Oskar Pastior's collaboration on, 47-48; poetic achievement of, 136-44; potatoes in, 139-40; sources for, 76n21; victimhood in, 143-44
authenticity, 145, 200, 201n7

autobiography, fiction and, 110–11, 113–14
autofiction, 4–5, 110–11, 114

Banat Swabian community: Herta Müller's distance from, 76n22; influence of, on Herta Müller, 58, 60–65, 75n18; peasant wealth in, 62, 74n13; as research object, 73n9; statistics on, 73n8
belonging, temporality and, 265–66
Berevoiești Case, 81n43
Berlin, 45–46, 63, 75n19
Bernstein, Charles, 246
betrayal, 17, 42, 91, 92
Biemel, Rainer, 148n8
Binder, Rodica, 197
Blecher, M., 40
body, 213–27
Bossert, Rolf, 5, 38, 92
Bozzi, Paola, 186, 189
Brandt, Bettina, 231, 237, 271n4
Brucan, Silviu, 95

cacophony, 245
Cărtărescu, Mircea, 82n46, 100
ceașca de moca. See *Mokkatassen*
Ceaușescu, Nicolae: ducks associated with, 259–62; and economic crisis, 94; eye of, 157; impact of, on language, 2–3; opposition to, 95–96; quoted in *Im Haarknoten wohnt eine Dame*, 168–69; regime of, 59, 78n29, 94–97; and retreat into *Nischengesellschaft*, 88

Center against Expulsions, 8, 11n2
Center for Exile, call for, 11n2
Charter 77, 77n26, 80n37
Christie, Ian, 237
Churchill, Winston, 148n5
Clifford, James, 232–33
collage poems: "Als der Abriss des Mondes," 35; as artwork, 156–57; body parts in, 159–60; border escapes in, 167; construction of, 179–80; deciphering of, 155–56; *Der Wächter nimmt seinen Kamm*, 160–66; detail and, 156–57; *Die blassen Herren mit den Mokkatassen*, 161, 174–79, 192–96, 233–41; *Este sau nu este Ion*, 196–99, 241–49; experimental prose and poetry in, 5–6; Hannah Höch and, 202n15; Herta Müller's use of, 230–31; humor in, 170–71; "Ich gehöre daheim," 34; "Im Gefälle zwischen," 33; *Im Haarknoten wohnt eine Dame*, 167–73; "In meinen Schläfen," 154; inspired by Herta Müller's mother, 30; language in, 178–79, 249; Lyn Marven on, 200n3; "Milch ist der Zwilling," 32; origin and development of, 156–60; for Oskar Pastior, 26; overriding reality in, 173–74; playfulness in, 171–72; sound in, 231–33; syntax of, 232; technique for, 100; truth in, 173–74; as *Vitrine*, 185–86, 199; word constructions in, 172; word sounds in, 171–72
collectivization, 61–62, 74n12

Communism, 59, 62–63, 72n4, 72n6, 83n49. *See also* totalitarian government
community, identity and, 18–19
commuters, 74n14
context, objects and, 210, 212–13
Cornea, Doina, 95, 96–97
Critique of the Power of Judgment (Kant), 112
Csejka, Gerhard, 38, 79n33
Cubism, 232
Culler, Jonathan, 238

Dadaism, 235, 245
"Das Limit prahlt" (Müller), 239–41
Decree 187 (1945), 148n6
Deletant, Denis, 92–93, 96
De Man, Paul, 113
deportation of ethnic Germans: Decree 187 and, 148n5; in "Die Anwendung der dünnen Straßen," 188–90; in *Die blassen Herren mit den Mokkatassen*, 194; discussing, 49–50; in *Este sau nu este Ion*, 198; impact of, 201n5; influence of, on Herta Müller, 186–88; overview of, 130–32; records and publications concerning, 132–33; Winston Churchill on, 148n5
Der Fuchs war damals schon der Jäger (Müller), 82n45, 181n16
Der König verneigt sich und tötet (Müller), 99–100
"Der Löffelbieger sagt" (Müller), 190
Derrida, Jacques, 17

Der Wächter nimmt seinen Kamm (Müller), 160–66
detail, 119–20, 141–42, 156–57, 210, 220–21
devil's circle, 16–17, 27–28
"Die Anwendung der dünnen Straßen" (Müller), 186
Die blassen Herren mit den Mokkatassen (Müller), 161; analysis of, 174–79, 231; artistic process in, 180; body parts in, 175; *Mokkatassen* in, 192–96; songs in, 235–36; sound in, 233–41; as *Vitrine*, 186
dignity, 29–30, 57, 70–71, 146
dispersal, 184–86, 192
Drückender Tango (Müller), 75n18

eccezionale normale, 58–59, 71n1
Eddy, Beverley Driver, 109, 127, 258, 272
Edelweiß, 190–91, 194–95
"Einmal anfassen—zweimal loslassen" (Müller): and Andreas Huyssen's conceptions of temporality, 254–55; and categories of temporality, 253–54; confrontations with *Entstehungsgeschichten* in, 255–65; ducks in, 259–62; establishment of location in, 267–68; future in, 269–70; overview of temporality and, 252–53; shoplifting in, 268–69; significance of objects in, 208–09, 211; temporality and belonging in, 265–66
Eke, Norbert Otto, 231–32
Elias, Norbert, 220

ensemble of relations, 222–23
Entstehungsgeschichten, 255–65, 270
"Ernest zicea" (Müller), 197–98
Este sau nu este Ion (Müller): analysis of, 231; *Mokkatassen* in, 197–99; as overstepping language barrier, 196–97; sound in, 241–49; as *Vitrine*, 186
"Este sau nu este Ion" (Müller), 244–49
ethics, poetics and, 110, 125–26
ethnocentrism, 239
ethnographic allusion, 232–33
ethnography, sonority and, 247

fantasy, 124–25
fear: body and, 213–14, 218; friendship and, 91, 92; institutionalization of, 96; nightgown associated with, 257; resistance to, 102–03, 269
Federman, Raymond, 111, 116
fiction, autobiography and, 110–11, 113–14
Foucault, Michel, 222
Frauendorfer, Helmut, 80n39
Frevert, Ute, 188–89, 200
friendship, 42, 90–92, 166–67
"Frühstück mit geschäumter Milch" (Müller), 158
futurists, 232, 233

Gauss, Karl-Markus, 146
"Gegenstände, wo die Haut zu Ende ist" (Müller), 221–25
German-language books, smuggling of, 69, 80n40

German-language poets, 38–39
German rural communities, 62–63, 74n15. *See also* Banat Swabian community
Germany, 3–4, 63, 80n40, 131, 201n5
Glajar, Valentina, 100, 106n11, 109, 186
Goma, Paul, 77n26, 80n37, 95
grace, loss of, 190, 199
Grass, Günter, 49, 188
Grenzgänger program, 149n13

Haines, Brigid, 109, 119, 221, 271, 283n5
handkerchiefs, 15–16, 20, 23–27, 29–30, 104
Havel, Václav, 72n6
Heesen, Anke te, 193, 194, 199
Herztier (Müller): betrayal in, 91, 92; body and objects in, 101, 210, 212–18; conclusions on, 104–05; as exposé of Securitate, 5; friendship in, 90–92; isolation and loneliness in, 97–100, 105; osmosis in, 219–20; overview of, 89–90; reality in, 100–102; resistance in, 102–04; rural conformity in, 76n23; totalitarian regime in, 93–97
Herztier (term), 103–04
Heute wär ich mir lieber nicht begegnet (Müller), 214, 218
Höch, Hannah, 202n15
homeland, 60, 72n7, 236, 244–45
horizon motif, 225–27
Huyssen, Andreas, 254–55, 271n4

"Ich gehöre daheim" (Müller), *34*
identity, 18–19, 60–70
image(s): in *Die blassen Herren mit den Mokkatassen*, 235, 236–37, 239; in "Este sau nu este Ion," 247; in Herta Müller's works, 117–19, 233; production of, 123; sound and, 231; temporality and, 255–60; of words, 139
imagination, 110, 112–15, 121–25
"Im Gefälle zwischen" (Müller), *33*
Im Haarknoten wohnt eine Dame (Müller), 167–73
Infra Noir, 41–42
"In meinen Schläfen" (Müller), *154*
innocence, loss of, 190
Ion (Rebreanu), 244–46
island metaphor, 75n20, 99

Johannsen, Anja K., 193, 202n10
July Theses, 78n29

Kandler, Matthias, 132–33, 149n9
Kant, Immanuel, 112
Kirsch, Roland, 5, 92
Klotz, Volker, 194
Köhler, Andrea, 146
Köhnen, Ralph, 210, 221
Koschorke, Albrecht, 225, 226, 227
Krämer, Theodor, 177

labor camps, 47–49, 76n21, 137–39, 188
language(s): in collage poems, 178–79, 249; in "Das Limit prahlt," 239–41; gap in, 119; of Herta Müller, 1, 2–3; Herta Müller on, 101–02, 165; Herta Müller's relationship with, 198–99; as homeland, 60, 72n7; in *Im Haarknoten wohnt eine Dame*, 169–72; outmoded, 195; overstepping barrier of, 196–97; reference of, 115–16
Lautmalerei, 237
Leitner, Anton G., 155
Letter of the Seven of April 1989, 80n38
Lévinas, Emmanuel, 122–23
libel, 22
Liiceanu, Gabriel, 78n28
Lippet, Johann, 38
Literaturhaus, exhibits and events at, 45
loneliness, 87–93, 97–100, 105
Löw, Martina, 223–24
Luca, Gherasim, 42

Marven, Lyn, 109, 180n2, 187, 194, 200n3, 248, 258, 271n5
Marxism, 67, 78n31
Matz, Uncle, 16, 26–27
Mein Freund Wassja (Biemel), 148n8
memory: bites of, 185, 198; missing links in, 186–88; and *Mokkatassen*, 188–92, 199–200; objects and, 184–86, 209, 213; of Oskar Pastior, 201n7; reassembling of, through speech, 196; spaces as products of, 224; temporality and, 254–55; trauma and, 200n2; truth and, 185
metaphor, 115–16. *See also* island metaphor

metonyms, 15–18
"micro-politics of resistance," 119–20
Midgley, David, 213
migration, urban, 64–65, 74n14
Mihăilescu, Vintilă, 78n30
"Milch ist der Zwilling" (Müller), 32
mobility: in *Atemschaukel*, 190–92; conclusions on, 199–200; in "Die Anwendung der dünnen Straßen," 188–90; in *Die blassen Herren mit den Mokkatassen*, 192–97; in *Este sau nu este Ion*, 197–99; and missing links in traumatic context, 186–88; overview of *Mokkatassen* and, 184–86
mocha cups. See *Mokkatassen*
modernist writing, 117
Mokkatassen: in *Atemschaukel*, 190–92; conclusions on, 199–200; in "Die Anwendung der dünnen Straßen," 188–90; in *Die blassen Herren mit den Mokkatassen*, 192–97; in *Este sau nu este Ion*, 197–99; overview of mobility and, 184–86
montage. *See* collage poems
Moromeții (Preda), 73n11
Müller, Herta: as autofictional writer, 4–5; beginning of career of, 1–2; departure of, from Romania, 3–4; and language, 1, 2–3, 101–02, 165, 198–99; mother of, 15–16, 20, 186; Securitate file on, 69–70, 73n10, 81nn41–42; song lyrics written by, 42; view of, on humanity, 220; view of, on literature, 117–19

Müller, Inge, 177
Müller-Guttenbrunn, Adam, 79n34

National Council for the Study of the Securitate, 82n43
Naum, Gellu, 41–42, 181n16
Naumann, Michael, 146
Niederungen (Müller): osmosis in, 219; publication of, 1–2, 43–44, 45; review of, for secret police, 75n16; surveillance following, 61, 63
nightgowns, 209, 255–60, 262–64
Nischengesellschaft, 88
normal exception. See *eccezionale normale*
Nr. 657 (Kandler), 132–33, 149n9

objects: associations between people and, 158–59; body and, 102–03, 213–18; body and space and, 221–27; as connection, 27–28; in *Herztier*, 101, 210, 212–18; imagination and, 114, 121–22, 127n8; mobility and, 184–85; prominence of, in Herta Müller's works, 193–94, 208–13; temporality and, 255–65
Olsson, Anders, 146
omission, 117–19
Ortinau, Gerhard, 38, 79n33
osmosis, 214–15, 218–21
outmoded vocabulary, 195

Pacepa, Ion Mihai, 95
Pastior, Oskar: in *Atemschaukel*, 136–37; and atonement, 191; collabora-

tion with, 47–48, 133–35, 145, 187, 201n7; collage for, 158–59; Ernest Wichner on, 46–49; handkerchief given to, 24–26; literary translation and, 39–40; as Securitate informer, 50–52, 76n21, 83n49, 150n21; visit to labor camp with, 188, 198; on "word images," 139

peasantry, wealth of, 62, 74n13

perception: automated, 208, 215–18, 221; invented, 112–15, 158; spaces as products of, 224–26

performative, 238, 239

photomontage, 157–59, 165. *See also* collage poems

poetics, ethics and, 110, 125–26

postmodernism, 122

poverty as escape, 15

power, 95, 97–100

Preda, Marin, 73n11

Quintilian, Marcus Fabius, 247

Radisch, Iris, 201n7

Rady, Martin, 95

Rebreanu, Liviu, 244

receptivity, loss of, 211

Reisende auf einem Bein (Müller), 157–58

relations, ensemble of, 222–23

Renneke, Petra, 194, 195, 202n14, 237

resistance, 102–04, 119–21, 268–69

"resistance through culture" strategy, 66–67, 68, 78n28, 78n30

rhyme: assonance, 176, 177–78, 235; in *Die blassen Herren mit den Mokkatassen*, 175–78, 236; in "Einmal anfassen—zweimal loslassen," 265; in *Im Haarknoten wohnt eine Dame*, 169–71, 174; internal, 175–78, 235, 236; pure, 177–78

Ricoeur, Paul, 115, 116

Romania: economic crisis in, 94; in *Este sau nu este Ion*, 198; ethnic separation in, 38–39; German rural communities in, 74n15; Germany's treaty with, 131, 201n5; languages of, 2–3; literary and art scenes in, 42; literary translation in, 39–41; peasant wealth in, 62, 74n13; rural fiction in, 61–62; solidarity in, 95–96; writing reforms in, 241–43

Romanian intellectuals, 72n4, 72n6, 77n27

Romanian language, 198–99, 240–43

Romanian-language poets, 38–39

Romanian Library, 40–41

Romanian Period: Aktionsgruppe Banat's influence on, 65–70; Banat Swabian community's influence on, 60–65; overview of, 57–59, 70–71

Romanian writers, dissident, 66–67, 68

Roth, Wilhelm, 146

Sartre, Jean-Paul, 121–22

Scherenschnitte, 160, 163–65, 167–68, 174–75

Schiff, Christopher, 235

Schleich, Thomas, 44

Schmidt, Rose, 146–47
Securitate: Aktionsgruppe Banat and, 42–44, 65–66, 68; attempted recruitment into, 2, 21–22, 43; collaboration with, 69–70, 75n17, 80n39; destroyed documents of, 81n43; exposure of, 5; file of, on Herta Müller, 69–70, 73n10, 81nn41–42; Literaturhaus events and, 45; methods of, 92–93, 209; novels discussing, 82n45; Oskar Pastior as informer for, 50–52, 76n21, 83n49, 150n21; rumors spread by, 22–23; surveillance categories of, 77n25
"seeing-as," 123–25
self-extension, 120
self-intensification, 120
Semprún, Jorge, 60, 185, 244
Shklovsky, Viktor, 208, 218
shoplifting, 268–69
shyness, 214–15
silhouette cutouts. See *Scherenschnitte*
solidarity, 95–96
Söllner, Werner, 51
space(s), 207–08, 218–27
spacing, 223–24
speech, writing and, 17–18, 28–29
stair parts, 23, 104
stealing, 267–69
Stieber-Ackermann, Hedwig, 132–33
subjectivity, 124–25, 267–68
surfiction, 111–12, 116–17
surrealism, 15, 41, 230, 233, 234–35, 237, 245, 271n4

surveillance, 70–71, 73n10, 75n17, 77n25, 81n42, 82n45, 207
synthesis, 223–24

Temeswarer Schriftsteller Vereinigung, 91–92
temporality: Andreas Huyssen on conceptions of, 254–55; belonging and, 265–66; in "Einmal anfassen—zweimal loslassen," 252–53, 269–70; and *Entstehungsgeschichte*, 255–65; and establishment of location, 267–68; Herta Müller's dissatisfaction with categories of, 253–54; and shoplifting, 268–69
totalitarian government: crimes and power under, 99–100; effects of, on friendships, 166–67; Hannah Arendt on, 87; in *Herztier*, 93–97; loneliness under, 87–90, 105; loss of innocence and grace under, 190; resistance to, 220–21; rhyme and, 169–71. See also Communism
Totok, William, 37, 38, 43, 67, 79nn32–33, 201n6
transfinite, 104–05
Transylvania, 201n5
trauma, 5, 59, 60, 98, 102, 110, 180n2, 187, 194, 199, 200nn2–4, 201, 220, 255
trauma theory, 109, 255, 257–58
Tudoran, Dorin, 77n27
typography as speech, 233

überendlich. See transfinite

"Voicu," 2
vowels, 238

Wagner, Richard, 37, 43, 44, 67, 79n33, 79n35, 101, 148n7, 201n6; Aktionsgruppe Banat and, 38, 76n24, 79n36; arrest of, 79n33; characters based on, 5, 91–92; departure of, from Romania, 3–4; on Herta Müller and Oskar Pastior, 150n21; trajectory of, 79n35
Warnock, Mary, 127n8
Weber, Georg, 187
"Wenn drei Straßen staubig auf dem Rücken schlafen" (Müller), 194–95
Wertheimer, Jürgen, 231
White, John, 100
Wichner, Ernest: Aktionsgruppe Banat and, 79n33; on Aktionsgruppe Banat and Securitate, 42–44; on Berlin and Romanian writers, 45–46; on collaboration of Oskar Pastior and Herta Müller, 47–48; on ethnic separation in Romania, 38–39; on events at Literaturhaus, 45; on first impressions of Herta Müller, 36–37; on Gellu Naum and Infra Noir, 41–42; on Herta Müller and Aktionsgruppe Banat, 37–38; on Herta Müller receiving Nobel Prize, 52; on influence of *Atemschaukel*, 49–50; on influence of Oskar Pastior, 46–47; on literary and art scenes in Romania, 42; on literary translation, 39–41; on Oskar Pastior as Securitate informer, 50–52; on photo of Herta Müller and Oskar Pastior, 48–49; on staying in touch with Herta Müller, 44–45; trip of, with Oskar Pastior and Herta Müller, 188, 198
Wittgenstein, Ludwig, 112
Wittstock, Erwin, 150n18
"word images," 139
World War II, 63–64, 75n20
writing: as betrayal, 17; Herta Müller on, 101; modernist, 117; speech and, 17–18, 28–29; tragic ambivalence of, 113
writing reforms, Romanian, 241–43

Zentrum gegen Vertreibungen. *See* Center against Expulsions

www.ingramcontent.com/pod-product-compliance
Lightning Source LLC
Chambersburg PA
CBHW021820300426
44114CB00009BA/251